PERFORMING FEMINISM
AND ADMINISTRATION
IN RHETORIC
AND COMPOSITION STUDIES

edited by

Krista Ratcliffe
Marquette University

Rebecca Rickly
Texas Tech University

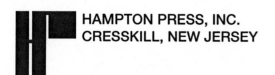

HAMPTON PRESS, INC.
CRESSKILL, NEW JERSEY

Printed in the United States of America

Library of Congress Cataloging-in-Publication Data

Performing feminism and administration in rhetoric and composition studies / edited by Krista Ratcliffe, Rebecca Rickly
     p. cm.
  Includes bibliographical references and index.
  ISBN 978-1-57273-784-6 (hardbound) -- ISBN 978-1-57273-785-3 (paperbound)
    1. English language--Rhetoric--Study and teaching--United States. 2. Writing centers--United States--Administration. 3. Feminism and education--United States. I. Ratcliffe, Krista, 1958- II. Rickly, Rebecca.
  PE1405.U6P38 2009
  808'.0420711--dc22   2008047692

Hampton Press, Inc.
23 Broadway
Cresskill, NJ 07626

CONTENTS

ACKNOWLEDGMENTS

Becky and Kris would like to thank all the contributors to this collection and all the people at Hampton Press, especially Barbara Bernstein who first expressed confidence in this project. We would like to thank all our colleagues who have helped us conceptualize, challenge, and perform feminist administration. And we would especially like to thank rhetoric and composition pioneer Win Horner whose voice, in tough times, echoes in our ears, exhorting us (just as, early in her career, her husband Dave had exhorted her): "Don't let the bastards get you down."

INTRODUCTION

Actions Un/Becoming
a Feminist Administrator:
Troubled Intersections of Feminist
Principles and Administrative Practices

Krista Ratcliffe

Rebecca Rickly

Performing Feminist Administration in Rhetoric and Composition Studies articulates multiple tactics that rhetoric and composition scholar-teachers may employ to perform feminist administration.[1] The idea for this book emerged at the 2003 Feminisms and Rhetorics Conference in Columbus, OH, when we were drinking coffee, reminiscing about graduate school days at The Ohio State University, and commiserating about current administrative duties. We had recently redesigned first-year writing programs at our respective institutions.[2] But, interestingly, we found ourselves talking not about program design, but rather about the tensions we noted between our deeply held feminist beliefs and our daily administrative duties. Among other things, we talked about balancing day care and day jobs, about being perceived as moms on the job, counseling young female teaching assistants in their search for classroom authority (especially in situations when their authority is challenged by undergraduate men), and trying to make contentious issues, such as gender's intersections with race, class, age, or technology, visible in a program-wide curriculum. More selfishly, we questioned whether the tensions we noted between our deeply held feminist beliefs and our daily administrative performances engendered actions un/becoming a feminist administrator.

This question, spurred not by guilt, but by a genuine desire to improve our performances as feminist administrators, led us to express a desire for an administrative primer for performing feminist administration in rhetoric and composition studies. Granted, the past decade has witnessed an ongoing scholarly conversation about feminism and administration within educational circles and within rhetoric and composition studies. Education scholarship[3] includes publications on feminist theory, feminist practice, and feminist leadership. Rhetoric and composition scholarship[4] exposes how feminists have administered writing programs,[5] writing centers,[6] learning centers, and other university sites, many doing so at their own peril within institutions that value publication more than administrative service. However, because no one book has focused solely on performing feminist administration in rhetoric and composition studies, the idea for this collection emerged as a means to fill that gap.

This collection's focus is unique because it analyzes how performing feminist administration is complicated by the politics of multiple locations: (a) administrative locations, (b) institutional locations, and (c) cultural locations.

The first location—administrative location—is an important consideration in performing feminist administration because rhetoric and composition faculty often find themselves impressed into all kinds of administrative service, not just writing program administrator work. Thus, contributors were invited to write from different administrative locations (e.g., writing program administration, writing center administration, writing across the curriculum administration, departmental administration, higher administration, and national administration as journal editors or organization officers).

The second location—institutional location—is an important consideration in performing feminist administration because administrative location is always complicated by institutional status or rank (i.e., whether the administrator is a graduate student, adjunct faculty, untenured faculty, or tenured faculty, either associate and full professor). Thus, contributors from a variety of these institutional locations were invited to discuss how the power differentials of these locations affect their performing feminist administration.

The third location—cultural location—is an important consideration when performing feminist administration because administrative and institutional locations are always inflected by cultural locations, such as gender. Thus, contributors were invited to address how gender intersects with other cultural categories, such as age, class, race, institutional reputation, and so on, in their performances of feminist administration.

This collection's focus on performing feminist administration from a variety of administrative, institutional, and cultural locations enables contributors to analyze the often-troubled intersections of feminist principles and administrative practices. To explore these troubled intersections, contributors make the following moves in their chapters:

- Identify issues of concern,
- Share experiences and contextual knowledge,
- Theorize these experiences in light of feminist thought and practice, and
- Offer pragmatic recommendations for performing feminist administration.

It is important to note, however, that contributors do not all agree on their feminist principles or their administrative practices: Indeed, a strength of this collection is that the chapters challenge one another and, we hope, readers.

Given this focus, this collection forwards three claims about performing feminist administration. First, gendered issues still exist within rhetoric and composition studies, thus validating the need for performing feminist administration. Second, all feminist administrative performances are historically and institutionally situated, yet the examples in this collection may serve as models that readers may adapt for their own situations when deemed appropriate. Third, the dominant trope that emerges for performing feminist administration is oxymoron (i.e., the ability to keep two conflicting ideas in one's head at the same time and to engage that conflict as a springboard for productive feminist action).

THEORETICAL GROUNDING: LOCATION AND PERFORMANCE

This collection's focus on administrative, institutional, and cultural locations is inspired, in part, by Adrienne Rich's concept of a politics of location and, in part, by Judith Butler's theory of performativity.

In "Notes Toward a Politics of Location," Adrienne Rich posits the concept of a politics of location as a materialist feminist stance that holds both feminists and feminist theories accountable for the situatedness of their own knowledge production. More than a naive standpoint theory that assumes all members of a cultural group experience life similarly, Rich's politics of location starts with the body, a particular body (her own), as it occupies multiple cultural locations that are both communal and particular (i.e., not only does she inhabit the cultural multiple locations women, American citizen, half-Jewish, mother, lesbian, poet, etc., but she also experiences these cultural categories and their intersections in particular ways that form her own particular identity; 212–213). Although Rich acknowledges common socialization that women (and men) encountered in the United States in the last half of the 20th century, she emphasizes that her politics of location are a reflective praxis through which a person may learn to recognize and analyze not just her common socialization, but also his particular identifications with that socialization—identifications that, in turn, shape his or her identity. When such recognition, analysis, and articulation render socialization visible, possibilities emerge for a person to reinforce, revise, and/or interrupt the socialization.

If we lay Rich's politics of location alongside Butler's theory of performance, then Rich's reinforcing, revising, and/or interrupting may be read as performances of identity. Both Rich and Butler would agree that names (e.g., *woman, white, U.S. citizen, WPA*) are associated with already-existing, yet mutable, cultural scripts (i.e., scripts for gender, scripts for race, scripts for nationality, scripts for writing program administration). But Butler further explains how a person's performing such scripts constructs a person's identity. For example, in terms of gender, she describes the performance of such scripts as "the repeated stylization of the body, a set of repeated acts within a highly rigid regulatory frame" (*GT* 44). From this theoretical stance, identity is not grounded solely in a person's preexisting interiority, but rather emerges in a person's conscious and unconscious performances of cultural scripts, which function as "highly rigid regulatory frame[s]" (44). From this theoretical stance, identity is not a fixed essence that precedes performances but rather is an on-going construction that emerges via performances (25). From this theoretical stance, agency and restrictions on agency arise not solely from individual will, but rather from whatever acts are allowed (or disallowed) within cultural scripts; more importantly, because such scripts are internalized within a person's body through identifications and disidentifications, agency arises from gaps that emerge when such internalized scripts collide with each other and/or with a person's bodily experiences (*GT* 187). Thus, a person's performances generate an endless play of (dis)identifications that continually constructs a person's identity.

With Rich and Butler in mind, contributors to this collection challenge themselves and readers to recognize and analyze multiple performances of feminist administration (particularly the collision of feminist principles and administrative practice) and, thus, perform their own scripts of feminist administration.

THE CONTRIBUTORS

This collection contains 14 chapters that examine how feminist administration may be performed in various administrative, institutional, and cultural locations within rhetoric and composition studies.

Part I. The Politics of Connecting Ethics, Theory, and Praxis

Part I questions how ethics, theory, and praxis converge (or not) when one performs feminist administration. In "What's Ethics Got to Do with It?: Feminist Ethics and Administrative Work in Rhetoric and Composition" (chap. 1), Carrie Leverenz identifies four key tenets of feminist theory —(a) standpoint theory, (b) care, (c) the concrete other, and (d) process, which she argues may inform administrative work in Rhetoric and Composition *if* these tenets are revised for current historical moments and particular locales. Rejecting the idea of a feminist administrative utopia (what *would* such a site look like?, she asks), Leverenz addresses three challenges to feminist administration: (a) institutionalized assumptions about what a good administrator is, (b) resistance from "concrete others," and (c) a woman's own assumptions about what a good administrator is. Echoing Leverenz's concern with utopian visions, Jeanne Gunner in "Checking the Source(book): Supplemental Voices in the Administrative Genre" (chap. 2), defines *administrative genre* as a site where writers are encouraged to promote a utopian vision (i.e., to "assume and reproduce an ahistorical space and a politics of political cleansing, leading to a utopian valorization of seamlessness, transparency, and a uniform *sensus communis*"). Although Gunner acknowledges her complicity in perpetuating this genre, she challenges it here by outing its partialness and searching for "supplemental ways of being in administrative roles," ways that are grounded in feminist theories, such as Gloria Anzaldua's. Echoing Gunner's skepticism of the administrative genre, Sibylle Gruber, in "When Theory and Practice Collide: Becoming a Feminist Practitioner" (chap. 3) questions whether the feminist theories that many of us hold dear (such as Rich's, Butler's or Anzaldua's) are actually productive grounds for feminist administration: Indeed, she provocatively argues that many of our best-loved feminist theories need to be revised given particular cultural locations and historical moments.

Part II. Performing WPA Work: Challenging Feminist Assumptions About Collaboration

Part II explores the role of collaboration in performing feminist writing program administration. In "Collaborative Writing Program Administration as Intellectual Inquiry" (chap. 4), Lynée Lewis Gaillet and Letizia Guglielmo (a tenured professor and a Ph.D. student/lecturer, respectively) argue that traditional feminist collaboration is a valid tactic for performing WPA work. Such collaboration, they argue, deemphasizes the service function of a first-year writing course and elevates the course as a site of knowledge-making for teachers, scholars, and administrators. More skeptical about feminist collaboration as it plays out between composition WPAs and literature TAs, Christine Farris (a tenured full professor) invokes in "The Maternal Melodrama of Writing Program Administration" (chap. 5) the Barbara Stanwyck character, Stella Dallas, as a trope representing the gendered and classed position of WPAs within literature-based English departments. Like good mothers, such WPAs may efface the disciplinary rigor of composition to smooth the way for first-time teachers, whose professionalization is then completed and claimed by colleagues in literature. To resist this Stella Dallas trope, Farris offers a collaborative model for WPAs and TAs that negotiates the aforementioned power differentials. Even more skeptical of collaboration than the two preceding articles, Ilene Crawford and Donna Strickland (both assistant professors who once were graduate student WPAs) claim in "Interrupting Collaboration: Feminist Writing Program Administration and the Question of Status" (chap. 6) that collaboration between faculty WPAs and graduate student WPAs, although useful, should be "tempered" by interruption, which they offer as a necessary trope for feminist administration in that it provides agency "to disrupt . . . the bureaucratizing of the affective." In "Three Models of Mentorship: Feminist Leadership and the Graduate Student WPA" (chap. 7), Julie Nelson Christoph, Rebecca S. Nowacek, Mary Lou Odom, and Bonnie Smith (all former graduate student WPAs) critique tensions that confront GWPAs and their collaborative work not just with faculty and undergraduate students, but also with nonadministrative graduate student peers. To negotiate such tensions, these coauthors also offer three tactics of mentoring: (a) friendship, (b) guidance, and (c) diplomacy.

Part III. Performing WPA Work: Challenging Institutional Assumptions about Gender and Agency

Part III demonstrates how performing feminist administration requires an agency for negotiating feminist and traditional assumptions about gender. In "A Tale of Two Tech Chicks: Negotiating Gendered Assumptions About Program Administration and Technology" (chap. 8), Amy C. Kimme Hea and Melinda Turnley (both assistant professors) reflect on their experiences not only as graduate student administrators, but also as tech chicks: From this dual position, they identify troubled intersections of administration and technology in WPA work, explaining that both sites have masculinist histories that have been subject to recent scholarly critiques. Within these dual critiques, Kimme Hea and Turnley offer WPAs (especially those less technologically savvy than they) ways to reimagine agency (i.e., ways to "complicate notions of technological mastery, which support deterministic, essentialist framings of agency and run counter to rhetorical, critical engagement with technology"). In "Managed Care: All-Terrain Mentoring and the 'Good Enough' Feminist WPA" (chap. 9), E. Shelley Reid (an assistant professor) defines how the intersections of her two administrative functions—untenured program director and teacher-mentor—intersect in ways that demand an agency for performing care. Consequently, she has learned to redefine *care*—"both personalized care and procedural justice"—in ways beneficial to both herself and the people she encounters daily. In "Defining Moments: The Role of Institutional Departure in the Work of a (Feminist) WPA" (chap. 10), Kathi Yancey (full professor) speaks across three different moments in her WPA career and reflects on the agency needed for institutional departure, which she defines as moments when she chose to leave not a WPA position, but an institution. She further reflects on the lessons learned from these moments, not the least of which being that such departures have "underscored [that] the agency I do have, . . . enhanced my work as a WPA, and through reflection, . . . brought a developing philosophy to my WPA work that in turn gives it a kind of coherence."

Part IV. Performing WAC and WC Work: Challenging Spaces in the University and in Feminist Theory

Part IV explores how performing feminist administration in WAC programs and in WCs provide sites for revising not only traditional spaces within the university, but also traditional spaces within feminist theory. In "'Where Else Should Feminist Rhetoricians Be?': Leading a WAC Initiative in a School of Business" (chap. 11), Kate Ronald, Cristy Beemer, and Lisa Shaver (tenured WAC director and graduate student assistant directors, respectively) contend that the tensions "between content and context, boldness and modesty, leading and serving" provide sites for articulating sometimes contentious relationships between feminism and administration, as exemplified by their WAC project at Miami University of Ohio. Moreover, they argue that traditionally masculinist sites, such as their business school, are precisely where feminist rhetoricians should be to challenge the means and ends of knowledge production at the university and in U.S. culture. In another challenge to masculinist traditions, in "Centered Women: Gender and Power in the Writing Center" (chap. 12), Carol Mattingly and Paula Gillespie (tenured writing center directors) revisit early notions of feminist theory, such as collaboration and nurturing, that undergird much early writing center work to argue that, in our current cultural moment, the writing center may serve as a site for extending "such early feminist values by complicating them and, perhaps, extending feminist principles into situations outside the writing center."

Part V. Performing Chair and Editorial Work: Challenging Institutional and Disciplinary Practices

Part V visits sites of administration other than WPA, WAC, and WC work where feminist administration may be performed in ways that revise institutional and disciplinary practices. In "Herding Cats: Feminist Practices and Challenges in Chairing an English Department" (chap. 13), Linda Hanson (a 13-year contract faculty who subsequently became a tenured faculty member and later chair of her department) discusses how the intersections of feminism, rhetoric, and writing pedagogy provided her with descriptors (e.g., *collaborative, inclusive, relational, faculty-centered, contextualized, dialogic, recursive, positive,* and *celebratory*) for feminist administration. These descriptors framed her work with colleagues to develop departmental community, reexamine departmental curriculum, and initiate more opportunities for faculty. Finally, in *"Computer and Composition Online:* Feminist Community and the Politics of Digital Scholarship" (chap. 14), Kristine Blair and Lanette Cadle (faculty journal editor and then graduate student assistant editor) explain how online journal editorship provides unique opportunities—via the submission process, active editing, and the promotion of open source scholarship—for feminist mentoring of men and women in their rhetoric and composition doctoral program at Bowling Green State University.

These chapters extend invitations for further research and online conversations. If you would like to contribute to these conversations, please visit our website at www.femadmin.org.

COMMON THREADS

When we reflected on common threads among contributors' chapters, we realized that the dominant trope for performing feminist administration is oxymoron—the ability to keep two contradictory ideas in one's mind and still function effectively. Although this trope is a time-honored definition of *intelligence*, as seen in Thomas Dewey's progressive theory of education, this collection demonstrates that oxymoron is also a time-honored presumption in performing feminist administration. Some oxymoronic linkages made by contributors focus on administrative mindsets: linking *grounding* and *flexibility* in feminist ethics, linking a *need for* and a *suspicion of* rhetorical theory as grounds for WPA work, and linking a *belief in* and a *skepticism about* existing feminist theories. Other oxymoronic linkages focus on administrative practices: linking *collaboration* and *interruption* in nonpeer administrative power dynamics, linking *silence* and *power* in women's gender-inflected identities, and linking *personal care* and *programmatic procedure* in faculty WPA's daily interactions with graduate and undergraduate students. The linkage that haunts all contributors' daily lives is the necessary linking of *mindsets* and *practices* (i.e., *talk* and *action*).

Together, contributors articulate oxymoronic linkages that expose troubled intersections of feminism and administration in rhetoric and composition studies. The contributors do not present these troubled intersections as failures or as opportunities for utopian solutions. Rather, they present these troubled intersections as sites of agency for challenging themselves, their colleagues, their students, their institutions, and the field of rhetoric and composition studies. Sometimes such challenges result in what the contributors consider productive results. Sometimes not. As such, this collection provides a rich, vital resource for graduate students, junior faculty, and senior faculty in rhetoric and composition studies. After all, scholar/teachers can administer only as well as we are prepared.

Ever aware of academic politics and the institutional constraints of promotion and tenure, contributors offer advice for navigating not just the competing demands of scholarship, teaching, service, and personal life, but also the troubled intersections of feminist principles and administrative practices—troubled intersections that arise when one performs feminist administration oxymoronically. Each chapter suggests that these three moves constitute actions becoming a feminist administration: (a) recognizing troubled intersections of feminism and administration, (b) struggling with these intersections, and (c) negotiating them again and again and again. Indeed, each contributor's performance suggests that these three moves constitute actions becoming a feminist administrator.

PART I

The Politics of Connecting Ethics, Theory, and Praxis

*Feminism has provided me with a great deal
of theoretical and practical support:
When I am in a tough situation, I ask myself
"what would a good feminist do?"
and that often gives me the answer.*

–Andrea Lunsford
(personal email)

1

WHAT'S ETHICS GOT TO DO WITH IT?

Feminist Ethics and Administrative Work in Rhetoric and Composition

Carrie Leverenz

A decade or so ago, when I was interviewing for my first academic job, I had an early lesson in the different ways one might view academic administration. It was a snowy day in early February, and I was being ushered around a large midwestern university by the English Department chair, a middle-aged man who was dressed in a full-length coat and drove a red sports car, very low to the ground. Although I wasn't interviewing for an expressly administrative job, it became clear during my visit that whoever they hired as an Assistant Professor of Composition would be expected to direct the writing program in short order. As a graduate student, I had done a fair bit of administrative work, and most of the colleges that interviewed me were clearly interested in my administrative experience. That was not a surprise. What did surprise me was the chair's casual attitude toward administration. "How hard is it to be Chair?" he asked, rhetorically. "All you have to do is figure out how to spend a million dollars." For my second lesson, fast forward 8 years and I am sitting across the desk from a Vice Provost trying to make my case that we should do a national search for a writing center director rather than advertise only locally. He tries hard to be sympathetic to my position while clearly preferring to fill the vacancy quickly. After all, he tells me, in his soothing Texas drawl, "What's administration but budget and personnel, budget and personnel?" More recently, a graduate student doing an independent study on writing program administration asked why the work we value so much is not always valued by the institutions for which we work. "We're the ones who make our jobs hard," I said. "What most institutions want writing program administrators to do is to put students in classes and hire teachers and deal with complaints. We're the ones who want to do more."

For feminist administrators, the urge to "do more" includes not just the goal of improving the programs for which we are responsible, but also the goal of changing the institution. This desire for change is not part of our official job description, but nevertheless informs the way we fulfill our official duties. If the institutions we worked in already operated on feminist principles, then such change would not be necessary. However, as the experiences I described earlier indicate, many academic administrators focus primarily on maintaining the status quo: staying on budget and hiring/firing personnel. If change is needed, it is most often depicted as a need for increased fiscal responsibility or an improvement in the national rankings. Although these changes might be beneficial, they are not the kinds of changes that feminists have historically advocated: social justice within (and without) institutions, valuing of difference, creation of programs that care for the whole person, and participatory forms of governance, especially the participation of those who have been systematically excluded or oppressed.

Administration, to the extent that it involves managing people with diverse needs and interests, necessarily involves ethics, the branch of moral philosophy that deals with the question of what constitutes right action toward others. In recent years, *ethics* has become a buzzword in many books and speeches about the role of the university. Perhaps in response to well-publicized critiques of higher education, books such as Rudolph H. Weingartner's *The Moral Dimensions of Academic Administration* have argued persuasively that institutions of higher education are ethically beholden to serve the public good, an implicit contractual obligation derived from their not-for-profit (and thus nontaxed) status (Weingartner 6–8). Weingartner acknowledges that prioritizing the public good can be difficult, in part, because universities are made up of professionals who value their autonomy. Academics are trained to think that they are doing good work when they advance their own careers and the knowledge base and status of their disciplines. Many academics would hesitate to describe themselves as part of a service profession.

Of course, many who end up in academic administration do so because they feel a professional responsibility or even a desire to serve others, but it does not take long to discover that the needs and interests of the multiple constituencies one serves often conflict. As Louise Wetherbee Phelps has pointed out, when WPAs, for example, must decide how to respond to the conflicting demands of students, teachers, the university, one's profession, and the community at large, they are operating in the arena of ethics ("Constrained"). Stuart Brown, in his essay "Applying Ethics: A Decision-Making Heuristic for Writing Program Administration," notes that "for contemporary WPAs, ethical conflicts dominate our professional lives" (157). Some obvious examples of ethical decision making include decisions about hiring and compensating writing teachers or the formulation of academic misconduct policies. Even such non-life-and-death matters as providing adequate computer resources or requiring instructors to use the same syllabus can present ethical challenges in regard to how best to meet people's needs. In each of these cases, an administrator's sense of the right thing to do may be constrained not only by competing interests of multiple constituencies, but also by tradition, by bureaucratic rules, and limited resources.

For the feminist administrator whose ethical principles may conflict with those of the still male-dominated, bureaucratic university, thinking too hard about the ethics of what she is asked to do may seem likely to lead not to a sense of agency and the potential for change, but to cynicism and despair.[1] As I argued in an earlier essay, however, theorizing about the ethics of our work can help save us from feelings of personal inadequacy as we come to a better understanding of the problem as one of conflicting ethical frameworks (Leverenz 113). By articulating our ethical principles — to ourselves as well as to others — we can begin to sketch out areas wherein we might act for change. Of course, talking about our administrative work in terms of ethics is likely to make others uncomfortable. In a meeting at my previous institution to discuss a proposal that would assign only new, untrained graduate TAs to tutor in the writing center I directed, I argued that it would be unethical to use the least prepared teachers to teach the least prepared students, at which moment I was immediately shut down by a senior male professor, who was indignant that I would call him unethical. I countered by saying that I was not calling him unethical, but merely stating what my ethical principles would not allow me to do. Although referring to the rightness or wrongness of actions in terms of ethics makes everything seem more personal, as a feminist administrator, taking our actions personally, taking personal responsibility for our actions, is necessarily a part of acting for change.

Feminist ethics, as a branch of feminist philosophy, comprises a large body of scholarship. My purpose here is not to present a comprehensive overview of feminist ethics theory, but rather to identify key tenets that might inform our administrative work.[2] Like all academic fields, the field of feminist philosophy is the scene of lively debate, making it impossible to state simply what it means to do feminist ethics. All of the contested issues within feminist theory—the nature of the female subject and of gender more broadly conceived, as well as the relation of gender to other social markers like race, class, sexual orientation, country of origin, and so on—have consequences for feminist ethics. Acknowledging that there is no single approach, Eve Browning Cole and Susan Coultrap-McQuin, in their introduction to *Explorations in Feminist Ethics*, nevertheless identify several characteristics of feminist ethics:

> [T]hey are grounded in a feminist perspective; they seek to challenge traditional, some would say "masculinist," moral assumptions; they frequently seek to reinterpret the moral significance of women's cultural experience as care-givers; they emphasize the importance of particularity, connection, and context; and they strive to reinterpret moral agency, altruism, and other relevant concepts from a feminist perspective. (2)

In the following, I discuss some of these principles in more detail as they apply to administration in Rhetoric and Composition.

STANDPOINT THEORY

It seems obvious to say that feminist administrators operate from a position that acknowledges the widespread oppression of women as a social group and seeks to overturn such oppression. Yet it is not so obvious to say what that means in actual administrative practice, where principles such as fairness and objectivity typically trump efforts to give support to members of a specific group. One WPA told me that she only recently realized that a lot of her responses to the teachers she supervises were affected by their gender. The fact that she realized the influence of the teacher's gender only after the fact, and that she felt vaguely uneasy about it, demonstrates how difficult it can be to bring together our feminist commitment to advance the interests of women and our administrative commitment to advance equally the interests of everyone whom we serve. Perhaps this is not surprising given that a focus on individual rights and equality have dominated discussion of ethics for hundreds of years. One important insight of feminist ethics is the recognition that any argument about ethical principles, even arguments about rights and equality, is necessarily an argument from a specific position. Moral values proposed to be universal or objective inevitably represent the values of the group proposing them; claims of universality typically come from dominant groups that think of themselves as the norm. In a well-known example, Carol Gilligan, in her 1982 volume, *In a*

Different Voice, exposed the way that Lawrence Kohlberg's moral development scale failed to apply to the women in her study not because the
women in her study were morally immature but because Kohlberg's scale
was derived from a study of White, male, Harvard students whom
Kohlberg likely thought of as the "norm" (or a norm that we should all
aspire to), but that clearly did not represent everyone.

This idea that there can be no universal moral code, that every moral
principle reflects a particular set of values and beliefs, is related to a controversial but still important idea within feminist philosophy, that of "standpoint" theory. Originally articulated as a critique of the ideal of objectivity
in science, feminist standpoint theory claims, in feminist philosopher of science Sandra Harding's terms, that "some kinds of social locations and
political struggles advance the growth of knowledge, contrary to the dominant view that politics and local situatedness can only block scientific
inquiry" (26). Nancy Hartsock, in "The Feminist Standpoint: Developing
the Ground for a Specifically Feminist Historical Materialism," identifies
five claims of standpoint theory:

> (1) Material life . . . not only structures but sets limits on the under-
> standing of social relations. (2) If material life is structured in funda-
> mentally opposing ways for two different groups, one can expect that
> the vision of each will represent an inversion of the others, and in sys-
> tems of domination the vision available to the rulers will be both partial
> and perverse. (3) The vision of the ruling class (or gender) structures
> the material relations in which all parties are forced to participate. . . .
> (4) In consequence, the vision available to the oppressed group must be
> struggled for. . . . (5) As an engaged vision, the understanding of the
> oppressed, the adoption of a standpoint exposes the real relations
> among human beings as inhuman, points beyond the present, and car-
> ries a historically liberatory role. (108)[3]

According to Harding, perhaps the most significant contribution of feminist standpoint theory is the commitment to "map the practices of power,
the way the dominant institutions and their conceptual frameworks create
and maintain oppressive relations" (31). As a principle of feminist ethics,
standpoint theory insists that we struggle to see how our views of ourselves, our work, and the work of the university have been shaped by those
in power, and that we then work to expose systems of oppression in the
university that benefit those in power at the expense of others. As Harding
puts it, "feminist standpoint projects are always socially situated and politically engaged in pro-democratic ways" (32). This commitment to making
institutions more democratic obviously extends to all oppressed groups:
people of color, underpaid workers, people whose religion or language or

sexual orientation leads to oppression by the dominant group. Feminist administrators have a special responsibility to identify the ways the university systematically limits the agency of these groups and to act for change. Again, such a responsibility is rarely in our job descriptions as WPAs or department chairs or deans. Indeed, our implicit responsibility to keep the machine running the way it has always run can seem to preclude such activism. Of course the desire to maintain business as usual is as much of an agenda as a desire to act for change.

Feminist standpoint theory, with its grounding in material conditions, also can inform administrative ethics to the extent that we acknowledge how our own experiences as women in the academy (not just our more general feminist commitments) inform our administrative practice. For example, those of us who have struggled to reconcile pregnancy, childbirth, maternity leave, and child care needs with life in the academy are uniquely situated to advocate for better policies. Hartsock warns against identifying the specific material conditions of some, but not all, women (e.g., pregnancy) as essential to a feminist standpoint, but she also notes that "[w]omen's activity as institutionalized has a double aspect—their contribution to subsistence, and their contribution to childrearing. Whether or not all of us do both, women as a sex are institutionally responsible for producing both goods and human beings and all women are forced to become the kinds of people who can do both" (113). Many institutions that lack adequate maternity leave policies do so on the grounds that such policies are unfair because not everyone is eligible for the benefit. Here is a classic case where the application of the principle of fairness results in the oppression of women who happen to be the sex that becomes pregnant, gives birth, and nurses infants. Is it fair that male academics do not have to choose between having an academic career and having a family? Yet without clear maternity leave policies or adjustments in the tenure clock, many academic women do feel compelled to delay or reject parenthood. Investigations of an institution's policies from a feminist standpoint can thus produce knowledge not possible from an "objective" point of view.

CARE

Perhaps the most frequently occurring term in feminist ethics theory is *care,* a term that officially entered feminist moral philosophy when Carol Gilligan concluded that the women she studied made moral decisions based on "an injunction to care" for others, rather than on "an injunction to respect the rights of others," as men often do (Gilligan, *In a Different Voice* 19). Nel Noddings, a philosopher of education, in her 1984 book, *Caring:*

A Feminine Approach to Ethics and Moral Education, goes beyond Gilligan's description of a specific group of women's moral experience to argue explicitly for the benefits of a moral education based on an ethics of care. Noddings identifies several key characteristics of an ethic of care. First, it is an act involving two actors — the "one caring" and the "cared for" (4). Second, it does not involve the application of general principles, nor can it be universalized. In Nodding's words, "my attention is not on judgment and not on the particular acts we perform but on how we meet the other morally" (5). Another feature of caring is that it involves the displacement of one's own interests and an attempt to apprehend the reality of another: "Caring is largely reactive and responsive" (14, 19). Caring also must be freely chosen; it cannot be coerced. As such, caring for another requires that one also care for oneself so that care for another can be for the other's sake and not for one's own sake. As Grace Clement notes, "unless a version of the ethic of care allows for the autonomy of the caregiver and the care recipient, the ethic of care will be deficient on moral and on feminist grounds" (21–2). When operating from an ethics of care, decisions and actions are thus motivated not by the protection of individual rights, the application of a universal principle like "fairness," nor by a calculation of the greatest good for the greatest number of people, but by the desire to act in a caring way toward this person or group at this particular time in this particular context. As a result, as Noddings notes, actions motivated by an ethics of care will vary from one instance to another: "Variation is to be expected if the one claiming to care really cares, for her engrossment is in the variable and never fully understood other, in the particular other, in a particular set of circumstances" (24).

Like standpoint theory, the "ethics of care" has not been without its critics. Although one goal of feminist ethics is to take into better account the lived experiences of women (which for many involves caregiving responsibilities), Noddings' concept of "care" has come under fire from feminists who accuse her of identifying caring as an (inherently) feminine behavior without considering the degree to which women have been socialized into their caregiver roles for the benefit of a patriarchal system. Nodding has defended her ethic of care by arguing that caring is not an inherently female quality and that both men and women need a moral education that teaches them to care. What has been widely accepted by feminists is Noddings' insistence that, rather than grounding moral decisions in abstract or general principles, ethical decisions should be made in the context of specific human relationships where feelings, not just rationality, play a key role (Cole and Coultrap-McQuin 2). Feminists committed to large-scale social change have questioned the feasibility of an ethic of care for national and international action given its focus on local and individual caring relationships. But scholar Sara Ruddick shows how an ethics of care could be relevant globally by using the concept of what she calls *maternal thinking* as the basis of a critique of militarism and war. Similarly, Joan Tronto extrapolates four elements of care—attentiveness, responsibility, competence, and responsiveness—that she believes can serve as the basis of ethical actions on a larger scale (Maihofer 390)

Granted, many feminist administrators already think of themselves as motivated by a caring attitude toward those whom they supervise and with whom they interact. Yet an ethics of care demands more; it demands that care be the dominant term in all of our interactions with others. For example, think of what it would mean to enact a plagiarism policy that is informed by an ethics of care. It means that rather than applying a straight rule—using the words of others without documentation results in an F in the course—each case must be considered individually, taking into account who the student is and what kind of work he or she has been doing, what the circumstances are around the specific instance of plagiarism, who the teacher is, what kind of assignment she has given, and what kind of teaching she has done. Whatever administrative decision is made by the WPA must balance care for the student's interests with care for the teacher and also must take into account the responsibility to care for the other students in the class. A plagiarism policy based on an ethics of care might result in different penalties for what looks like the same infractions, a move that, ironically, can appear unethical to those who believe one should objectively apply a universal principle. When we imagine an ethics of care on a larger scale, such as in tenure and promotion cases, it becomes clear how difficult this change would be in many institutions. Gone would be the single standard of a scholarly monograph and in its place would be a more complex assessment of professional work that might vary dramatically from person to person. Obviously, it is easier to apply an ethics of care in arenas where we as feminist administrators have primary responsibility and much harder in larger arenas where we must persuade others—our nonfeminist peers or upper administration—to act on the basis of an ethics of care. Yet our commitment to change motivates us to make just such arguments.

THE CONCRETE OTHER

Feminist ethics theorists have been influenced by multiculturalism and poststructuralism and by the work of lesbian feminists and women of color to see gender as only one category of difference that intersects with race, class, sexual orientation, nation, and so on, to produce a complex array of subject positions that are hierarchically arranged. Thus feminist ethics questions not just the immorality of gender oppression, but other kinds of oppression as well. In addition to countering oppression against groups marked as culturally different, feminists have also sought ways to value difference in the process of moral decision making. As Margaret Urban Walker noted, "Differently situated people will tend to have different moral problems or experience similar ones differently" (368). Feminist philosopher Seyla Benhabib likewise seeks an ethics that attends to differences in individual perspectives, but she also believes that such an ethics can result in universal principles that everyone can recognize as applicable to them. Benhabib rejects ethical theories that claim individuals can reason from some objective position outside of their personal history. She also rejects those theories that claim we can consider the perspectives of some "generalized other" by placing ourselves behind what philosopher John Rawles calls a "veil of ignorance," wherein we reason about moral principles by setting aside our actual social positions.

According to Benhabib, the setting aside of one's social position when theorizing about ethics is neither possible nor desirable because, "for the democratic citizen and economic agent, the moral issues that touch her most deeply arise in the personal domain" (Benhabib 185). At the same time, communities cannot be good or just if individuals consider only their personal interests. Rather than trying to imagine what it is like to be "the other," Benhabib insists that processes be put into place whereby differing voices engage in conversations about what will be shared moral principles. In her words,

> Neither the concreteness nor the otherness of the "concrete other" can be known in the absence of the voice of the other. The viewpoint of the concrete other emerges as a distinct one only as a result of self-definition. It is the other who makes us aware both of her concreteness and her otherness. Without engagement, confrontation, dialogue and even a "struggle for recognition" in the Hegelian sense, we tend to constitute the otherness of the other by projection and fantasy or ignore it in indifference. (167–8)

Such ethical processes of communication, referred to as communicative ethics or discourse ethics, depend on two conditions, according to Benhabib:

> (1) that we recognize the right of all beings capable of speech and action to be participants in the moral conversation—I will call this the *principle of universal moral respect*; (2) these conditions further stipulate that within such conversations each has the same symmetrical rights to various speech acts, to initiate new topics, to ask for reflection about the presuppositions of the conversation, etc. Let me call this the *principle of egalitarian reciprocity*. (Benhabib 29)

Perhaps the most obvious way to apply the principle of the concrete
other—with its instantiation via the principles of universal moral respect
and egalitarian reciprocity—is to include representatives of all affected constituencies in decision-making procedures. Especially important is the
inclusion of voices typically excluded. In how many institutions, for example, are adjunct instructors given any say in the policies that govern their
work? Adjuncts rarely have voting rights or serve on committees that
choose textbooks, design curriculum, set policies for instructors or students, and so on. Even more rare is the presence of adjuncts on committees
that determine adjunct salaries or benefits. Although feminist administrators can support unionization and collective bargaining for contingent
labor and other workers, in the absence of such efforts or even in institutions where such efforts have already been successful, they can still advocate for the inclusion of all voices. What about students? Should student
representatives also be included in the making of policies that affect them?
It seems that they should. Furthermore, working to include the voice of the
"concrete other" is not always a matter of seeking out the obviously
excluded. At one institution where I worked, the two tenure-track faculty
who served as the WPA and WC director and who together were responsible for training and supervising more than 100 graduate TAs were replaced
by the Dean with staff lines that did not have departmental voting rights,
thus giving these new administrators little say in a department where they
played an essential role. Given the difficulty of making any policy changes
in large state institutions, it would be tempting to simply denounce this situation as unfortunate but unchangeable. Yet feminist administrators' commitment to change, to care, and to include the voices of those "othered" by
the institution demands that we work against such policies.

All of us know women—or have been those women—trapped in
administrative roles whose agency is structurally limited. Recognizing these
limits as a form of oppression that benefits those in power, as standpoint
theory suggests, is a first step. Finding allies, especially feminist allies, willing to work for change is another. For administrators in such a position,
assuming as much agency as one can—asking to attend meetings, to be
informed about decisions, offering an opinion on issues that affect one's
work while continuing to make arguments about changing one's official
status—is another important step. Obviously, feminist administrators with
more agency (e.g., tenure) have a heightened responsibility to advocate for
increased agency for others even in the face of staunch resistance. In one
liberal arts college where I worked as both an adjunct and a full-time
instructor, a feminist chair worked hard to give part-time teachers voting
rights in the department. The transition wasn't easy for anyone. Part timers
(several of whom had worked in that capacity for 20 years) were used to
being excluded from department business and thus felt awkward attending

meetings and were hesitant to speak. Tenure-track faculty who had opposed their inclusion ignored their presence. But over time, having a vote gave those part-time teachers a reason to take positions on important department issues, and knowing that part timers could vote against their proposals made tenure-track faculty pay attention to the needs and interests of part-time teachers.

PROCESS

Postmodern theory also has had an impact on feminist ethics. If we accept the challenge that postmodernism poses to ethical reasoning, according to Zygmunt Bauman, then we must accept that postmodern ethics are characterized by (a) an inability to believe in the possibility of a nonambivalent moral code, (b) accepting that there are no innate moral principles, and (c) recognizing that moral decisions are often made in the face of contradictory impulses. In Bauman's view, modernist attempts to reason out an ethical dilemma by dividing it into parts, seeking agreement on terms and the rules that should apply in a particular case, result in an oversimplification of the kinds of complex moral problems we need to act on in the real world (9–11). For Bauman, however, the absence of universal or foundational principles of moral action does not mean a descent into relativism. Although postmodern ethics teaches that, whatever we do, we will never know that we are "right," the absence of certainty requires that we be even more ethically sensitive in the process of making decisions and reflecting on the consequences of those decisions.

Margaret Urban Walker makes explicit connections between postmodern and feminist ethics when she notes the degree to which feminist epistemologies "reject foundationalism that posits given, self-evident, or incorrigible bases of justification" and "urge us instead to examine actual practices of forming and fixing beliefs . . ." (368). Walker adds that this process of examining moral beliefs should be exercised in the context of groups, rather than by individuals alone. In her words, "Feminist ethics profits from viewing moral knowledge as a communal product and process constructed and sustained in interactions among people, rather than an individually action-guiding theory within people" (369). One goal of a feminist process of ethical decision making, then, beyond the inclusion of multiple points of view (especially less privileged points of view), is to make the process as transparent as possible. This may mean something as simple as reporting to constituents how decisions are made (and by whom) as well as what decisions are made. When I was in graduate school, graduate students were chosen to serve as senior faculty's administrative and research assistants by an unknown process that seemed to involve being plucked by some invisible hand into these privileged positions. Although as a graduate student I benefited from this invisible process, I had many competent friends who complained bitterly that they were never asked to serve in these prestigious roles. When I suggested that faculty write job descriptions, solicit applications, and conduct interviews, one faculty member expressed concern that she would then have to reject people, as if choosing a research assistant through an invisible process wasn't also a rejection of everyone else who was interested in the job. Although inclusive, transparent decision-making processes do make administrators more accountable for their decisions, it is this process of being accountable that makes the decision ethical, not just the outcome of the decision.

Equally important in a feminist process of ethical decision making is the commitment to revisit decisions to determine their effects and to make changes where necessary. In Walker's words, "This [process] allows us to see what our terms and arrangements really are, what it takes to sustain them, how their costs are distributed, and how habitable is the common life to which they lead, for people variously placed within it" (370). Although we as individuals can certainly reflect on the consequences of our decisions, Seyla Benhabib would remind us that doing so in the absence of those who are affected places us in danger of projecting, distorting, or ignoring the actual experience of those concrete others. Realistically, we cannot spend every minute of our day consulting everyone about how our decisions affect them, but we can build in regular opportunities for constituencies to respond to our efforts through staff meetings, surveys, and formal evaluations of our administrative work.

CHALLENGES TO FEMINIST ADMINISTRATION

It would be unethical to espouse these principles of feminist administrative ethics without also considering the difficulties—and risks—one is likely to face when attempting to enact them. First and most obviously, feminist administrative practice is complicated by institutional(ized) assumptions about what good administrators are like, assumptions based primarily on masculinist models. Although WPAs and others who work primarily with students and instructors who have the least power are frequently women, WPAs continue to struggle to see their administrative work valued, making them especially vulnerable to unstated assumptions about how the job should to be done. In 10 years of administration work at two different universities, my administrative work has never been formally evaluated in the way that teaching evaluations and peer-reviewed publications constitute criteria-driven evaluations of those other important parts of my job. Evaluations of the various chairs and deans under whom I have served also have been infrequent and informal and have not been based on explicit criteria. This evidence indicates that evaluation of administrative work often depends on local assumptions (or the assumptions of the next administrator up the ladder) about how to do that work effectively.

For example, in "Who's the Boss?: The Possibilities and Pitfalls of Collaborative Administration for Untenured WPAs," Eileen Schell describes the difficulties of enacting feminist administrative principles in the context of sharing administrative responsibilities with a male colleague, an experience that exposed unstated assumptions about how administrative work should be conducted. For example, the autonomous and authoritative decision making of her male colleague seemed to him to be more efficient than the process of taking the time to "mull over decisions and get multiple opinions" that Schell preferred (75).

Another problem that Schell experienced as a codirector is that students, teachers, and other administrators continued to see her as the primary caregiver of the composition program. As Schell reports,

> [G]ender stereotyping played a role in the perception that I was more nurturing and approachable and that I participated in reinforcing that stereotype with my attentive, caretaking behaviors. Feminist educational theorists and sociologists . . . have argued that such gendered response and role constructions often place academic women (especially untenured women) in the "double bind" of taking on disproportionate service and mentoring obligations when most need to be engaged in developing their own scholarship and teaching. ("Costs" 75)

As another female WPA put it in a survey on gender differences in writing program administration: "It's not so much our lack of status as our female conditioning to be very service-oriented, placating, and caring. These qualities cause us to attract responsibility, not rewards" (Barr-Ebest 66). Not only do these qualities cause us to attract responsibility, they also can lead to a loss of respect and authority in institutional cultures where being firm, tough, and independent are more highly valued as leadership qualities than are collaboration and caring. As Schell notes, the extra time and energy required to play the care-giver role inevitably takes time and energy away from the teaching and research that are often the more valued (or more rigorously evaluated) parts of our job, which is especially problematic for untenured administrators ("Costs" 74–5).

A second challenge to a feminist ethics of administration may come in the form of resistance from those concrete others whom we seek to include for their benefit and the benefit of the program. For teachers who have never been permitted to choose their own textbooks or design their own syllabus, the responsibility can be daunting. An increase in responsibility—even if it means more agency—typically results in more work. Adjunct instructors or graduate TAs who have been socialized by their lack of choice to put limited thought into their teaching may balk at what we deem to be a valuable freedom. Similarly, for low-paid workers who must supplement their incomes by teaching at various places, often at a distance from each other, the sudden invitation to serve on a committee or collaborate on a project may be perceived as simply more work without more compensation. In "Lessons of the Feminist Workplace," Louise Wetherbee Phelps discusses the complex challenge of creating a writing program based on feminist principles, during which time she experienced just such a reaction from those she supervised. As she describes it, "Many teachers in my program were angry, anxious, and resistant to expectations for professionalization" (312). She goes on to remark that,

> every aspect of my vision of a writing program as utopian project is questionable (and was immediately questioned) as both impractical and at least potentially unethical. In treating teachers as moral agents—adults—and providing opportunities for curricular control and leadership, I exposed them, perhaps involuntarily, to new risks and pressures while possibly exploiting their capabilities and energy without adequate reward. (313)

Even when disempowered employees embrace the offer of greater agency, the move can still be problematic. For example, I have known instructors hired into temporary positions who have been eager to participate in program or departmental service in the hopes that being a good citizen would increase their chances of being hired permanently, although no such opportunity existed. In this context, they would have been better off spending their extra time doing things that would help them get a permanent position, which in the current job economy means publishing. When there is no immediate chance that an instructor's working conditions can be improved, we should be careful how we articulate the benefits of fuller participation. Instead of requiring attendance at meetings (unless a stipend can be offered), we might instead ask for participation in the form of a survey or an e-mail exchange. We also can invite participation that will benefit contingent faculty in ways they value. If a part-timer wishes to advance her career or if professional development counts for merit evaluation, inviting contingent faculty to lead a workshop or participate in a conference panel may benefit them more than requiring attendance at workshops we lead. That means, of course, making an effort to know what kind of career each person we supervise wants. Even as we seek to include those with different experiences and perspectives, we need to be especially mindful of differing material conditions as well.

A third force working against the enactment of feminist administrative ethics can be our own assumptions about how to be a good administrator. As Amy Goodburn and I suggested in an earlier essay, sometimes it is the "bureaucrat within" that is the feminist administrator's worst enemy (Goodburn and Leverenz 290). In *As If Learning Mattered*, Richard Miller argued that it is naive to think that as administrators we can act for change within institutions without acknowledging that we are bureaucrats whose job it is to do the institution's bidding, which Miller argues is essentially bureaucratic work. We are not independent agents or resistance fighters but employees—often tenured, permanent employees. In his discussion of the disillusionment that many successful academics feel, Miller notes how James Scott's *Domination and the Arts of Resistance* applies: "If such a thing as 'false consciousness' may be said to exist, it is to be found not among the disenfranchised, as theories of dominant ideology would have us believe, but among those who have risen through the educational system and have come to believe deeply in its values" (R. Miller, *As If* 195). Having become successful academics and having been deemed worthy of leadership roles means we likely know a good deal about how to do what is asked of us and have thus inevitably internalized at least some of the institution's bureaucratic values. For example, when a faculty member at my graduate institution was denied tenure, in part, because most of his scholarship was collaborative, one of my feminist colleagues commented that, because he knew collaboration was going to be a problem, he should have done less collaborative work. This from a woman who had published collaboratively, had written a dissertation on collaboration, and espoused its value. As feminist administrators, we must be ever aware of this tension between our need to be successful in traditional terms and our desire to change those terms. It takes courage and vision to turn away from established measures of success and define success differently—to find as much satisfaction in achieving voting rights for part timers or establishing a more inclusive decision-making process as we do in that teaching award or publication in a prestigious journal.

If feminist philosophers like Margaret Urban Walker are right, and knowledge is created communally rather than individually, it follows that effective feminist work depends not on a single feminist administrator's actions, but on the actions of a network of others with shared interests. If no such group exists on your campus, consider creating one. Teach a women's studies course. Start a women's reading group. It is equally important to connect with other feminist administrators or academics outside your institution to share war stories (is there a less masculinist metaphor?) and to get an outsider's perspective on your own situation as well as to explore models of feminist administration in place elsewhere. Finally, continue to read and theorize about feminist ethics. It can be both comforting and motivating to see your concerns reflected in the words of others, but it also is important to continue honing your own process of critical reflection by exploring how current theories of feminist ethics do and should inform your administrative work.

2

CHECKING THE SOURCE(BOOK)

Supplemental Voices
in the Administrative Genre

Jeanne Gunner

In writing about the politics of performing feminist administration, a critical challenge is to resist the conventionally administrative approach to writing about administration. Such writing, cued by what can be identified as the administrative genre, is typically framed within a rhetoric that smoothes over questions otherwise raised by political and feminist critiques. The conventional rhetoric of administration tends strongly to the monological, the linear, and the teleological, and, in so doing, references and reaffirms a normative and model-bound epistemology. Hewing to its conventional models, the administrative genre privileges abstraction over the complexities of local material conditions. The sourcebooks, resources, and problem-solving guides that embody the administrative genre direct those who write within it to assume and reproduce an ahistorical space and a politics of political cleansing, leading to a utopian valorization of seamlessness, transparency, and a uniform *sensus communis*. A Platonic impulse tempered by an Aristotelian method: In the rhetoric of the administrative genre, the truth emerges from material experience cleansed of the individuating, stripped to an essence that is then posited as *the* essence within particular local conditions. The case study. The scenario. The problem–solution framework. The decision-making heuristic. Guidelines, statements, principles, and standards.

In this generic approach, material conditions are seen as concealing truth: "The empirical nature of administrative situations, decisions, and repercussions makes the case study quite suited for instructional purposes. There are no certainties, exact answers, or clean results" (Myers-Breslin xvi). Some ultimate truth, unsullied by the real, lies beyond the local: "Thus, readers seeking wisdom about administration will gain much from this approach, an approach that attempts to develop and understand the universal principles by a close examination of particular cases" (xvi). Even as it is mined, the local takes on a vaguely threatening power to engulf, and the appeal of its difference is to be tempered by larger community values: "While we should recognize that each situation is unique in its context and participants, we must also recognize the commonalities that unite us and the principles that guide us" (Carpenter 6). Some implied master discourse is at work, most obviously so where sourcebook authors struggle to resist invoking it. In the introduction to their edited collection, *The Writing Program Administrator's Resource: A Guide to Reflective Institutional Practice*, Stuart C. Brown and Theresa Enos write: "The nature of writing program administration is inclusive [. . . .] To encompass these sometimes competing roles requires people of unique character and training" (xvii–xviii). This uniqueness meets prior fixed practices, however, that compete with the value of difference:

> [. . .] We sought to develop a collection of articles [. . .] that would address fundamental practices and issues encountered by WPAs in their workplace settings. We felt that new WPAs especially need practical, applicable tools to effectively address the many differing, and sometimes competing, roles they find themselves in [. . . .] We found ourselves returning time and again to the recognition that WPAs come in all sizes, shapes, and colors. [. . .] (xvii-xviii)

The perception of heterogeneity runs counter to the generic conventions, and the generic convention of a dominant, instrumentalist model of the field is at odds with the competing desire to recognize and value the individual and local: "[The term] *Handbook* never felt quite right—too suggestive of brief, alphabetized entries. At various points, we considered calling the book an *encyclopedia* or a *field guide* or a *sourcebook* [. . .]. These genres, however, seemed too prescriptive" (xvii–xviii). The editors settle on/for the term "Resource" and the subtitle "Guide." The unique character and training of the individual is subsumed to established practice. The need for the tool and the law, the prescriptive, a patriarchal, normalizing impulse, takes precedence over the desire for diversity and inclusiveness. The bureaucrat within subsumes the ethic of care (Goodburn and Leverenz).

This conflict of parental models is not surprising given that a common warrant for the administrative genre is professional mentoring. The administrative genre intends to mentor those new to rhetoric-composition, guiding them along a natural professional path to administration, schooling them in the traditional curriculum of administration. Its precepts intended for edification of the young require a stable world, and so the genre seeks to erase the tensions and complexities of the political realities in which individuals are enmeshed. The ability to assume an untroubled authority and suppress difference are taken as hallmarks of professional maturity:

> "Trust yourself. You know more than you think you do," begins Dr. Benjamin Spock's *Baby and Child Care*, with the words that helped make this compendium of useful advice an American classic for half a century. [. . .]
>
> Handbooks of all sorts, whether manuals on how to rear children or repair cars or use standard grammar and mechanics or administer writing programs, are for newcomers—the uncertain, the insecure—as well as the confident who need a ready reference. [. . .]
>
> [. . .] Because the authors are experts, in the spirit of all handbooks, they straighten out the snarls and offer sensible solutions to the problems; they make even the most complicated of processes seem doable, the most convoluted of conflicts seem manageable. They proffer access, authority, and plans of action. (Bloom, "Moving Forward" ix–x)

The expedients of efficiency and efficaciousness rise above concern for inclusiveness and diversity as the best professional values. With the political administrative commonplace that the responsible, mature administrator is one who learns to work within the system to manage and reduce complexity established within a perpetuating genre, this political position is then allied with rhetorical expertise. Such expertise becomes a resource to be exploited. Through its mentoring warrant, the administrative genre thus promotes a rhetoric of efficiency and efficacy.

A version of Stanley Fish's "theory's hope" or the belief that theoretical projects can provide agency, the result is "rhetoric's hope," a belief in the smooth efficacy of the rhetorical. Fish charges that "[t]his kind of work—massive, encyclopedic, (rhetorically) magisterial—is as empty as it is ambitious and fails where it most wants to succeed: as a predictor and shaper of the future" (376). The very basis for the claim of the rhetoricity of administration is this plasticity of a universal administrative wisdom. Allying rhetorical expertise and administration neatly fits with uncritical efficiency and efficaciousness. Rhetorically adept administrators are not charged with critiquing, revising, or displacing the inequities of a system; they are promised instead enhanced likelihood of professional success within it. Critique and change become background concerns or deprivileged elements. The administrative guide first offers models that are abstracted from the local and material and, second, and contradictorily, strategies that are intended to reforge this erased connection to influence real-world situations. The process of abstraction-application erases the material realities of gender, race, class, sexual orientation, and unequal power relations of all orders. The problems that then constitute the work of administration have been vetted, and only those consistent with the prevailing norms merit case study status. Caught within a closed system of problem definition, rhetorical approaches to administration promise not to interrupt the normalizing function of the administrative genre.

"Models immobilize; that is their purpose, and that is the pleasure they provide" (Worsham 90): The administrative genre can perhaps be said to operate from an erotics of administration, if a perverse one—a patriarchal system that plays to the desire for stability and control. It rises above the individual body and its material conditions and promises the pleasures of a disembodied moral order. It is different from a masculinist administrative erotics, which is centered on the pleasure of power, domination, and hierarchy, evident in the metaphors of casual cruelty that typify its discourse— "Oh him, he's not a problem, we can hold his feet to the fire"; "Let him try it—he'll be cutting off his own hands"; we'll "break the back" of this proposal; and we'll "shoot that one down." Such comments, taken from my own staff meeting notes, map the world in familiar ways and reflect a familiar ideology historically tied to the White male body. The erotics of the WPA administrative genre resists a material orientation, attempting to arrive at an idealized equality above actual material conditions, constituting a faux-feminist utopian agenda that operates within the patriarchal.

An experienced author of the administrative genre, I write not as some innocent who seeks a more morally and politically correct status set against the complicitous. My work appears in sourcebook and resource, which means I have modeled, essentialized, and systematized, cleansing the representations of administration of temporal, political, and cultural depth. The genre calls for this—it calls it out. How might we write or act differently as an administrator—performing the administrator as supplement, a voice of "subversion and social critique," a "soul in limbo" introducing "ambiguity and tentativeness" (Janangelo 12-14) into administrative work, "interrupting" (Crawford and Strickland, chap. 6, this volume) its essentializing discourse? I am not seeking to correct or condemn the writing of others in this genre, nor to repudiate my own, but to find the ambiguities, to interrupt serene narratives of administrative wisdom and success, to introduce a note of tentativeness to phallogocentric claims of administrative modeling, the sourcebook as "a bible for writing program administrators" (Olson, "Foreword" ix). This is an attempt not to theorize a feminist administrative utopia, which seems inevitably to require a denial of history and presentness in a material moment. Instead, I am in search of supplemental ways of being in administrative roles—ways of "thickening" the conventional instrumentalist approaches. To hear "for whom?" in narratives of "what works"; to recuperate the "scattered practices" (de Certeau 48) that can render the hegemonic more visible; to recognize the spatialness as well as the linearity of the moment; to be grounded in daily political struggles (Cushman); and to perform administrative work at the borderlands that overlap the center.

Resist stopping at reflection. Many of the essays in the administrative genre call for conscious reflection on administrative work. *Reflection* is a problematic term. It suggests repetition within a system of representation. By itself it seems not to provide a means of interrupting the system. It remains specular; it does not provide for restructuring the antecedent. It promises a multiplicity whose variation lies still within a closed system. Consider Louise Phelps' essay, "Turtles All the Way Down: Educating Academic Leaders," in *The Writing Program Administrator's Resource: A Guide to Reflective Institutional Practice*. This essay illustrates the difficulties of reflective administrative narratives that depend on a model in which apparent differences are ultimately ordered by a relational structure, cleansing the administrative scene of history and politics.

Throughout the essay, Phelps invokes an ecological, dialogical, activity system notion of administrative knowledge. Addressing the issue of professionalization, for example, one topic in a broader discussion of administrative leadership, Phelps emphasizes the value of "local, context-dependent, impermanent knowledge" ("Turtles" 14):

> At any historical moment when paradigms are unstable, there are not two but many ideas and ideals in play, including both normative and distorted versions of established ideologies and their utopian counterparts. By adopting a strictly dichotomous approach to professionalism and power with graduate students, we misrepresent the complexity of the environment they are entering and predetermine their choice between stereotyped oppositions, instead of encouraging the open-minded inquiry that would develop more nuanced positions and unfold heterogeneous, unforeseen options for participation and identity. (16)

This heterogeneity of knowledge and experience is subject to an organizing system, however, a leadership model fashioned as a "fractal structure, with irregular patterns of leadership repeated at smaller and smaller scales of organization" (5). In an effort to become "equal partners in reform rather than futile resisters or passive objects of it," faculty must "[develop leadership] programs designed to operate seamlessly throughout a faculty career from graduate school to senior leadership roles" (4). Heterogeneity is to be at once accommodated and managed by the plasticity of the heuristic; the

fractal model promises to provide "an integrated practical model for developing leaders that addresses the full range of needs, settings, and interde-
pendencies implied in a fractal theory of leadership" (6).

Phelps acknowledges that the administrative leadership model she supports is not intended to be a means of resistance. She has interrupted narratives that treat the use of power as always the equivalent of oppression and
has championed the idea of the responsible use of power within institutions. Her essay calls for "workable concepts of legitimate authority and
constructive power" that can lead to "ways to understand the morality of
power, like technology or rhetoric, as not intrinsic but lying in its contextual definition, distribution, and use. What is needed is an ethical ideal that
envisions responsible, strong leadership as a conceptual possibility, not an
oxymoron" ("Turtles" 19). What remains problematic is the separation of
an ideal of leadership—a model or even "multi-modal models" (8)—from
the system for which they serve as tools of reproduction. The fractal model
as it is treated in the essay seems to float above historically specific and
material conditions of a particular field, location, and era, rendering difference as always *only* local. An overarching system towers above the particu-
larity of the historical moment, the embodied instance. One result is valorization of a fractal equality: The leadership, the power, of one position
exists in emblematic relation to power exercised at all parts of the institution. Some may be situationally and temporally more equal than others, but
even such power-heterogeneous participation can, in this model, be seen as
constructing a valid system of power sharing. As an abstraction, the fractal
model allows for multiplicity, a "friendly pluralism" (Villanueva 263) forming a unified mosaic. It is not unlike a representative democracy, with
power theoretically spread throughout the members even as it is locally
concentrated in elected officials. Unfortunately, it is also not unlike totali-
tarian structures (*Arbeit Macht Frei*), colonized lands (the jewels in the
crown), and the subordinated female (submit graciously to your husband).
The claim in each case has been that the subordinates share power through
their subordination in the power of the system that engulfs them. The fractal model, in material form, is as likely to sponsor overt or velvet domination as union organizing. In its synthesizing claim, it deploys a political
self-cleansing mechanism through the dismissal of particular inequities as
too local, too idiosyncratic, to be meaningful.

This cleansing function applies to both the model administrator and the
viewpoint of his or her subject. Individual difference from the model is to
be suppressed in accounts of administration. Further, the model implies a
mechanism of self-surveillance:

> I think university administration is an honorable profession. Most of
> the administrators I have worked for and with are very smart folks,
> trying their best to make the institution a better place with increasingly

limited resources. [. . .] Of course, there are some university administrators who ought not to be in that position, who by virtue of the Peter
Principle have reached their level of incompetence or who are more
interested in their own careers than in the good of the institution [. . . .]
But if you really feel that *all* administrators are by virtue of their positions difficult, devious and unethical, then certainly you shouldn't consider being one. (If you really feel that way, my guess is that you will
also have difficulty working with administrators as a WPA.) (McCleod
114-15)

Difficulty, conflict, resistance: these are anti-efficacy. Or they may be naturalized as inevitable working parts of activity systems: "While acknowledging conflict, difference, inequity, fractured purpose, and self-interested
motive in the play of activity, we can eschew binaric, static theories of
power and instead teach WPAs how to see themselves as vital centers of
energy within networks of numerous participants in power" (Phelps,
"Turtles" 28). As Crawford and Strickland argue in relation to collaborative administrative models, difference and conflict are "undesirable" elements problematically foregrounded in materialist analyses of administration. Difference and conflict work against the ideal of seamlessness and
transparency, the untroubled realm of the *sensus communis*.

Model-making of this sort, with which the administrative genre is so
replete, is one reason for the conventional ahistorical discourse of administration. In *The Practice of Everyday Life*, Michel de Certeau argues that the
"objects of our research cannot be detached from the intellectual and social
'commerce' that organizes their definition and their displacements" (45–46).
Building models requires the extraction and abstraction of practices, with
the effect that they claim an efficaciousness that is illusory and mask their
role in reproducing the system they claim to change. The desire to make
difference and conflict an unthreateningly dissonant part of a larger har-
monic pattern is an ahistoricizing move. Phelps calls for us to move beyond
dualistic thinking, represented by the literature–composition split, for
instance, because "outside our own 'academic village' this question is fundamentally boring, parochial, and essentially a matter of academic turf. . . . I
would like to get to genuine questions about how writing program administrators can work within institutions to enhance education" ("Institutional
Logic" 157). Labeled as a professionally local binary, the material inequalities that result from the historically unequal professional status of literature
and composition are reconfigured as only material and can only bog down
the effort to work at the level of the model. Foregrounding the complexity
of the local threatens to interrupt the truth of the model: "The more contingency, the less predictability, and the less power an axiomatically derived
theory possesses. Thus the instinct of theoreticians is usually to explain
away contingency and, with it, eventful temporality" (Morson 620).

In "Taking Dictation," Donna Strickland demonstrates how "the 'feminization' of composition teaching [. . .] functions to empower some and disempower others" (46): It "signals a complex intersection of cultural values, a process that tends to relegate women to the lowest levels of the academic hierarchy while simultaneously elevating the primarily white, native-born teachers as keepers of correctness and racial propriety" (470). The administrative genre participates in this process by misrecognizing its pedagogic function as a feminist move and by allying itself with the administrative equivalent of mechanical correctness, the universal truths of the sourcebook/resource guide.

Can we imagine instead an administrative *écriture feminine?* How might we write about the politics of administration in ways that recognize material complexity, the historical nature of experience, and the temporality of space and occasion? How might we mobilize a rhetoric for an administrative *new mestiza,* in Gloria Anzaldúa's terms, who "learns to juggle cultures," who "operates in pluralistic mode—nothing is thrust out, the good the bad the ugly, nothing rejected, nothing abandoned. Not only does she sustain contradictions, she turns the ambivalence into something else" (79)? How can we compose outside the sourcebook, recognizing, in Audre Lorde's words, the illogic of working from within the normative system it reinforces:

> What does it mean when the tools of a racist patriarchy are used to examine the fruits of that same patriarchy? It means that only the most narrow perimeters of change are possible and allowable [. . . .] *For the master's tools will never dismantle the master's house.* They may allow us temporarily to beat him at his own game, but they will never enable us to bring about genuine change. (110–12)

The conventional administrative genre collections have a place in the market, first, and in the WPA culture, and simple resistance or rejection is an unhelpful binarized response. Perhaps more hopeful and helpful is what might be called a *rhetorical supplement*—a strategy of reading and administering.

Those of us who are "in" administration—and all of us subject(s) of/to administration—are well—and inevitably—positioned to "thicken" the discourse of administration, to layer into local conversations, exchanges, policies, and practices alternative discourses that help supplement, and perhaps in instances, disestablish the claims of administrative discourse as programmatic efficiency, as containing, disciplining, and structuring how we think and write about administration and about what it is we help administer. Developed within a patriarchal, White-privileging system, the modeling function and instrumentalist trajectory of administrative discourse disestablishes resistant, supplemental voices if we accept it as the professional linguistic code. In local, real terms, we are likely always to have to engage in and with the dominant discourse. But in local, real terms, we can complicate discussions with a much thicker discourse to interrupt the model-bound genre that claims a moral high ground above the material world. Supplemental discourses are open to us, drawn from feminist theory, especially including the discourses of feminists of color, and from critical theories that privilege the temporal, the daily political realities over the grand narratives of administration.

I have used the term *erotics* to include the implicit desires apparent in patriarchal administrative values and the administrative genre as I have considered it here. It is a term that might be useful in exploring what feminist administration might desire because it lets us supplement the conventional values of certainty, closed systems, dominance, indoctrination, disciplining, ostensibly ahistorical, and apolitical stances to encourage a different way of seeing and being in administrative work. It allows the desire for difference without requiring a new model and a model's attendant constraints. It welcomes voices, we can hope, that are marginal and critical without casting them as children to be guided by their more knowledgeable and powerful elders (another facet of the boss compositionist). It can privilege the possibilities and complexities of the daily local realities, where, as Ellen Cushman argues in a chapter entitled "Language and Power in the Everyday," even apparently oppressive social structures can be successfully challenged with oppositional ideologies" through "daily interactions with gatekeepers" (230).

Cushman's perceptive analysis of how the inner-city residents she observed found agency within oppressive conditions offers a compelling sense of the value of critical readings of daily experiences in the moment, in their presentness, as well as of reflective critique and exploration of new strategies:

> Institutional languages developed in a [. . .] process where residents learned vernacular skills in their neighborhood, deployed them in gatekeeping encounters, then evaluated their language back home. Individuals learned to work with institutions by listening to the stories of other area residents who had returned from their interactions with wider society's public servants [. . . .] They became socialized into institutional language through direct instruction, observation, and practice. When the time came, residents were well prepared to gather, select, and deploy their community-based language abilities and transfer these to their interactions with gatekeepers; it allowed them to blend together institutional structures and their own agency to gather resources and respect from institutional agents. [. . .] [I]ndividuals questioned, assessed, honed, and celebrated, their linguistic tactics.

> Institutional language skills involved residents in critical and strategic
> negotiations of the everyday political workings of institutions. (xiii)

The residents supplemented the official code with an array of less privileged
ones, and they did not limit their rhetorical strategies to those serving the
dominant group. They recognized the possibilities that lie in the local. As
de Certeau puts it, "Beneath what one might call the 'monotheistic' privilege that panoptic apparatuses have won for themselves, a 'polytheism of
scattered practices survives, dominated but not erased by the triumphal
success of one of their numbers" (48).

To foreground the potential power of discursive heterogeneity, we
might consider rereading and supplementing the administrative genre from
within equivalent local frames. Lynn Worsham has written about the value
to composition theory of resisting "an inscription of a specific content"
(88), the "require[ment] to be systematic, theoretically consistent, and
politically transparent" (90). Worsham cites Luce Irigaray's etymological
tracing of "concept" as a capturing, a seizing, a rape, and critiques the
impulse of model-making: "Academic language is [. . .] specialized: It is a
way of speaking and thinking that captures and appropriates an external
reality through models and concepts. [. . .] [A]cademic language immobi-
lizes thought through the limits imposed by concepts, models, and methods" (90).

An administrative *écriture féminine* calls for difference, for inclusion of
the profane along with the sacred, the official. It is not mere resistance, but
an opening up, a tolerance for ambivalence and uncertainty—for the stances
that the administrative genre most systematically seeks to erase. It counters
with an erotics of risk and foregrounds the "impermanence of knowledge"
that Phelps ("Turtles" 14) and others recognize, but seek to tame, privileging contingency rather than the seamless whole of the model. It shifts our
attention from the principle to the local moment, interrupting the genre's
implicitly teleological narrative in favor of the thickness of the moment. It
encourages what Gary Saul Morson has called "sideshadowing," an awareness of contingency in each moment, so that "the future is experienced as
open and the present possesses real presentness, in which the weight of
chance and choice may lead to many different outcomes" (600). Such
awareness extends to the past as well, in that sideshadowing enables us to be
aware of what Morson terms the *vestigial*—the awareness of what might
have been, how different contingencies might have delivered us to a different present, and how conscious attention to current contingencies might
enable us to imagine other futures. The interruption of administrative narratives refleshes out the moment in this way, helping to add the critical
voice to administrative discussions—as has happened in revisitings/
supplementations of collaborative administration or placement testing,

recovering the historicity of practice encompassed into model through the ahistorical renderings of the administrative genre. Such moments of recovery call attention to the thick possibilities of the present.

Sideshadowing administrative discussions, we represent the porousness of borders. Nedra Reynolds notes the "seduction of movement" offered by travel to new lands, even as she calls for recognition of its "material side" ("Who's" 542), a strategy for introducing alternate frames in administrative work. The totalized student to be administered, for example, can be clothed in concrete form, drawn from real experience, openly presented, rather than pathologized as challenged, developmental, or labeled with some other foreigner metaphor, and can even speak for him or herself to open up discussions from provincial home to borderland spaces, countering the "confined spatiality" (551) of the administrative genre. Anzaldúa's description of the mestiza offers this kind of spatialized rhetorical heterogeneity:

> [La mestiza] has discovered that she can't hold concepts or ideas in rigid boundaries. The borders and walls that are supposed to keep the undesirable ideas out are entrenched habits and patterns of behavior; these habits and patterns are the enemy within. Rigidity means death. Only by remaining flexible is she able to stretch the psyche horizontally and vertically. La mestiza constantly has to shift out of habitual formations; from convergent thinking, analytical reasoning that tends to use rationality to move toward a single goal [. . .] to divergent thinking, characterized by movement away from set patterns and goals and toward a more whole perspective, one that includes rather than excludes. (79)

The mestiza/o administrator listens for difference (Ratcliffe, "Rhetorical Listening" 203) and interjects it, interrupting the patriarchal script of administration to supplement it, in all its practices, in local situations and in the professional discourse on administration.

As with Jane E. Hindman's critique of academic discourse, administrative discourse "entextualize[s] an abstract body of knowledge and disembody[ies] the individual writer because it requires gestures to those methodologies, subjects, territories, genres, structures, stylistic conventions and—of course—ideologies of our discipline" (100). The administrative genre represented by the sourcebook works against the potential to aspire to more than the machinery of efficiency. A feminist politics of administration can restore us to ourselves, can tie the political once again to the personal. The sourcebook is a handy accompaniment to the managed university and, as such, is likely to continue its generic dominance. But it can be made to invoke its own partialness, to call out its own supplementation.

3

WHEN THEORY
AND PRACTICE COLLIDE

Becoming a Feminist Practitioner

Sibylle Gruber

I wanted to write a straightforward and traditional (feminist) chapter where I discuss the challenges I encountered when I tried to incorporate my strong feminist principles into the WPA position I held. I wanted to let everybody know that it was far from easy to institute changes to the first-year writing curriculum. I wanted to conclude with specific strategies that I used to engage in proactive feminist practices, clearly redefining how we see our role as WPAs and redefining how our role is perceived by our constituents. It would have been easy, and it would have been one version of the truth—streamlined, palatable, uplifting, and in line with other explorations of the trials and tribulations of WPAs. Yet, as Jeanne Gunner (chap. 2, this volume) so aptly points out, this administrative genre is nothing but a utopian vision. Although I have contributed to promoting this genre in the past, I have come to realize that my performances as a feminist administrator are infinitely more complex, contradictory, and much more situated in the historical, cultural, and institutional locations than is assumed by the feminist, postcolonial, postmodern, and other theories to which I subscribe.

I do not mean to suggest that theory and research do not affect practice and that practice does not influence and guide research and theory. I believe in and promote feminist principles, and I consider myself a feminist teacher and scholar. Yet similar to Marcia Dickson, I cannot claim "a perfect model of feminist writing programs administration" because, as she points out, "there is none" (140). My contribution to this collection affirms that performing feminist administration often contradicts the theoretical principles of feminist thought. I am influenced by and depend on the administrative goals and perspectives—the specific situation—in which I perform my administrative work. My discussions on my ideological leanings and my theoretical perspectives on gender, race, class, literacy, nationality, or sexual preferences change drastically depending on whom I talk to and the purposes for talking to them.

In the following pages, I look at specific incidents from my administrative experiences to point out that the theoretical principles that guided my practices as the WPA can be—and often are—compromised by the practical needs of first-year students, the GTAs, the instructors, the administrative assistant, the department chair, the dean, the provost, the president, and also my own. I use Jane Flax's concept of toleration for ambivalence and resistance of structure ("Postmodernism"), Dickson's, Hildy Miller's, and Amy Goodburn and Carrie Shively Leverenz's feminist principles of collaboration and sharing of authority, as well as Hesford's call for reflecting on the historical and discursive construction of power to show that the theories we identify with have to be carefully evaluated and adapted to the realities of the positions we occupy.

In other words, I show how established and accepted hierarchies, and our perceptions about the place of these hierarchies, play out in specific situations. I provide examples from my work with the GTAs where I can exert power—hierarchical, shared, or dialogic—and from my work with the upper administration where power—hierarchical mostly—is exerted over me. Working as a WPA, I argue, requires a multilayered approach to theory and practice, where both theory and practice are hampered and influenced by the particular needs of the individual and the community and by the individual's and community's positions in an institutionally sanctioned power structure. I suggest that we expand on the theoretical frameworks intended to guide us as feminist practitioners. Maybe it is time to be ambivalent about the practicality of the theories we try to apply to our practices, and maybe we need to use our practices, although theoretically flawed and inconsistent, as the basis for working out a new theoretical basis of feminist practices.

HOPING FOR THEORIES: WHEN IS THE TRUTH NOT ENOUGH?

I did not grow up with American feminist thought. I did not even know it existed until I moved to the United States in my 20s. But when I was first introduced to feminist theories, I was convinced that Gloria Anzaldúa,

Audre Lorde, bell hooks, and Judith Butler had read my developing mind and spoke The Truth about life, women, and women's objectified positions in the United States. Since my initial introduction to these feminist thinkers, I have continuously broadened my knowledge base on feminist thought and principles. My perspectives have become more complex, and I have started to question some of the underlying assumptions of feminist theory. But I was still ready to succumb to my penchant for proving that the undoable is doable, and that I could apply clearly defined feminist theories to my work as a WPA. I told myself that I would follow Flax, who so ardently argues that feminist theories "should encourage us to tolerate and interpret ambivalence, ambiguity, and multiplicity as well as to expose the roots of our needs for imposing order and structure no matter how arbitrary and oppressive these needs may be" ("Postmodernism" 56). This notion is what I emphasized in many of my previous articles: the need to move away from patriarchal power structures and embrace postmodern concepts of multivocality, multiaccentuality, and heteroglossia. I wholeheartedly questioned unification and consensus, and I emphasized the need for accepting and recognizing the multiple identities and multiple realities we occupy.

I thought I would show that I believed in and applied—maybe not successfully—Dickson's feminist model of administration to my situation. As she puts it,

> A feminist model . . . is more concerned with doing away with hierarchies than with perpetuating them. The feminist form of administration I envision allows for the blurring of the lines of authority and control. A feminist administrator becomes one of a group of instructors (not the *leader* of a group of instructors) that creates a collaborative program that considers human stories, issues, and abilities—before, during, and after creating departmental policy decisions. Such a WPA forgoes the illusion of control, sits neither at the top of the pyramid nor at the center of the circle and in effect, trust the other members of the department enough to turn over the asylum to the inmates. (148)

Goodburn and Leverenz's explanation of feminist principles of management would be perfect as well. They consider "nonhierarchical collaboration, shared leadership, and the recognition of multiple sources of authority" (277) as important elements of a feminist administrative style. Hildy Miller adds "the integration of the cognitive and the affective" to these principles.

I thought to expand on Wendy Hesford's comments that "feminist teachers and activists in the academy must recognize how power and resistance are historically and discursively constructed at the crossroads of social differences and must use this knowledge to develop more reflective and democratic learning and writing communities" (148). I could have shown that the practices I instituted had become a "formidable challenge to the status quo" (Bishop, Wendy, "Learning" 501). It would have been simple—and truthful—to claim that I shared responsibilities with graduate teaching assistants (GTAs), the one-year instructors, and the administrative secretary. I also could have easily established that I taught just these principles in the practicum course that GTAs are required to take. In other words, I could have underscored my strong feminist beliefs in subverting patriarchal power structures, bureaucratic obstructions, and hierarchical principles. I could have foregrounded theory, and I could have shown how I applied these theories in my position as an administrator. It would have been a glimpse into one of the realities of my administrative self. Unfortunately, the other realities got in the way, and my skeptical side prevailed.

I could not ignore that my positions as a teacher, administrator, and researcher are by no means straightforward, and that there are other truths to be told. For example, my approach to teaching, administration, and research is not always as proactive as I intended it to be. I realized that I can not claim to apply feminist theory, feminist principles of leadership, and feminist pedagogy to all—or most—of my everyday situations. Often the administrative environment I worked in led to practices that, as a theorist and researcher, I would not have supported. In fact, I might have opposed some of the practices if I had not experienced the administrative situation first hand. I recognized that in an ideal setting I would thrive on the interdependence and equal emphasis put on theory, research, and practice. In such a setting, I would not lead and I would not control. I would use my personal power to empower others. I would encourage resistance. I would tolerate ambivalence. I would encourage reflection. Yet, as an administrator, I have become more aware that theory and research can easily be severed from practice. I can provide theoretical arguments and show through research that we need to use critical pedagogy, that we need to underscore feminist theories, that we need to practice Marxist ideologies, and that we need to implement critical technological literacy in our teaching. However, it becomes more difficult to apply these principles in a specific classroom setting and in a specific administrative environment that is restrained by established (and sometimes fossilized) situational and institutional circumstances.

PERFORMING WITH GTAS: CONTEXTUALIZING ADMINISTRATIVE LOCATIONS

I started to administer the university-wide writing program at my institution after the previous administrator quit midyear. I had not planned on taking on this position for another 5 years at least, but circumstances prevailed.

There I was, surrounded by dissatisfied TAs who felt overworked and undersupported, weary faculty who felt dragged into the middle of it all, and a department chair who had invested heavily in the previous WPA. I knew I was getting into a volatile situation, but I was hoping that my training in composition studies and my strong commitment to feminist ideologies and critical technological literacy would benefit the program and see us through the transition. I was tempted to follow Dickson's advice that "the only way to direct a program is to let the individual program shape itself according to the beliefs of the people who make it up and existing power structures of the institution in which it is located" (147). I also quickly realized that I had agency and that I would be—because of the situation of this particular position and my own situation—the one doing most of the shaping.

As the WPA, I was responsible for the first-year writing requirement, the sophomore writing course, and the WC. The WPA trains the GTAs, observes them on a regular basis, teaches a practicum course, oversees the WC, works with the administrative assistant on budget issues and scheduling requests, works with the chair, talks to students about curriculum and grade concerns, and writes regular reports to the chair, dean, and provost. From my perspective, it would have been a relief to be part of a collaborative endeavor, where the WPA work would be shared among many constituents. Instead, I "played into the hierarchy," as Anne Ruggles Gere puts it, by accepting a position where the WPA is a "single individual responsible for diverse components" (127) that encompass the writing program. I was the administrator in a hierarchical model, "exercising concentrated authority over curriculum and program policies" (Gunner, "Collaborative" 254). The budget cuts and hiring freezes did not allow for a situation where administrative duties could be shared and where the WPA could work with a WC director, a practicum teacher, or a WAC specialist. I was aware that I would not be in a situation where I could brainstorm ideas with faculty colleagues who would then work with me on implementing these ideas. If I wanted to share authority, I needed to figure out ways in which the 40 GTAs and the two instructors who were on a 1-year contract could become more involved by collaborating with each other and with the WPA.

The GTAs at my institution are predominantly enrolled in a 2-year master's program. Their commitment to the writing program is strong, but they also know that they will only be teaching for 2 years, with the second year spent looking for jobs or doctoral programs. Many of them want to know what they will be teaching from one day to the next, and most want to be supplied with lesson plans that they can follow pretty closely. The anxiety level about being in the classroom for the first time is usually high, and knowing what they will be teaching helps many to be more confident in front of their students.

My goal was to find a middle ground that would address the need for structure, but would also provide ways of sharing responsibilities and authority. In practice, this meant that I needed to figure out how to approach my position. I thought I could split responsibilities and roles—be the nurturing facilitator, the traditional administrator, and the collaborator. The following sections show how my vision materialized, especially when I was searching for community, when I asked GTAs to take on responsibility for revising the custom reader, when I revised the curriculum to include the readings chosen by the GTAs, when returning GTAs were asked to teach workshops on specific topics they considered most pertinent to new GTAs, and when faculty in other areas of the department were tapped to be GTA mentors.

PERFORMING IN (FEMINIST? ANY?) COMMUNITIES: WHERE IS EVERYBODY?

Before I took on my administrative position, I saw the GTAs in the hallways and thought of them as quite a happy group. They were friendly when I talked to them, and they would answer questions about teaching with a cheerful, "It's going fine. The students are great!" Nobody mentioned any conflicts or problems. I only found out about the high levels of frustration and dissatisfaction when I started to work with them as the WPA. They brought up lack of administrative and faculty support, lack of collegial support, curricular problems, difficulties understanding the assignments, concerns about the readings, departmental splits based on graduate emphases, time-management problems, bitterness about office space, and quarrels about overhead projectors. Most of the GTAs' complaints did not evolve around lack of input in curricular decisions, but a concern that they were not being told what to teach and how to teach it. In a sense, they saw themselves as being given too much agency without being given the tools to understand how to take advantage of their agency, which translated into a lack of direction and rapidly increasing anxiety levels. My initial instinct— based largely on my propensity for order and structure—was to find a solution for each problem, and I was hopeful that some concerns could be alleviated more easily than others.

After taking a few deep breaths and reminding myself of Hesford's admonition that power and resistance are social constructions that needed close examination, I realized that I would not be able to find a simple solution for every problem. Instead, GTA frustration seemed to be an expression of a broader and more fundamental problem. Most of them were frustrated because, as they put it, "there is nothing we can do about it." GTAs did not think they could change their position in a hierarchical system or the structure of the program that seemed determined by those with higher academic degrees. In other words, the way control, power, and dominance were exercised—the way things were done—did not allow for their input. They had complained to the chair, but that only led to further top–down decisions. In the end, they were just lowly GTAs doing a lot of work, but receiving little recognition.

How could I counter existing hierarchical and authoritarian practices to ensure that GTAs could assume "agency in order to work and hope for social change" and to work against "masculinist codes of academic discourse," as Reynolds so succinctly put it ("Interrupting" 58)? How could we create a positive space that would move us toward a common goal while providing room for difference, ambiguity, and debate to move beyond the existing impasse that kept everybody guarded and doubtful about the new semester? Because I believe, as McNenny and Roen have argued, that "without collaboration, we are reduced to social isolation and alienation" (qtd. in Yancey and Spooner 48), I envisioned this positive space as collaborative, cooperative, participatory, and interdisciplinary, where we could engage in effective and useful discussions.

I realized that I could easily do away with hierarchies because I was the one who controlled these hierarchies in the first place. Despite encouraging apparent democracy, I also realized that I was still in a position were I could—and did—control in how much collaboration and dialogue we would engage. This seemed especially pertinent because I was acutely aware that my position as a woman administrator could lead GTAs to mistake my intent of providing a collaborative and nurturing environment as an excuse for not knowing how to be an administrator who can control the situation at hand. I found Michelle Payne's comments on women in the classroom pertinent to my position as an administrator in charge of 40 GTAs. As she puts it,

> A female teacher's authority, though endowed by a degree and the university, is tenuous no matter which pedagogy she embraces. And if teaching is a matter of persuasion in the classical rhetorical sense, then women may have a more difficult time being taken seriously by their students when the very fact of their gender undermines their ethos. As much as I wish this weren't the case, my power and authority—my effectiveness as a teacher—is dependent on how much power and authority my students grant me (in addition to the support the administration grants me). (408)

Payne's words reflect my own experiences as a teacher, and her comments could easily be applied to my role as an administrator. No matter what my approach, in the end, I wanted to persuade the GTAs that working together and forming a collaborative community would enhance their teaching experiences and their experiences as graduate students. I wanted to make sure

that taking on agency and participating in decisions made about the readings, assignments, and curriculum as a whole would provide a venue for
such collaborative activities. However, if the GTAs decided not to grant me
the power and authority to change the old system, we would not be able to
arrive at anything new, different, and, from my perspective, better.

But I was lucky. The GTAs were hopeful that any change to how
authority and power had been distributed in the past would be a positive
step. We had discussions about their major concerns, which included long
venting sessions. More important, after the different voices were heard, we
moved to the next step in what could almost be called an administrative and
pedagogical therapy session. Many of the GTAs admitted that complaining
would not solve the situation, but that they also needed to reflect on the
roots of the problems they faced and that they needed to take action to
institute changes.

It was easy for them—and also for me—to blame the administration
for any discord and dissatisfaction. The administration presented the traditional power structure. It presented a road block that we could not control
and did not know how to resist at this point. But the GTAs had more difficulty to also look at the divisions in their own ranks and to work on being
more inclusive, willing to share, and willing to help. I considered this especially important because, as Janet Miller so aptly puts it, "it is within the
activities of our daily lives, in the gatherings in the hallways and classrooms
and offices and counseling cubicles of school buildings where our forms of
emancipatory research and pedagogy must take place" (172). I wanted to
use this Freirean approach to critical awareness and conscientization to
provide GTAs with the beginnings of agency. I hoped they would realize,
to use Freire's words, that society—or approach to authority, academic
conventions, and a composition curriculum—is "something unfinished, not
. . . something inexorably given; it has become a challenge rather than a
hopeless limitation" (13). But how could we focus on the importance of
sharing lesson plans and readings, discussing successful or problematic
classroom interactions, taking advantage of disciplinary knowledge of colleagues, and the stories that second-year GTAs had to share about their
first year teaching composition if many of the institutional values contra-
dicted the importance of these principles? Even my position in the hierarchy suggested that individual control and power superceded the commitment to team efforts and collaboration. Even if I wanted to, I could not
deny that I was making most of the decisions, including the decision to
encourage GTA collaboration.

I might have contributed to what Hesford calls a "more reflective and
democratic" GTA community by encouraging them to engage in dialogic
interactions with each other and discussing their experiences in their offices
and in the hallways. It was a success in many ways, but it would be too
easy to simply claim that I fully embraced democratic principles in my own

interactions with the GTAs. Throughout the process, the GTAs and I knew that my position in the hierarchy of the institution provided me with an authority in the eyes of my superiors and in my own eyes that they did not possess. As a result, I remained on the periphery of this community, not able or willing to surrender socially constructed hierarchies for dialogic collaboration. Although I like to claim—in theory—that I see myself as part of (not as a leader of) a group of GTAs and instructors, in reality the group and I knew that my position provided me with leadership roles and responsibilities that they could not, and did not want, to take on.

PERFORMING FEMINIST PRACTICES: WHO DECIDES WHAT STUDENTS READ?

Collaboration can happen. I experienced it myself. To change the reader, GTAs formed a reader committee that collected comments and complaints about the current reader from their colleagues and first-year students. The GTAs were used to the environmentally focused reader, but few of them seemed to enjoy teaching it. Nobody seemed to feel that their composition class represented Marilyn Cooper's ideal environment for student learning: "challenging, engaging, rewarding in the sense of giving a feeling of worthwhile accomplishment" (14). Instead, students and GTAs seemed to go through the motions, with complaints surfacing from time to time. Although students complained, the reader remained in place for a number of years. It represented the powers of the university administration and the WPA—those who were interested in presenting the university as an environmentally oriented institution—and the powerlessness of the GTAs and students—those who needed to teach (and were taught) the curriculum and who are traditionally not able to institute change. The new reader no longer focused on environmental issues, but approached the environment from cultural, political, gendered, social, economic, and historical perspectives. GTAs collaborated on this effort; they polled their colleagues and students to find out what topics and readings would best fit the needs of those who teach and those who take the course.

Collaborating on putting together the reader was an almost picture-perfect example of how I became, for a short time, "one of a group of instructors" who "turn[ed] over the asylum to the inmates" (Dickson 148). But even in this case, the GTAs and I knew that I needed to approve the readings. They knew that I was interested in feminist and critical pedagogy. Lucky for them and for me, our interests coincided, and it was easy to move the reader through the appropriate channels for publication. How would I have reacted had the reader committee chosen articles that I considered inappropriate for a first-year writing program? Would I have been able to continue sharing authority or would I have taken control of the situation without taking the efforts of the committee into consideration? I would like to think that I would have encouraged further explorations, but I am glad that I did not need to find answers to these questions.

UN/PERFORMING FEMINIST PRACTICES: WHAT IS IN A CURRICULUM?

I had to rethink and adjust my theoretical principles when it came to curricular innovations. I inherited the program's rocky history. The traditional two-semester sequence that focused on the teaching of literature disappeared before I was hired. The program shifted to one 4-hour course that focused on teaching rhetorical principles and teaching writing as a process. I heard many stories that recounted the events leading up to this change, some applauding the new direction that the WPA had envisioned, and some lamenting the fall of civilization. The various WPAs tried their best to fulfill the vision of the program's originator, but dissatisfaction with many of the facets of the program had started to surface over the years.

From my perspectives as a theorist, this was fertile ground for exploring dialogic collaboration, which, according to Dickson, is "more concerned with doing away with hierarchies than with perpetuating them" and which allows for the "blurring of lines of authority and control" (148). Yet, as a practitioner who needed to have a curriculum in place by the beginning of the semester, I also questioned the practicality of shared responsibilities and multiple authorities in all instances of revising a first-year curriculum. I knew that I needed to work out a compromise that took into consideration university-wide administrative needs, GTA needs, student needs, and my own multiple roles as WPA. In broad terms, I needed to decide how I would handle the authority and power that I undeniably had over others. I found that if I clearly delineated my roles and those that the GTAs would take on, we could come to an agreement on how collaborative our curricular restructuring efforts would be. The procedures did not always follow the theoretical foundations of traditional feminist principles and the principles of decentered WPA work. In some cases, theorists writing without the situation-specific practical restraints in mind might see the approach I took as controlling and hierarchical, contributing to what Gunner sees as a division between curriculum and teachers and, in effect, "minimizing the role that all faculty should play in program direction" ("Decentering" 8).

I know that I did not encourage the GTAs to rethink their apathy and unwillingness to work collaboratively on the curriculum and syllabus revisions. GTAs were not interested in sharing this responsibility. In other words, the culture of the institution and my own situation were not conducive to this approach. It seemed that they wanted to know what was expected of them as teachers, and they wanted to be given the fundamental elements. In this case, it was the syllabus that they could revise to a certain extent, but that served as their point of reference.

Much of the GTAs' need for a structured approach was based on their experiences of nonstructure, which was not based on any theoretical perspective, but which was mostly the outcome of an unsuccessful attempt at revising the curriculum while the semester was underway. I knew the history, and I could have created a collaborative environment where all decisions could have been made in dialogic fashion and where multiple voices could have been heard and incorporated in curricular decisions. But I never questioned their need for method and organization. Quite to the contrary, I encouraged it. I appreciate and usually support Jane Flax's argument that we should fight against our propensity to impose order and structure, however arbitrary this need is ("Postmodernism" 56). But I also knew that, in this specific situation, where 40 GTAs needed to be trained within a 2-week period prior to the beginning of the semester, I wanted to make sure that the basic framework was in place. In some respects, this framework could be seen as arbitrarily imposed by the WPA, where the need for structure undermined a possibly more messy effort in collaboration and teamwork. In other respects, it could be seen as taking on the responsibilities of the WPA, who wanted to provide a well-conceived structure for GTAs by incorporating established theories into the curriculum. Either way, the practical need for a serviceable curriculum outweighed my concerns about abandoning my feminist principles of fostering collaboration and sharing responsibilities.

RE/PERFORMING FEMINIST PRACTICES: WHO TRAINS AND TEACHES WHOM?

In many ways, it is easier to provide venues for GTA leadership when such leadership almost inevitably leads to positive results. For example, I could carry out my conviction that feminist and critical theories are cornerstones of GTA–WPA interaction in the training of new GTAs. For this 2-week orientation program, which familiarizes new GTAs and reacquaints returning GTAs with the curriculum, multiple authorities and shared responsibilities work very well. Returning GTAs provide team-taught workshops for new GTAs on topics ranging from teaching specific rhetorical skills, classroom management, grading, connections between readings and assignments, to managing graduate student status and instructor responsibilities. It provides authority and encourages professionalism in the returning GTAs, necessitates their familiarity with the curriculum, and provides new GTAs with role models for diverse teaching styles.

All in all, the workshop approach encouraged many of Goodburn and Leverenz's principles of feminist administration. It underscored collaboration and foregrounded the various abilities of the returning GTAs. It also encouraged new GTAs to recognize their colleagues as authorities, and it showed them that leadership is shared. Despite these elements, it did not necessarily move toward a more ambiguous interpretation of authority and structure, nor did it emphasize the need to question and resist traditional power structures. The role of the WPA was still firmly in place. The workshops provided new GTAs with the tools to follow the established structure. Any questions and concerns were fielded by me, and I was the one who observed, checked, and oversaw the efforts of the GTAs. In some ways, I was, as John Trimbur puts it, "invariably implicated in acts of surveillance that constitute both staff and students as 'docile bodies' " ("Writing" 142). Of course I did not want to see them as compliant and obedient for the sake of keeping a tried-and-true formula in place. But Trimbur's words show the difficulties of interpreting my efforts of creating collaborative workshops as a means to undermine any system, whether arbitrarily structured or intentionally disarrayed.

SHARING FEMINIST PERFORMANCES: TRUSTING MENTORING RELATIONSHIPS?

One element of the program that could have led to questioning the WPA's power and authority was a faculty mentoring program that supported GTAs in their teaching endeavors. They did not always feel that the WPA could help them with their concerns, especially if those concerns resulted from the way the writing program was administered. This certainly means that the WPA needs to be able to let go of a WPA-centric approach and also acknowledge the expertise and valuable input that other faculty can provide. Although we might sometimes disagree with the pedagogical and theoretical approaches that faculty not trained in composition studies might take, the involvement of other faculty can provide a strong alliance needed to remind the university community of the importance of composition. It can move the WPA away from being the lone voice when defending the program's existence or the importance of GTAs. Furthermore, if we insist on working by ourselves, we might run the risk of "dispensing authority in a top-heavy fashion, no matter how collaborative or student-centered we seek to make our teaching or administrative styles" (Gunner, "Decentering" 13).

When we started the faculty mentoring program, I was not sure what the outcome would be. I was aware of Goodburn and Leverenz's experiences and struggles with restructuring a writing program according to feminist principles of leadership. It would be too easy to claim that I embraced the concept of decentering authority and encouraging GTAs to consult with faculty about the readings, pedagogical approaches, or curriculum. Instead, I worried whether this approach would be seen as abdicating authority instead of creating agency for GTAs. Would other faculty and university administrators see me as a female administrator who could not run a writing program efficiently? Would GTAs consider my efforts in promoting dialogic collaboration as just another way of putting more work on them? In other words, would a fledgling and floundering feminist model of reorganizing leadership to include shared commitment and multiple authorities work in this particular setting?

The faculty mentoring program did not subvert my authority—shared, dialogic, or hierarchical—as a WPA. GTAs chose faculty mentors from a list of volunteers at the beginning of the semester, and most of them contacted their mentors and promised to get in touch when they needed help. However, only a few met with their mentors during the semester. The reasons could have been many. It could have been that the mentoring program was not structured well enough and meetings were not required. GTAs could have found their peer interactions sufficient or more useful than interacting with faculty. They could have had difficulties scheduling time, or they could have gotten too busy with their teaching responsibilities and their responsibilities as students. Whatever the reason, faculty mentoring was an option that was mostly utilized in cases of emergency. If they needed to consult with their mentors, they knew whom to contact.

Providing a faculty mentoring program coincides with one of the characteristics that Dickson sees as an important characteristic of a feminist administrative structure: "a commitment to provide ample support and mentoring services for all levels of participants" (152). The mentoring program fulfilled this need, although the collaboration took on a slightly different form. Instead of interacting with their peers, GTAs were encouraged to look for input from faculty members whose authority had been established through their many years of teaching, their status as faculty in the department, or simply their age. The relationship and collaboration, in this case, were much more hierarchical. However, GTAs, although they requested faculty mentors, were not forced to interact with them or consult them if they decided against it. This approach seemed to provide them with the agency that they lacked during the previous administration, and it encouraged them to become more proactive in their endeavors as TAs.

Although it was not an ideal implementation of feminist principles, I could follow many of the theoretical tenets. I could focus on the position of the GTAs, and I could emphasize the well-being of the GTAs. It could have become a power struggle between the GTA and the faculty mentor, with the faculty mentor evaluating the performance of her mentor. But we followed Hildy Miller's suggestion of seeing mentors as "supporters" instead of "supervisors" (85). On the whole, however, the concept of a supportive mentoring program hardly impacted the program's established structure. Mentors did not work with me on implementing collaborative improvements to the program. Instead, faculty worked with the GTAs on a microlevel, using their knowledge and teaching experiences to help them work within the system. My position, the curriculum, and the pedagogical foundations for teaching writing were not questioned or challenged.

PERFORMING WITH ADMINISTRATORS: LOCALIZING ADMINISTRATIVE CONTEXTS

Gary Olson's 2002 comment that "Writing program administration is one of the most difficult, most demanding, yet least rewarded positions in today's English departments" (Preface xi) was largely true for my situation. Disciplinary conversations about WPAs' roles abound with stories of conflicting responsibilities, burnout, institutional marginalization, and relegation to a "mere" service function (Leverenz; Tom Miller; Peeples; Schuster; Ward). WPAs across the country still struggle to gain institutional support and the support of colleagues for work that is stigmatized as intellectually inferior. Managing budgets, promoting the program across campus, hiring and training instructors, and evaluating staff are hardly ever considered glamorous, and research efforts that look to improve first-year writing programs, discuss community outreach endeavors, or look at the literate practices of college students are often considered less vigorous and acceptable to tenure and promotion committees than theoretical explorations found in traditional academic research. When we add feminist pedagogical practices and leadership principles to the mix, it becomes even more challenging to be accepted in an academic setting, where power, authority, and control are exerted by the few over the many and where individual progress supercedes shared responsibilities and team efforts.

Much of what I did as a WPA involved working with GTAs, who, from a hierarchical perspective, reported to me and who saw me as the person with power and in control of their teaching destinies. Collaborative efforts and efforts to share authority—successful or not—were mostly initiated by me. It was my decision whether and in what ways I wanted GTAs to participate in programmatic decisions. These decisions were closely connected to my ideological leanings. My feminist principles shaped my thinking, my research on critical literacy shaped the curriculum, and my connections to the computers and writing community influenced my perspectives on how to approach technology in the writing classroom. Even if my theories had to be amended by the practical realities in which I performed my job, theory influenced my practice. Depending on the situation, I tried to emphasize collaboration and shared authority. I tried to incorporate critical literacy skills into the curriculum. I tried to provide venues for technological literacy that would underscore the pedagogical principles of the writing curriculum.

When I worked with administrators whose positions put them above me in the hierarchical bureaucracy of academic institutions, it was much harder to make decisions based on my theoretical principles because often my principles—from the administrators' perspective—had little bearing on the administration's goals and objectives. For example, even if I would have preferred dialogic collaboration with the department chair or the dean, I could not force them to share my preferences. Even if I would have liked to question decisions made by the administration, many times I could not even get close enough to the source of the decision to make an impact. Instead, I was largely dependent on how these administrators wanted to interact with me based on accepted institutional norms. This almost inevitably depended on how they perceived my position as a WPA, a woman, a rhetoric and composition scholar, a troublemaker, or a faculty member willing to take on the role of an administrator.

PERFORMING CRITICAL PEDAGOGY: WHO DECIDES?

In my case, I reported to the department chair. The department chair can get involved as much or as little as he or she wants. The WPA who I succeeded worked closely with the chair. From the outside, it did not seem to be a dialogic collaboration, but instead a hierarchical arrangement where the chair decided on the curriculum, how the budget was spent, and how to suppress dissent in the ranks. One of my conditions for taking on the WPA role was noninterference from the chair in matters of curriculum and budget decisions. Yet, interference reared its head when the newly and collaboratively developed reader found its way to the desk of the chair. Too controversial, too liberal, too biased, and too contentious were only a few of the objections. Parents wouldn't want their children to read about the pros and cons of gay marriage. What could we have been thinking? It did not matter that the GTAs had brought in articles that addressed multiple perspectives. What mattered was that the writing program did not need any kind of controversy; if even one student went to the dean, provost, or president, it would reflect poorly on the program's success.

I did not have an opportunity to engage in dialogue with the chair or explain the theoretical foundations of the reader. I was reminded of Richard Miller's comments about WPA work that "there is nothing so dependable in this line of work as disappointment, rejection, defeat" ("Critique's" 7). I was certainly disappointed and almost conceded defeat after being told that I had overstepped my authority. I questioned whether a male WPA would have experienced the same interactions. It was difficult to respond to the chair's comments partly because I considered them uninformed and partly because I had to readjust how I saw my supervisor and how I wanted to be seen by him. Was he in charge of my academic destiny? Did I want to be loyal to my chair and accept his accusations of overstepping my authority? Did I want to fight back and undermine his authority over me? Laura Micciche put it nicely when she explained Mara Holt's feelings of alienation from her administrative work. In my case, "powerlessness, isolation, and self-estrangement" seemed to struggle with stubbornness, loyalty to the GTAs, preserving my own identity in this hierarchical system, and standing up for my belief in teaching critical literacy skills through a wide range of readings and exercises. I decided that my loyalties were to the GTAs and the writing program first and to the chair a distant second.

I did not retract the reader, but instead wrote a memo—the first of many memos to come—to put the readings in context. I began by pointing out that the new reader addressed the many aspects of the writing process from multiple perspectives. The readings, I explained, were purposely chosen for their usefulness in teaching summary, analysis, rhetorical appeals, and argument. They also would challenge critical thinking skills by addressing issues of gender, race, class, ethnicity, sexuality, and, ultimately, the construction of identity from an ecological perspective. The readings, I argued, looked at the effects that discourse has on all environments: classroom, political, electronic, ideological, historical, economic, and natural. It strongly supported students' critical reading and writing processes.

I avoided the chair's office for many weeks. We went ahead with the reader, and I made sure to incorporate positive GTA and student responses in any report I wrote. We did not have outraged parents at our door, nor did we experience increased student resistance and complaints. But the interactions certainly caused me sleepless nights. I did not feel empowered by my opposition to the chair. Rather, I felt conflicted about the role I was playing. Using Hildy Miller's terms, I used masculinist practices and became the general or the statesman (83) defending my troops and resisting invasion from a foreign power, knowing full well that the invading power's weapons were superior to my own and that in case of an ensuing conflict the little territory of the WPA could easily be conquered. I understand and appreciate the concept that, as hooks says, "all knowledge is forged in conflict" (*Teaching* 31). I would hope that Susan Jarratt also referred to interactions with administrators when she points out that "recognizing the inevitability of conflict is not ground for despair but the starting point for creating a consciousness in students and teachers through which the inequalities generating those conflicts can be acknowledged and transformed" ("Feminist Pedagogy" 119). But I doubt that anything that transformative happened. Although there was an uneasy truce, we did not progress to seeing authority as a "messy pluralism" where we can "resurrect authority and make it more democratic, better suited to voices of both consensus *and* conflict" (Mortensen and Kirsch 569). I was not willing to give up or negotiate my authority even if it was only perceived authority. In Ed White's words, I refused "to accept the condition of powerlessness" (108) and gained power that I did not even know I could gain.

PERFORMING TECHNOLOGICAL LITERACY: AMBIVALENCE AND ENTHUSIASM

Another imposed element in the curriculum that did cause consternation and resistance—from the GTAs and from me—was the full integration, starting in the fall of 2002, of technological literacy into the curriculum. Although I am an ardent supporter of teaching critical technological literacy, I was reluctant to impose a standardized approach that mostly focused on functional skills supported by the university administration. However, because the first-year writing course is the only required course on this campus, the administration considered it the ideal setting for their fledgling technology requirement. I considered it a great challenge in terms of (a) combining the required functional skills with the relevant critical technology skills, (b) working with students who had different technology backgrounds and different learning styles, and (c) GTAs who had different levels of comfort with computers. As the WPA, I needed to figure out a compromise or, in Micciche's words, I needed to "navigate the murky waters of institutional hierarchy, where decisions to create any sort of change are seriously constrained, where daily existence requires pragmatic, sometimes morally problematic decisions, where one's ability to act on one's conscience or one's political ideals is seriously compromised" (442). In some ways, I felt like one of Hildy Miller's "figurehead monarchs of make-believe realms" (81). I was taking on the responsibility of instituting a campus-wide requirement without much power to refuse the honor.

In the end, we were pragmatic. The writing program incorporated technological literacy skills. However, instead of focusing exclusively on the functional aspects—the how of computer use—we also underscored the critical aspects—always asking why, who, and when? Additionally, we moved to the rhetorical, making sure that students could practice the how, why, and who by foregrounding their own work as producers of multimedia literacy. For GTAs, this task seemed overwhelming and out of the realm of teaching writing. As a computers and writing scholar, I could easily see the connections between technology and writing instruction, but I had to find ways to present these connections to the GTAs, and the GTAs had to be able to make the same connections in their classrooms. They had to encourage students to work on increasing their technological literacy, and they had to convince them that technological literacy incorporates functional skills as well as culturally and socially situated analytical and critical reading/writing skills.

Much of this top–down approach easily could have ended in GTA and student resistance. Although not all GTAs embraced technology in their classrooms, they took ownership of the technology aspects after I asked them to collaboratively create technological literacy modules that drew on the strengths of all group members and that focused on incorporating critical reading and writing skills. Each group felt responsible for the success of the module they presented. Although anxiety levels were still high throughout the first year, GTAs felt ownership over the modules despite the initial top–down approach. They were quite proud of their achievements. The modules worked well, and students' measurable technology skills improved. I am also proud of this achievement. I know we still have a long way to go to ensure that students become exposed more fully to the critical technology skills emphasized by Cindy Selfe and to the rhetorical technological literacy addressed by Stuart Selber in *Multiliteracies for a Digital Age*, but we made sure that we participated in shaping how technological literacy is taught in the writing curriculum.

Surprisingly, this administrative stipulation of integrating technology into the curriculum led to some of the most feminist-oriented interactions. We questioned, resisted, collaborated, shared, and cooperated to make it work. We became an administrative structure that followed closely the concepts outlined by Hildy Miller:

> With the self seen as inter-relational and personal power enhanced by empowering others, such a community is marked by collaboration and cooperation. Rather than striving to develop uniform and universalized rules, feminist communities tend to produce flexible decisions arising from experiential contexts. Ideas are tentative, and thus subject to alteration as contextual needs change. While not all members of a communi-

ty need to agree on all details, there is generally basic consensus on important points. (84)

My role in this instance had slightly shifted with the GTAs. They seemed to recognize the difficult position of the WPA who had little control over the technology integration, but who had to make the appropriate changes to the curriculum. I could not institute this change by myself. We were dependent on each other's support and willingness to entertain the idea of uniformly taught technology skills in a writing course. We decided to use the modules developed initially as a testing ground for students' abilities and GTAs' comfort with teaching technological literacy. We found ways to connect the functional with the critical and rhetorical, and we helped each other to acquire the same functional, critical, and rhetorical skills that we asked of our students.

SHARING SANITY

In a recent article on the rhetorical future of English departments, Tom Miller tells his readers that "those of us who administer composition programs, writing centers, or other 'service units' are used to being treated as idiots as we struggle to explain our work to our colleagues and the public" (34). He quotes Berube and Nelson, who discuss "a kind of idiot savant academic culture that assumes any idiot can do administration and only an idiot incapable of scholarship would agree to do such menial work (24)" (34). I appreciated Tom Miller's bluntness. Yes, indeed, I often had the suspicion that others saw or treated me as a mentally challenged member in an otherwise sane institution. But from time to time, I saw myself as the only sane member in an otherwise irrational environment who has learned to live with irrationality, absurdity, and silliness. But I know that there was some truth to my colleagues' perceptions, and I know that my sanity was often ready to make room for the ridiculous.

When I became the WPA, I thought I could create working environments that adapt feminist leadership theories and principles and that I could keep my sanity by sharing responsibilities, collaborating at all levels, tolerating ambivalence, and resisting structure and order. But I could only keep myself sane in my day-to-day reality by carefully choosing the right moments for dialogic collaboration and team efforts, for using my position of power as a hierarchical advantage, for imposing order and structure, and for opposing or working with the administration. When I look at postmodernist, modernist, structuralist, feminist, postcolonialist, womanist, or cultural theories, I run the risk of seeing myself as the idiot who doesn't only take on administrative duties, but is also incapable of making up her mind about the theories that best describe her practices. To keep my sanity, I have learned to see myself as a bit of everything, using my theoretical foundations to create a working environment that fits the needs of the many constituents whom I serve and to whom I report. What I suggest, for our sanity's sake, is to ground our theories more fully and honestly in the realities of our practices. In other words, it would be useful to know that our practices do not fall short of the theoretical guideposts, but that the theoretical guideposts sometimes fall short of understanding our practices.

PART II

Performing WPA Work

Challenging Feminist Assumptions About Collaboration

Develop a sensitivity for the problems and emotions of others and a thick skin about your own.

–Carolyn Miller
(personal email)

4

COLLABORATIVE WRITING ADMINISTRATION AS INTELLECTUAL INQUIRY

Lynée Lewis Gaillet

Letizia Guglielmo

The work of WPAs is often strangely defined and dual in nature. As Rita Malenczyk explains, WPAs are not administrators in the same ways deans and college presidents are. She argues "that the difference between a WPA and a dean or a higher-level manager is that WPA work, like the work of more traditional academic disciplines, is grounded in research and scholarship and is ultimately intellectual and pedagogical rather than managerial" ("Fighting" 18). Unfortunately, most college deans and presidents do not recognize this distinction. Consequently, much WPA scholarship attempts to define and legitimize the unique intellectual work and role of the WPA position. An important body of scholarship examining WPA work as intellectual inquiry has emerged in response to scholars such as James Sledd ("Why") and Marc Bousquet ("Composition"), who characterize WPAs as "boss compositionists" and declare these middle management positions unnecessary. We think the greatest potential for intellectual inquiry lies in the collaborative nature of writing program administration.

In this chapter, we argue that collaborative administration, when negotiated carefully, has the capability to move writing programs away from a primary identity as a coordinator of service courses and toward a new type

of institutional system with multiple purposes, functions, and activities tied
to integrated student, teacher, and administrative research. When WPA
work is viewed as intellectual inquiry, writing programs have the potential
to become powerful institutional systems that foreground the localized collaborative work of writing teachers, researchers, administrators, and students within (and outside) the university. However, we must remember
that this kind of intellectual inquiry—work that blends teaching, research,
and service—is inextricably tied to institutional politics. Institutional forces
require WPAs and TAs to examine issues of professionalization and subjectivity, theorize about the politicized positions they hold, and think of
themselves (in many cases) as agents for institutional change. In this chapter, we offer brief reviews of literature addressing collaborative administrative practices and intellectual inquiry, blended with our own local experiences engaging in these processes.

Although the first-year writing course became a staple at most institutions by the 1970s, the idea of a writing program began to develop much
later. Jeanne Gunner explains that the first-year writing course "was sepa-
rated from a general English department curriculum and [. . .] characterized as much if not more by administrative practices than by a set of
coherent disciplinary offerings" ("Ideology" 7). As faculty (most trained in
literary and linguistic studies) became interested in writing instruction as a
legitimate and distinct field of study, research emerged concerning composition curriculum and pedagogy. Teachers/scholars/administrators working in writing programs began the kind of intellectual study that led to
program revision—and, in the process, stepped on quite a few toes. Often
upper level administrators did not want to financially support emerging
programs, and literature faculty (who rarely taught first-year writing, but
wanted to dictate the content/pedagogy of those courses) viewed composition instruction as an intellectually subservient activity—service courses
appropriate for TAs, adjuncts, and newly hired faculty to teach. As
Edward M. White reminds us, a WPA's struggles against the elitist oppo-
nents of writing programs often stem from issues of composition's legiti-
macy as a field and from larger divisions within departments, where literature instruction is valued over the service provided by Rhet-Comp faculty
(111).

Irene Ward suggests that another "possible source of conflict can be
personal values and ethics. [. . .] Academics may hold negative stereotypes of leaders" (55), an impression that determines both how one may
approach the WPA position and how others tolerate WPAs. Faculty and
upper level administrators often conclude that WPAs have little connection to what takes place in the classroom and to students in first-year
writing courses. In many programs, the majority of teaching is done by
GTAs and adjunct or temporary faculty, from which, critics argue, the

WPA is dangerously disconnected. Bousquet goes so far as to suggest that completion of the Ph.D. in English, particularly in Rhet-Comp, coincides with the end of teaching because many of these students will go on to professorships that involve little time in the classroom, especially in the first-year writing classroom, and much more time spent theorizing ("Waste Product"; see also Sledd, "Why"). These assumptions, however, overlook what Richard Gebhardt describes as "macrolevel teaching," potentially the most significant work in which a WPA will ever take part ("Administration" 35). Gebhardt argues that the managerial duties, for which both Sledd and Bousquet have criticized the position of WPA, are merely the "tools for macrolevel teaching, not the heart or soul of program administration" (36). In fact, the WPA position enables committed writing instruction faculty to engage in work that lies at the heart of writing instruction: collaboration and epistemic reflection. Solitary WPAs dedicated only to the advancement of institutional policies, those detached from curricular issues, disciplinary scholarship, and local exigencies, ultimately do become "boss-compositionists" at many institutions. Conversely, collaborative WPA work can improve the quality of teaching, resulting in visible outcomes of intellectual inquiry, but often extracted at the price of institutional peace. Placement exams, holistic scoring, class caps, expanded enrollment, portfolio assessment, curriculum revision, assessment standards, teaching with technology, and so on require collaboration among composition teachers, other faculty, department chairs, deans, and provosts, with WPAs initiating and supporting these kinds of institutional changes. This kind of leadership requires collaborative effort based on feminist administrative models.

COLLABORATIVE MODELS OF WPA WORK

Commenting on the unique position of the WPA, Marcia Dickson claims that no single, ideal model of writing program administration exists, that the only productive models come from collaborative faculty governance (140). Dickson lists the following attributes of feminist administrative structures:

1. a willingness on the part of the WPA to relinquish control over the word—dictating official policy;
2. a heavy emphasis on collaboration;
3. an agreement to assign duties according to ability rather than according to title or rank—diversifying rather than delegating authority;

4. an ongoing conversation about the projects in which the faculty is engaged: teaching, research, and administration;
5. a workshop and a forum atmosphere that allows for experimentation in teaching and research;
6. a commitment to provide ample support and mentoring services for all levels of participants; and
7. a constant and steady system of rewarding excellence and effort. (152)

Dickson claims these program characteristics facilitate trust among program members, stress "moral and ethical issues" as well as "rational and logical" ones, and allow for "freedom to act upon good ideas" (152). Finally, she asserts that it is not "power a WPA needs to control a writing program" but rather "the ability to step back and let the program grow through the concerted efforts of the members of the community rather than by insisting that it conform to rigid and cripp[l]ing policy" (153). Her notion of collaborative administration is shared by compositionists who believe that "the only way to direct a program is to let the individual program shape itself according to the beliefs of the people who make it up and existing power structures of the institution in which it is located" (147). Working against overly patriarchal and traditional WPA structures, Dickson argues that feminist administration blurs hierarchical distinctions of authority while making room for conceptions of a "collaborative program that considers human stories, issues, and abilities—before, during, and after creating departmental policy decisions" (148).

Often initiated by WPAs "to make alliances or co-directorships or other creative programmatic hybrids with colleagues," collaborative models, explain Diane Kelley-Riley, Lisa Johnson-Shull, and Bill Condon, become necessary for junior faculty members working to protect themselves as they approach tenure (129). Although collaborative models do not always conform to traditional power structures, they do support current societal developments in communication, allowing for "a high level of interaction among individuals and groups" (130–32). With a WPA to initiate and facilitate the collaborative process, the resulting "flatter structure," as opposed to the top-down construction of most administrative processes in the university, "accommodates collaborative working relationships; promotes information sharing and shared decision making; responds to problems, input, and initiatives; and expands/extends not only to those within the writing programs, but also to those who are affected by them" (133, 135). Additional benefits of these revised models include increased cross-curricular teaching opportunities, additional occasions for service across campus through consulting, and greater potential for WAC initiatives (Johnson-Sheehan and Paine 203). Each of these collaborative structures combines the efforts of faculty toward the singular goal of effective writing instruction, underscoring the individual contributions of members in a "decentralized and democratic" structure and building on collaborative processes inherent to work in composition studies (Kelley-Riley, Johnson-Shull, and Condon 139).

One of the most notable collaborative arrangements in writing program administration relies on the efforts of full-time faculty and graduate students. Beyond advancing the benefits of a decentered structure, these models offer greater opportunities for mentoring and for the professional development of graduate students as they attempt to make the transition from graduate school to professorships. Drawing from their experiences as collaborative directors, Suellynn Duffey et al. claim that these structures "can foster critical self-reflection [. . .] establish a community of teachers," and facilitate identify formation (80).

As noted by other authors in this book, negotiating power within these administrative arrangements/structures comes with its own challenges, yet it is precisely this continued negotiation that Ratcliffe, Rickly, and contributors to this collection identify as *feminist*. Commenting on the potential power struggles that may result from "collaborative efforts between teachers with different amounts of institutional power" (66), Margaret K. Willard-Traub argues:

> [F]ormal opportunities [to engage in administration and assessment] would not only help to improve the quality of teaching and of learning; opportunities for graduate students to theorize the politicized nature of their positions within the institution would help serve the aims of scholarship as well, providing emerging scholars with occasions for the kind of epistemic reflexivity that Pierre Bourdieu argues for in support of the pursuit of disciplinary knowledge. (68)

Perhaps the most significant benefit resulting from collaborative administration, as illustrated by the experiences of Susan Popham, Michael Neal, Ellen Schendel, and Brian Huot (working together as both GTAs and program administrators), is the increased opportunity for significant reflection leading to alternatives to traditional administrative hierarchies. Working as a group, the members were able "to emphasize the intellectual nature of the work that WPAs do," asserting that it is "through administrative action that we can also enact and advance disciplinary knowledge" (21, 23). Having found a way to combine successfully theory, practice, and program policy, Popham et al. assert that writing programs benefit from collaborative reflection that leads to revision in policy and curriculum and informs the intellectual work of WPAs (28).

A COLLABORATIVE MODEL OF ADMINISTRATION
AT GEORGIA STATE UNIVERSITY

I (Lynée) was the WPA at Georgia State University (GSU)—a large Ph.D.-granting institution located in the heart of downtown Atlanta—from 1999 to 2004. Prior to taking over this position, the first-year writing program was administered by a sole director and driven by an exit exam. My predecessor was the first holder of the position trained in rhetoric, and he laid the groundwork for eliminating the exit exam and acquiring technological resources for the program. When I took over (the first woman in recent history to hold the position), I was fortunate enough to negotiate—with great assistance from my department chair—an associate WPA position, hired from the existing pool of visiting instructors within the English department. In addition, I established an assistant WPA position—held by a TA. At the time, we had 100 TAs and 10 instructors/lecturers who regularly taught first-year composition.

The newly formed collaborative team completely revamped the existing program: defining and sequencing the two first-year writing courses, adding TA training components, establishing a mentoring program for new TAs, and crafting a supplemental text for students. We also established professional development workshops for graduate students. According to Jeanne Gunner, "Collaborative administration entails ideological critique, a restructuring of institutional power, and, in practice, a sharing of authority" ("Collaborative" 254). She explains:

> In general terms where labor and responsibility are shared, where administrators have some degree of authority over their particular duties, and where the various "heads" meet to consider the program as a whole rather than individually reporting "up" to a single person in charge [. . .] we can say a collaborative writing program exists. (255)

Gunner describes three common collaborative writing structures—flattened hierarchies, professional training tracks, and rotational collaboration (258). Like many of the programs referenced previously, the administration of our revised first-year writing program blended traits from all three of the common collaborative structures described by Gunner.

Flattened hierarchies are "the 'textbook' type of collaborative structure in which individual faculty members take on individual duties, sharing the work and consulting as a group to direct the program" (Gunner, "Collaborative" 258). At GSU, the WPA (tenured faculty member), an associate WPA (a lecturer), and an assistant WPA (graduate student) each have specific responsibilities, but the director is ultimately in charge of reporting to the department chair and other committees/administrators outside the department. In "Politics and the WPA: Through and Past Realms of Expertise," Doug Hesse tells us that regardless of whether we like it, WPAs must be both politicians and rhetoricians (41). Citing debates in WPA scholarship over the roles WPA authority should take, Hesse explains that WPAs must adopt both the perspective of "having considerable authority and decision-making power (White)" and "more overtly democratic or collaborative arrangements (Gunner)" because of the many spheres in which WPAs work (43). Within departments, Hesse encourages a collaborative model of WPA authority. If teachers are enlisted in decisions, they are then invested in writing policies and practices. However, when working within administrative structures outside the department, Hesse suggests WPAs must "act with a decisiveness that may exceed their democratic sensibilities" (43). This model held true during my tenure as a WPA at GSU. Along with the WAC director, the WPA is called to account for writing practices and assessment to committees outside the English department, although decisions affecting curriculum, TA training, assessment, and so on are made in consultation (by committee) within the writing program administration office.

Professional training tracks are programs that "employ teaching assistants as part-time administrators, and not all such programs can be considered actually collaborative—they may be completely hierarchical. [. . .] Graduate students may work in teams to design and teach/facilitate practica, working with less experienced peers on pedagogy and curriculum for freshman writing courses, or they may run the writing center" (Gunner, "Collaborative" 258). At GSU, we have an assistant director who is an advanced graduate student. In addition, our experienced graduate students are paired with new TAs for their first year of teaching. Graduate students organize our day-long professional development colloquiums and lead many of our required teaching seminars, which are offered weekly. Recently, we created a committee to assess our first-year writing program that consists of graduate students who currently teach first-year composition. Working in conjunction with the WAC and WPA directors, they are charged with creating rubrics for assessing the courses, detailing the materials to be collected from individual teachers, setting the timetable for collection, and so on—a truly collaborative venture with considerable outcome affecting program review and our SACS visits.

Rotational collaboration means "sharing the established program positions by having faculty rotate through them is another form of collaborative administration. The arguments for such a system include preventing WPA 'burn out,' allowing for change through change of directors, helping administrators balance scholarly and administrative work, and enhancing a sense of shared responsibility for program design" (Gunner, "Collaborative" 259). We are just entering this phase of collaborative administration at GSU. I was the first WPA at my school trained primarily in composition and publishing about WPA work. Together with the associate and assistant directors, we made many changes in our program—changes that brought our training of TAs and discussions of mentoring/professional development in line with national standards and practices. I do not want to lose this progress. I also do not want to permanently leave administration, but I felt the need to take a break after 5 years. In addition, I moved on to another administration assignment—executive director of the South Atlantic Modern Language Association (where I also engage in collaborative administration). An experienced colleague, also committed to collaborative research and administration, has taken over as WPA and brings experience in administration (department and WC), TA training, and curriculum development to the position. Before officially making the transition, she served as my chief advisor and was quite familiar with the existing program. The associate WPA working with me stayed in the position and provided additional continuity for the transition. With a rotational arrangement completely supported by our department, I am not opposed to rotating back into the position in the future.

Those of us involved in collaborative administration at GSU found that we avoided the overwhelming burnout facing so many of our colleagues at other institutions because we shared the work burden and had each other as reliable sounding boards for ideas and complaints. Perhaps the greatest advantage to collaborative administration for us came in the increased opportunities to pursue both individual and collaborative research projects. Of course, there are some disadvantages to collaborative program administration. Not all departments allow collaborative program administration, and in some instances, when the work is dispersed, not all participants are credited by department or college P&T committees. Problems also arise when personalities conflict, nontenured faculty run programs and receive no institutional rewards, or program improvements are phased out when administration changes. Still the unique opportunities for intellectual growth through these collaborative arrangements ensure that WPAs can pursue scholarly projects while also serving the writing program and department as a whole.

WPA WORK AS INTELLECTUAL INQUIRY

As Gunner and Shamoon et al. make clear, the varied responsibilities of the WPA—a newer breed of administrator—make classifying and even identifying their work a difficult process. Although tenure and promotion comes with its own intricate system of awarding credit, the nature of a WPA's work often leaves the candidate at the whim of promotion and tenure committees, which may reward only traditional research and scholarship. Beginning with Richard Bullock's *WPA* article, "When Administration Becomes Scholarship: The Future of Writing Program Administration," numerous articles, book collections, and conference presentations, "theorize the importance of recognizing and valuing the work of the WPA" (Gunner, "Identity" 39; K. Bishop 42). From the outset, a WPA may face opposition during the tenure process simply because of a foundational tie to rhetoric and composition and a marginal status that reinforces its characterization "as a service void of real intellectual work and real disciplinary content" (Fox 91; Tiernan 164). Consequently, those faculty who choose to teach composition are generally regarded for providing a service rather than promoting intellectual work—the "real" work of the university (Schuster 331). Comparing the plight of a compositionist to that of Boxer in Orwell's *Animal Farm*, Schuster argues that "composition specialists [. . .] [are] generally required to do more than their fair share of minding the farm" (332). Combine Boxer's grim fate with the accepted belief that "administration—including leadership of first-year writing courses, WAC programs, writing centers, and the many other manifestations of writing administration—has for the most part been treated as a management activity that does not produce new knowledge and that neither requires nor demonstrates scholarly expertise and disciplinary knowledge," it is easy to imagine why tenure review may be an uphill battle for a WPA (WPA 366; see also Anson and Brown).

Compositionists such as Gary Olson argue "that rhetoric and composition *already* is an intellectual discipline," one that is "more than a service to the university (though it is certainly that), more than a field devoted solely to improving writing pedagogy (though it is that too), and more than a stepchild to literary studies" ("Preface" xii, xvi). Because knowledge is created through much of a WPA's reflective work, Yancey and Morgan assert that this work "has epistemological value," a value that warrants its consideration as part of the intellectual work of the university (92). It is precisely this belief that prompted the WPA council's creation of standards for "Evaluating the Intellectual Work of Writing Administration" to "refigur[e] writing administration as scholarly and intellectual work, [. . .] worthy of tenure and promotion" (WPA 366).

Overwhelmingly, compositionists argue that much of the inequity in judging the work of a WPA comes from issues of representation: "our work remains invisible because we lack effective ways of making it comprehensible to those within and outside the field" (K. Bishop 45). Simply labeling a WPA's work as service, argue Weiser and Rose, discounts "its application to teaching and its potential for research and for theory development" (186) and makes necessary the creation of a process through which the WPA can "*articulate* what it is that [he/she does] [. . .] in ways that are comprehensible to our departments, to our institutions, and to, indeed, the discipline of English studies generally" (Tiernan 171; see Hult). The impending problem, however, with effective representation has much more to do with the established model for judging intellectual work—a kind of positivist research standard borrowed from the sciences—that views theory and practice as binary opposites and results "in the traditional academic separation of research, teaching, and service" (Weiser and Rose 186). For example, Julia Ferganchick-Neufang's study on "gender-specific problems in the writing classroom" fails to fit the model of traditional academic research, yet its subjectivity and ability to respond to local exigencies make it particularly relevant to composition studies and characteristic of the WPA's required, yet devalued, work (19, 22).

Fortunately, as "part of the conventional lore about teaching reform, especially at research universities," the work of Ernest Boyer can help to reinforce that a WPA's work, carefully combining scholarship, teaching, and service, is in fact intellectual in terms that committees across the university will understand (Hesse, "Understanding" 306; WPA 371). Blending all four categories of Boyer's model—discovery, integration, application, and teaching—WPA "work is intellectual: it requires specific expertise, training, and an understanding of disciplinary knowledge" (WPA 370; see Cambridge and McClelland; Roen et al.; and Hult). As a theorist, "a reflective agent seeking explanations of phenomena and situations in order to understand them better and to act on that understanding in a particular context for a particular purpose," the WPA combines theory and practice while creating knowledge (Weiser and Rose 183). Working to address the situations at hand, rather than simply theorizing the universal, WPAs move from "institutional critique" toward inciting "institutional change" (Ferganchick-Neufang 23; Fox 93).

Early on, scholars such as Bullock and Hairston depicted the WPA as "an isolated figure battling for recognition of his or her work, program, and discipline," yet this "unitary WPA" seems to disregard the inherently collaborative nature of writing programs and composition studies (Gunner, "Identity" 39). The potential for collaborative administration, as Popham et al. assert, "to emphasize the intellectual nature of the work that WPAs do" (21) and for collaborative research to "[allow] for the dialogic co-construction of knowledge" (Jablonski 179), makes a move toward collaborative structures that is both logical and necessary for success in writing program administration.

WPA WORK AS COLLABORATIVE INQUIRY AT GSU

My (Lynée) areas of scholarly research include the history of writing practices and contemporary composition theory and pedagogy. Although knowledgeable in the field, like most WPAs of my generation, I received no formal training in program administration nor specifically researched writing program theory or practice before taking over this position—immediately upon becoming tenured in my department. Having adopted a publish-or-perish mindset for the previous 5 years while working toward tenure, I knew I did not want to abandon my publishing goals in lieu of administrative work, and I also needed help and advice ASAP from experienced administrators in revising the existing program. As I expanded my interests in composition theory to include concentrated research in writing program administration, I found many avenues for blending my research in the history of rhetoric with WPA scholarship. At the time, I also was teaching both the required TA training course and a publication class for graduate students. My need to engage in intellectual inquiry so that I could function in an administrative position for which I was not trained, combined with my interest in the professionalization of graduate students and lecturers, led to several collaborative research projects involving the newly established WPA team, first-year writing teachers, and other faculty members. Because we were all new to WPA work, intellectual inquiry (a task with which we were all familiar) became not only a necessary labor to quickly gain disciplinary knowledge, but a unifying activity as well.

Redesigning our large, urban first-year writing program to include TA training and curriculum/assessment changes took the combined efforts of many people and resulted in numerous collaborative research projects.[1] Initially, I worked with the associate and assistant WPAs in researching other large urban, public college programs similar to ours. We collected data concerning sequencing the two first-year courses, TA training, and division of authority. As a result of our findings, we instituted weekly mentoring meetings (led by teachers within our program). The TAs submitted abstracts for proposed sessions (to gain experience writing conference abstracts). The proposals were then vetted by the administrative team and, if approved, slated for presentation. In addition to classroom observations of all TAs, we initiated a mentoring program for TAs new to GSU, whereby experienced TAs mentored incoming teachers. When the pairings worked well (and we took great pains in matching instructors), new TAs learned about teaching in a relaxed and personal way. Experienced TAs learned to articulate their own teaching philosophies and practices and could put this collaborative/leadership experience on their curricula vitae.

Next, we took on the university-approved curriculum in an effort to replace the literature driven curriculum with courses grounded in argumentation and/or civic rhetoric; seven of us piloted ethnography-based courses designed to introduce first-year students to civic rhetoric. The participants in this program became disciples for this approach, collaboratively designing and leading mentoring workshops exploring the theory and pedagogy supporting this pedagogy. We converted many TAs and set up a kind of support group for sharing information, contacts, and assignments that promoted the study of local, civic rhetoric. This pedagogical approach, based on primary research, provided many opportunities for directors, teachers, and students to engage in collaborative research and writing. The WPA team presented our findings and experiences at local and national conferences and also wrote up our research and experiences for (both individual and joint) publication.

To financially support program changes, the WPA team and several teachers collaboratively edited a research supplement, packaged with our required handbook. The proceeds were used for operational expenses and to provide travel and research grants for the TAs. Over the years, thousands of dollars were awarded for travel and pedagogical research projects, but, most important, these self-generated funds provided a necessary means for instilling a sense of professional development among the teaching staff. Subsequent members of the collaborative WPA team produced a text for the required Regent's Exam course, which fell under the auspices of the first-year writing program. Revenue from this project provides continued support for teacher research and travel.

Faced with an upcoming Southern Association of Colleges and Schools (SACS) visit, interested teachers were asked to participate with the writing program directors to devise assessment outcome documents and evaluation instruments. These resources were, of course, presented to the SACS team, but also were also published on the GSU website and disseminated to all teaching faculty as a model for other divisions (creative writing, literature, education) to emulate. In addition, many experienced instructors worked with the WPA team to develop the GTA Handbook, contributing assignments, research, and student writing samples. Another ad hoc team comprised of teachers and administrators developed the guidelines and assessment rubrics governing the teaching portfolios required of all TAs—setting a higher standard than the one adopted by faculty in the department. As a result, our TAs report being fully prepared for job interview questions concerning their teaching and also have on hand required teaching documents necessary for job applications. The administrative team also worked diligently to reform the hiring and promotion practices of lecturers and instructors, putting into the institutional record revised documents and publishing/presenting our experiences nationally.

CONCLUSION

Feminist models of collaborative administration create space for innovative leadership, draw on the strength of individual faculty members, allow opportunity for building problem-solving strategies, encourage experimentation, and foster mentoring. Collaborative administration also allows program directors and teachers to engage in pedagogical research explicitly tied to institutional politics and local exigencies. This kind of intellectual inquiry produces better local programs, offers teachers a vested interest in program goals, and provides professional development opportunities for administrators and teachers to blend their research, teaching, and service interests.

ADDITIONAL RESOURCES

See below select collaborative presentations and publications incorporating profiles of writing instruction. These works grew out of collaborative administration practices at Georgia State University. In addition, dozens of individually authored presentations and publications were produced by those of us involved in first-year composition instruction and administration at GSU. Not included in this list are numerous collaboratively produced and disseminated reports, accreditation documents, assessment guidelines, and scoring rubrics.

Bell, Kim, Michelle Eble, and Lynée Lewis Gaillet. "Literacy and TA Training or What do Literature-Trained TAs Really Need to Know About Rhet/Comp to Teach First-Year Writing?" Western States Composition Conference. Tempe, AZ. October 2001.

Eble, Michelle, and Lynée Lewis Gaillet. "Informing the Discipline of Technical and Professional Communication: Rhetoric, Moral Philosophy, and Civic Engagement." *Technical Society Quarterly* 13 (2004): 341–54.

_____."A Model of Collaboration: Mentoring Writing Instructors in a Metropolitan Institution." Mentoring Special Interest Group. Conference on College Composition and Communication. Chicago. March 2006.

_____."Nineteenth-Century Education of the 'Other': Mechanic's Institutes, Dissenting Academies, Women's Schools, and Public Lecture Series." South Atlantic Modern Language Association. Roanoke, VA. November 2004.

_____."Public Literacy and Rhetorical Intervention: Composing the Civic Life." Conference on Composition and Communication. San Antonio. March 2004.

_____."Research Doesn't Have to be Boring (for You or Your Students): Ethnography in the Composition Classroom." Georgia Conference of Teachers of English. Savannah. February 2001.

_____, eds. *Stories of Mentoring*. Forthcoming Parlor P.

_____."Telling Stories of Mentoring." Conference on College Composition and Communication. Chicago. March 2006.

Gaillet, Lynée, and Letizia Guglielmo. "Collaborative Writing Administration as Intellectual Inquiry." Writing Program Administration Conference. Chattanooga. July 2006.

Grabill, Jeff, and Lynée Lewis Gaillet. "Writing Program Design in the Metropolitan University: Toward Constructing Community Interfaces." *WPA: Writing Program Administrator* 25 (2002): 61–78.

Lamb, Mary, and Lynée Lewis Gaillet. "Faculty Insider/Out: Non-Tenure Track Teaching Positions at Georgia State University." In progress.

_____. *Reading in Composition Studies*. Proposal under review at Parlor Press for the *Lenses on Composition Studies*, edited by Susan Hunter and Sheryl Fontaine.

Lamb, Mary R., and Marti Singer. *Successful Regents' Essays: A Sourcebook for Writers*. 2nd ed. Boston: Houghton Mifflin, 2005.

Lamb, Mary, Robert Krut, and Lynée Lewis Gaillet. "Visiting Voices From the Edge: Institutional Critique and Temporary Composition Labor Force/Administration." Writing Program Administrators Conference. Grand Rapids. July 2003.

Singer, Marti, Cara Minardi, and Dan Vollaro, eds. *First Essays: A Peer Approach to Freshman Composition*. Plymouth, Michigan: Hayden-McNeil Publishing, 2007.

Singer, Marti, Mary Lamb, Marc Pietrzykowski, and Melissa McLeod. *Resources for Instructors*. 2004. Atlanta, GA: GSU Department of English, 2005.

Sugarman, Tammy, Laura Burtle, Lynée Lewis Gaillet, and Michelle Eble. *An Introduction to Pullen Library at Georgia State University*. 1999. 2001. 2002. Fort Worth: Harcourt Brace, 2003.

5

THE MATERNAL MELODRAMA OF WRITING PROGRAM ADMINISTRATION

Christine Farris

I've spent the best years of my life on you.
A woman wants to be something else besides a mother, you know.

—Stella Dallas

In the 1937 King Vidor film, *Stella Dallas*, Barbara Stanwyck plays Stella Martin, a young woman who crosses class boundaries to seduce and marry mill boss, Stephen Dallas, an upper class young man temporarily slumming in her small town. Over time, they drift apart, as Stephen, increasingly critical of Stella's lower class tastes, relocates to New York and comes back into his own. Stella asserts her independence as a brash, good-time gal, all while making sacrifices to raise their daughter, Laurel, alone, only to relinquish her to Stephen when she reaches adolescence. While Stella has had a few laughs with Ed Munn, an old flame down on his luck, her estranged husband has become reacquainted with Helen, now a wealthy widow with two sons. Eventually Stephen and Stella divorce. Stella's motherly love and work are brushed aside. It goes without saying that, despite the closeness of mother and daughter, Stephen and his new wife can provide Laurel with life's real advantages. In the film's classic final scene, Stella stands in the rain, outside Helen's grand house, eager for a glimpse of her daughter's society wedding. Her tearful eyes shine not with bitterness, but with the satisfaction of a job well done.

Bracketing ideological reprehensibility for a moment, what is it that is so appealing about this film? Perhaps the maternal martyrdom of Stella Dallas, resigned to near bag-lady status as long as her daughter's needs are met and her success assured, reminds me of the position of women WPAs in English departments, especially those working at research universities in the shadows of large doctoral programs in literature. If this is not the sort of department with which you are familiar, count your blessings. If you work in some sort of rhetoric and composition wonderland, then maybe I'm not talking about you—or I'm not talking about you yet.

After preparing graduate students to teach first-year writing in workshops and seminars, the WPA typically releases her charges to teach independently or with other faculty colleagues, who are perhaps more likely to privilege scholarship and job placement in literature over a career centered on composition and pedagogy. The "other parent" may even attribute the teaching abilities of graduate students to their scholarly or innate talents, ignoring the influence of the WPA, rendering it, along with composition, as invisible as Stella Dallas' childrearing. Even graduate students who go on to become excellent teachers and designers of courses may not view the first-year writing curriculum, composition studies, or pedagogy as intellectual work tied to expert knowledge and to a specialized field. Particularly if their doctoral emphasis is literature and not rhetoric/composition, they may view such work as natural, domestic preparation easily effaced, internalized, or even claimed entirely as their own as they move away from first-year writing into other teaching assignments and the competition of an academic job search.

Enculturation—internalizing our values and practices as they come into their own—is, of course, what WPAs want for the next generation. While graduate students enter our programs unfamiliar with or even resistant to teaching, if we are successful, we convert our expertise about college students' reading and writing practices into an accessible, transportable teaching "lore." Having laid the groundwork for that future ascent, WPAs may find that they become, like Stella, watchful bystanders as graduate students move up the social ladder from low-culture composition to high-culture matters if and when the absent literature parents reemerge to claim them. Perhaps the melodrama of the self-sacrificing, working-class mother as heroine (or pawn) in the patriarchal system can shed light on the situation of the women WPAs serving the literature-driven English department, in that both are caught up in similar struggles between duty and identity. I want to suggest, however, that women WPAs may be well situated to negotiate the seemingly conflicting demands of supporting new teachers and defending a professional identity that is still anchored in the authority of composition studies.

But first a flashback to our story. As a young wife and parent, Stella Dallas faces contradictory demands. Not wishing to interfere with her husband's chances for advancement, Stella does not leave the mill town and go with her husband to New York. Although her staying behind finishes off what is left of their marriage, the fun-loving Stella does not want to give up her old friends. She is in a bind, not unlike that of the WPA who seeks a separate identity for herself and for composition studies that involves more than just TA training and domestic servitude to literature. Nevertheless, Stella takes pride in the duties of motherhood. She sends Laurel to the best schools, sews her fancy dresses, and plans birthday celebrations that fizzle when the snooty parents of Laurel's friends will not allow them to attend. Stella's maternal responsibility to provide the best for Laurel eventually takes over her desire to be a part of Laurel's social ascent. Finally, in a parody of herself, Stella feigns disinterest in her daughter, pretending to prefer partying with her old drinking buddy, Ed, in order to ensure that Laurel, ever loyal to her mother, will agree to go live with her father.

Helen, the new Mrs. Dallas, sees right through Stella's deception. Although Helen is as refined as Stella is tacky, she also is a mother. When Stella writes to Laurel that she will have to live with her father because she has decided to join Ed at his new job in South America, Helen recognizes the ultimate maternal sacrifice. Nevertheless, in keeping Stella's lie to herself, Helen ensures that the social order remains intact. Conveniently, Stella will not be in the country to attend Laurel's marriage to the college chum of one of her sons. Charitably, Helen asks her butler to keep the drapes of the picture window open during the ceremony, should Stella happen to be among the spectators on the sidewalk.

A writing program director, in "mothering" new instructors, also makes sacrifices and paves the way—downplaying not only her own identity, but composition's, as she shares ready-made syllabi and materials, overlooks mistakes, and makes teaching problems go away. Consequently, she smoothes over the rigor and complexities of what is, at first, more anxiety-producing than rewarding to new graduate student instructors. In doing so, she may affirm the perception in academia that teaching is burdensome and distracting labor, never one's "real work." At the same time, with no apologies, her colleagues are evaluating the rigor of those same graduate students' performances in scholarship. Final satisfaction, like Stella's, may come primarily from a WPA's private perception of her long-term influence on the future professoriate—at least those who will come to care about teaching.

Of course, it is impossible to distinguish the perception of the woman director of composition from the perception of the field in general. Despite attempts to reconfigure it intellectually and politically, composition is tied to gendered images of home and family, inseparable, as Susan Miller points out, from the figure of the composition *teacher* as paradoxically both a comfort and a powerful disciplinarian, who enables practice in what will count later in life ("The Feminization" 47–8). This characterization can be extended to the composition *director,* who also serves as both nurturer and disciplinarian to first-time teachers. Determining curricula and panoptically overseeing classes, she is the mother who restricts the academic freedoms of individual instructors even as she introduces them to a teaching world heretofore unknown. Like Stella Dallas, uninvited to the wedding, the composition teacher (and, by extension, the WPA) is, says Miller, "a culturally designated 'initiator,' similar to a temple priest or priestess who functions to pass along secret knowledge, but not to participate freely in a culture that depends on that knowledge" ("The Feminization" 48).

Characterizations of the marginalized gender and class status of composition are commonplace both within and outside the specialization—"sad women in the basement," milkers of the department cash cow, "comp droids" who "beep and whir and grade" endless stacks of papers, performing the dirty work that no one else wants to do. Not surprisingly, writing program directors typically characterize themselves as victims, sometimes, as Donna Strickland points out, too easily conflating their position with that of the writing instructors over whom they have power ("The Managerial" 53). Needless to say, there are more published accusations than confessions of comfortable "boss compositionists," as James Sledd once called them, who manage exploited teaching labor, but never teach writing themselves (Ferry 249). Across genders, parenting analogies abound in narratives documenting the unfortunate (or fortunate) accidents by which WPAs entered writing program administration, some thrown unexpectedly, like Diane Keaton in the film *Baby Boom* or, more recently, Kate Hudson in *Raising Helen,* into instant parenthood, which of course changes their lives forever (for such WPA narratives, see Diana George's *Kitchen Cooks, Plate Twirlers and Troubadours: Writing Program Administrators Tell Their Stories*).

That some academics "take to" the job of teaching or administering composition is discussed in an even more essentialized fashion by those who have no intention of doing it. Cary Nelson, as many in composition have been quick to point out, confesses that he would now find composition teaching "demoralizing and intolerable" and that he could never "grade hundreds of composition papers . . . as carefully and thoughtfully" as his graduate students do (qtd. in R. Miller, *As if* 200). In the guise of praise for those whom he presumes to save from "comp droid" hell, Nelson manages to separate himself from composition, make the age-old connection Margaret Marshall observes between effective teaching and "the natural nurturing work of women with little intellectual dimension" (140), and, as Richard Miller points out, "propose changes that will improve the employment possibilities of his graduate students without imperiling his own position of privilege" (*As if* 200). Nelson's is a revealing slip: He positions demonized composition teaching at the center of his reformist project on behalf of graduate students, with whom he identifies. Composition teaching is what he least desires to do. Thus, the ultimate indignity experienced by this generation of English academics looking for jobs is having to teach writing more often or for longer than Nelson had to do it. Institutional critics like Nelson and Michael Bérubé, in decrying the collapse of the job market in English, characterize the composition industry in their own "melodrama of educational reform" (R. Miller, *As if* 202) not just as labor-intensive, but as dreadful, unskilled domestic work emblematic of the rise of the corporate university and the demise of the scholarly life of the mind. As more students are admitted to a university less concerned with providing a liberal arts education and more interested in delivering the most cost-effective product to the student consumer, "we will all," Bérubé once proclaimed apocalyptically to my department, "end up working for composition." The role of the pundit or prophet in this reformist melodrama, Richard Miller maintains, is to serve as "the academy's moral conscience," the good-guy critical intellectual versus the bad-guy bureaucrats who have brought the university to ruins (201).

Of late, many compositionists responding to the institutional critics avoid the feminized initiator or nurturer stereotypes of the composition teacher and administrator concerned with the welfare of students, preferring to spar with the tough guys, casting themselves as wiser, even more realistic men on whom nothing is lost. Suggestions from both within and outside the field that composition has constructed the need for its services (Crowley; Guillory) or that specialists profit from managing contingent laborers whose conditions have not improved, of course, invite, if not bully, compositionists to respond. The first line of defense is typically an argument for the complicity of all faculty, not just those connected with composition or administration, in a university that has always been a bureaucratic enterprise, one that, in fact, has only supported a life of the mind for a rare few.

One exception to the defensive masculinist discourse is Doug Hesse, who, reverting to the parenting metaphor, writes of his father as a role model for the WPA as a stoic, responsible, self-sacrificing provider. Citing not Stella Dallas as his movie counterpart, but James Stevens, the butler played by Anthony Hopkins in *The Remains of the Day*, Hesse writes that he came to realize too late, like Stevens, that in emulating his father's conscientious fulfillment of his domestic duties, he may have sacrificed building relationships ("Politics" 47). Similarly, in his 2005 CCCC Presidential Address, "Who Owns Composition?", Hesse preferred to combine personal experience with an overview of the public perception of writing, rather than directly take on composition's detractors.

For the most part, however, the male response to criticism of composition has centered on appropriation of the economic analysis that calls the critics' bluff: If indeed the university at large *is* more interested now in composition than literature, why not accept the market realities of composition's service and hire as teachers of writing not conscripted, disinterested English graduate students, but the most qualified from disciplines including, but not limited to, English (see Harris, "Meet the New Boss"; R. Miller, "Let's Do the Numbers")? Richard Miller argues that disciplinary expertise at the doctoral level in rhetoric and composition is not necessary for the delivery of writing instruction, a recommendation that his critics believe aligns him with those who would "preserve the centrality of literary studies (by denying the value of composition theory)" (Fitts and Lalicker). Miller's main purpose, however, particularly in his book *As if Learning Mattered,* is to expose the soft utopic underbelly of the "prophets of doom," literary studies-based reformers who, he says, are more interested in positioning themselves as intellectuals outside the bureaucratic system, idealizing the life of the solitary scholar, than they are in rebalancing a hierarchy in English or participating in genuine reform of a system that, ironically, would require elaborate bureaucratic plans and managers for any kind of follow-through (*As if* 202–3).

Although I am generally in sympathy with criticism of faux radical reform proposals, I am struck by the extent to which many of the responses like Harris' and Miller's seem to depend on an image of the WPA as a male figure. There is a combativeness in most of the responses to those who would ignore, blame, or sell out composition in their critiques of the academy. Also, men are doing most of the talking. Even if the arguments of books like Richard Miller's or Gerald Graff's *Clueless in Academe* critique grand pronouncements on academia, preferring instead institutional and curricular change at the local level, they participate in the largely masculinist polemic that grabs attention in professional journals, at conferences, and on the backs of book covers: "In the wake of theory, in the wake of feminism, post-colonial criticism and all the rest, what is a liberal arts education supposed to be about? How should teachers teach?" (Graff). In a 2005 CCCC session, all-male panelists debated whether we are we at "the end of composition."

Continuing in a tradition of combative discourse that includes Ed White's "Use It or Lose It: Power and the WPA," WPA work can be constructed not as domestic, but as powerful and public, not just for the good of a program, but so that WPAs don't get played for fools, wooses, or Mr. Moms. Should composition continue as literature's bitch—this scholarship is, in effect, asking—or should we embrace our bureaucratic power?

Efforts to legitimize the WPA's professional status and identity, says Alice Gillam, codes the ideal WPA as male and the female as "dystopic" ("Taking" 67), resulting inevitably in "an economy of values in which the most 'public' professional acts are deemed most important and the more 'private' trivialized" (68). Thus, Gillam claims, "in-house work with students and teachers is 'insubstantial' while negotiating budgets with deans is 'substantial'" (68). Women's private labor is "dismissed as unimportant and as evidence of unprofessional status while the stereotypical public labor of men—winning battles and running things—is associated with professional achievement and recognition" (68).

Is there a way to transform the gendered WPA binary: invisible, under-appreciated, melodramatic women's work versus the combat of the shrewd warrior? How might we do this in relation to the larger disciplinary and institutional melodrama of the academic intellectual enslaved by bureaucrats who trade in composition piecework?

Louise Phelps complicates the discussion of gender in composition with the reminder that any feminist critique of disenfranchisement is, of course, also a "utopian vision of empowerment," in which women have opportunities for leadership and influence ("Becoming" 291). At the same time, she says the feminism of WPAs hovers, passive-aggressively between the "need for power and the distaste for it" (304), an observation also made by Ed White about WPAs in general, who often prefer "just to stay with a conviction of our own powerlessness, amply affirmed by the deans and department chairs who (it appears) have real power" (5). Phelps prefers to read "the meaning of composition's gendering" as not fixed, but something that can be re-imagined and transformed (290).

More recently, Donna Strickland points to what she terms the *managerial unconscious* of those who, in their reimaginings of new roles or alliances, fail to acknowledge their own power in conflations of composition teaching with composition management, "as if the entire field were marginalized because those who teach it—as opposed to those who specialize in it—are economically and ideologically marginalized" ("The Managerial" 47). Strickland singles out Joseph Harris' argument that composition's professional status is less important than ensuring that undergraduates are taught well in their writing classes as an example of how a "position of privilege" permits the forgetting of the extent to which WPAs benefit from composition's professionalism. Harris suggests forging class alliances built around a shared desire for "more direct control over our curricula and staffing—within departments of English or, if need be, outside them" ("Meet" 57).

Strickland is right that the sense of victimization felt by composition specialists and WPAs contributes to a glossing over of the material conditions under which composition gets taught. I would maintain, however,

that both literature and composition—specialists, bosses, and pundits all—
manage to conflate their marginalized or imperiled positions in the academy
with those of the progeny with whom they identify and hope to launch in
successful careers. That need not stop us, however, from imagining different
roles for composition vis-á-vis the rest of English studies, new alliances
with faculty not usually responsible for pedagogy or writing instruction or
new configurations of authority in the programs we administer.

In the last several years, I helped design in my department a second
pedagogy seminar in the teaching of literature and culture to follow and
build on the composition pedagogy seminar. Faculty teaching the seminar
collaborate with experienced TAs in the conception, design, and teaching of
a first-year course that integrates literature, culture, and composition.
These collaborations are now part of our ongoing efforts to redistribute
labor, dissolve binaries, and unify the teaching of reading and writing in
ways that need not be disconnected from or threatening to instructors'
scholarly interests (see Farris "Stars"; Farris and Favret). I admit that passing on the TAs to the rest of the faculty for work on pedagogy has given
me more than one "Stella Dallas moment," in which I felt rather like Stella
preparing Laurel for the world she cannot enter herself, that the groundwork I had built with TAs in their first year had been erased. Dwelling on
such thoughts eventually forced me to consider how I might do more with
my disciplinary identity and expertise than defend territory and selflessly
launch successful teachers. It has been my sense all along that the graduate
student perception of composition begins immediately when they see so
few tenure-track faculty in the first-year writing classroom and when they
realize whose capital is tied to pedagogy and undergraduate needs. Most of
my efforts concentrated on the design of curricula that theoretically and
ideologically attempted to bridge the divisions in the department primarily
through shared methodologies. For instance, our composition curriculum,
has, for over a decade, borrowed extensively from cultural studies in our
approach to the teaching of analytical writing (Farris, "Too Cool for
School"). Perhaps I had been, like Stella, overdressed in her polka-dots,
never the "real thing." Although many graduate students are familiar with
cultural studies from their own coursework, the approach makes for a more
complicated and stressful teacher preparation and requires that the WPA
continuously sell the aims of the first-year course to new instructors.
Nevertheless, my procedures for TA preparation had pretty much
remained the same.

Several years ago, I decided to dispense with the eight second-year TA
consultants who complemented the TA orientation and fall proseminar by
mentoring and meeting regularly with consultees in small groups. I opted
instead for four assistant directors with more years of teaching experience,
charging them with redesigning the first-year writing curriculum from

scratch. While I listen and advise in daily meetings for a month in the summer, the standard syllabus and materials we use in orientation are now mostly theirs. When the assistant directors came to the conclusion that first-year students lacked a context for much of the gender, race, and class analyses they read, we decided to include assignments centered on the historical analysis of photographs and films. In the past, the syllabus materials having to do with representation in popular culture were always variations and updates of what had originally been mine. Now I see my aims for the course in the sequence of skills, but only traces of my original assignments.

I do not mean to imply that I am not occupying a position of privilege as an appointed WPA and tenured full professor, working with assistants holding temporary positions, or that I am abdicating my position, as some have argued Stella Dallas does in the film's final scene (Williams 316). But having designed much of the curriculum and materials and having introduced new groups of 30 to 40 teachers to them for 16 weeks, the assistants' role has changed from middle manager (often perceived as spy) to an expert on much more than damage control. If the new instructors have difficulty with the curriculum, the assistant directors are part of analyzing why; they do not just pass that difficulty on to me. They now have a greater investment in the program that comes with having to justify, not just explain or oversee, what was formerly always the WPA's cross to bear.

I believe I withheld this responsibility from all my assistants in the past, in part, because they were still relatively new to teaching and because I wanted to protect them from conflicts—call it maternal self-sacrifice. I also admit to a certain possessiveness regarding my specialty. I now find that I can actually share my expertise better if I reverse the script and function as a consultant to them. Assistant directors from various English doctoral specialties who are given more intellectual, as well as supervisory, responsibilities can participate in the work of integrating literary and cultural studies with composition and thoughtful pedagogy. If nothing else, they are helping to transform the beliefs of former generations that the teaching of writing is something one always moves up and out of, as one would leave a mill town. It is also a way for graduate students to take professional development within the context of the current job market more seriously—as scholars, teachers, and administrators. For me, in my role as a WPA in this melodrama, it also is about being "something else besides a mother" without denying parental responsibility altogether to ensure the happiness and success of "the children." I imagine, however, that, like Stella Dallas' daughter, the assistant directors will eventually do very well for themselves.

6

INTERRUPTING COLLABORATION

Feminist Writing Program Administration and the Question of Status

Ilene Crawford

Donna Strickland

We would like to make a case for privileging *interruption* as a key value and practice for feminist WPAs. Although most existing accounts of feminist administration tend to encourage and define collaboration as quintessentially feminist, we note the status differentials inherent in writing program administration and question whether collaboration should be the measure of feminist action. Using materialist approaches to feminism to read our previous experiences as graduate student members of an administrative team and our more recent experiences as tenure-track administrators, we demonstrate why collaboration, although useful, needs to be tempered with a commitment to the performance of interruption. In particular, we argue that such performances are a powerful means to disrupt what we see as the bureaucratizing of the affective.

INTERRUPTION IN THEORY

During the 1990s, in the wake of a more general political turn in composition studies, a number of feminist and politicized WPAs began to theorize alternatives to the traditional masculinist model of administration. Collaborative writing program administration came to be privileged as a way of "decentering . . . their program" and creating a more "democratic structure" (Gunner, "Decentering" 7).[1] For some, this decentered approach to administration also has come to represent a feminist approach insofar as it overturns the more dominant, bureaucratic, and masculinist form of administration (Dickson; H. Miller). In the more dominant form of administration, one person is responsible for making decisions about the program, including decisions about who teaches and what is taught. In collaborative administration, by contrast, members of an administrative team share decision making. Jeanne Gunner, for example, describes the ideal program as one in which "the intellectual agenda and authority would come from a synthesis of informed instructors and the program they develop—it would be a group, or collaborative, entity, in need of a spokesperson or liaison, perhaps, but not a single position assigned total curricular responsibility or autocratic power" ("Decentering" 13).

However, although collaborative administration is more inclusive, it cannot erase real differences in status among team members. In practice, as Gunner also notes, collaborative teams often bring together tenured, non-tenured, and nontenure-track faculty, including GTAs. But despite these differences in status, when members of collaborative teams describe their experiences, their narratives tend to valorize inclusiveness to such an extent that status and power differences among team members are downplayed. For example, in one narrative from the spring 1998 issue of *WPA*, which was devoted to collaborative administrative arrangements, two tenure-track faculty members argue that, because of their collaborative administrative style, their graduate instructors "felt empowered to 'make it work' [during a crisis] *just as if they were in charge of the program*" (Meeks and Hult 9; italics added). In another narrative from this issue, a graduate student WPA feels that "when it comes to facing down the university's central administration, I, a female graduate student, and the tenured male director of the Freshman English program *share a vulnerability*" (Keller et al. 38; italics added). By linking tenured administrators to graduate student administrators with the "just as if," these narratives appear to overlook the material differences between graduate students and professors or between tenured and nontenured team members. In this second narrative, another female graduate student team member lists her impressive administrative experience, but then notes that, "although I have gained valuable administrative experience, I am not yet able to market this experience because I have not yet completed my degree" (Keller et al. 45). Although she may do the work "just as if" she were in charge of the program, this graduate student administrator is certainly not being paid "just as if" she were, nor had she, at the time, been able to move on to a more lucrative tenure-track position. In fact, it may well be that the time demands of administrative work were at least partially to blame for her unfinished degree. In practice, in other words, collaborative teams must often include members from different material circumstances—members who are asked to work with the program as if they have the same power as tenured faculty, even when that sharing of power materially benefits the tenured faculty more.

The erasure of material differences between members of collaborative administrative teams is symptomatic of the tendency in collaborative arrangements to not only ignore the material, but also to implicitly code difference and conflict as undesirable.[2] In many narratives, a lack of conflict is often a measure of how well a collaborative team is working. It is worth remembering, however, that the coding of difference and conflict as undesirable has been a major development of the capitalist workplace, a development that we want to critically examine.

Moreover, when difference is erased within collaborative teams that have identified themselves as motivated by feminist principles, this erasure may come into conflict with those same principles. From a materialist perspective, feminism is not primarily an identity, but a political activity. In the words of bell hooks, "Feminism is the struggle to end sexist oppression. . . . [It] is neither a lifestyle nor a ready-made identity or role one can step into" (*Feminism* 28). In the struggle to end oppression, feminists must confront, rather than obscure, conflict and inequality. Feminist participants in administrative teams, consequently, may need to confront differences in status by interrupting narratives that downplay difference.

We borrow the concept of interruption from Nedra Reynolds, who has argued for its value as a key feminist rhetorical strategy. Reynolds identifies bell hooks' interruptions at a Cultural Studies conference as exemplifications of this strategy. hooks objected to the way in which "the discourse of cultural studies as it was being constructed here was silencing certain kinds of people" (Reynolds, "Interrupting" 65). Her interruption was a call to action to those at the conference—a call not only to speak about transforming society, but to "break with behavior patterns that reinforce and perpetuate domination" (hooks, cited in Reynolds 65).

In a similar way, we would like to interrupt WPA discourse that downplays difference and conflict and, in so doing, places more value on the process of collaboration than on the political work of resisting oppression. In particular, we wish to break with the affective patterns that reinforce inequality and oppression. We begin by telling two stories that took place when we were GTA members of a collaborative administrative team. Experiencing and retelling these events as GTAs and later as tenure-track faculty have taught us that pursuing a materialist feminist agenda while participating in administration requires that we place difference and conflict between different faculty constituencies at the top of our agenda. Now that we are doing our WPA work from the location of the tenure track, our materialist perspective also has helped us see how our acculturation into WPA work was in large part about being socialized to do a certain kind of gendered emotional management. This chapter represents our effort to consider how feminist WPAs can create alternative models with their colleagues and resist this socialization.

INTERRUPTION IN PRACTICE

Decisions a department makes about how to fund its graduate students have an immediate impact on the material lives of those students. One year prior to the first story we tell, the Graduate Policy Committee of our department revised the requirements for funding graduate students. Rather than routinely giving all doctoral students 4 years of funding, the committee decided to tie the renewal of each year of funding to progress toward the degree. In addition, a fifth year of funding was offered for the first time as a reward for making 4 years of significant progress. The possibility of a fifth year of funding was of immense help to many GTAs in the department. GTAs in this department, as in most English departments, "assisted" no one, but taught a 2/2 load of mostly composition courses in addition to taking two courses. This heavy teaching load inevitably delayed GTAs' progress, and many ended up as part-time lecturers in the department after their fourth year. However, one year after the new fifth-year policy was implemented, this same committee made the sudden and unexpected decision to discontinue the possibility of fifth-year funding. Some members of the committee believed that graduate students were taking advantage of the new policy. Specifically, they alleged that dissertation committee members were falsely claiming that their students had made the required progress when, they further maintained, few if any graduate students were actually completing the fifth-year funding requirements—two chapters of the dissertation by the end of the fourth year.

The day this edict was handed down, our collaborative administrative team was scheduled to assemble for our weekly meeting. At this time, four of the five team members were graduate students. Only Alice Gillam, the coordinator of composition, was a tenured professor. Two members were in their fourth year of funding and so were directly impacted by this sudden change in policy, while another member was in her third year and so would be in the same position the following year. They would lose their fifth year of funding despite the fact that they were on track to make the required progress toward the degree. If they opted to become a lecturer once this GTA funding was exhausted, they would need to move from teaching two to teaching three course sections per semester to earn the same wages—increasingly hazardous conditions for finishing a dissertation. The loss of teaching assistantships also would mean the premature end to administrative work. When we came together for our weekly meeting, then, several of us were shocked and deeply upset at this sudden news. Most of all, we were angry at "them" for doing this to "us." We felt that the supposed abuses cited were exaggerated, and we felt that the change in policy was unethical given the difficult job market.

As our coordinator, Alice was in a complicated position. Although we did not confront her directly with the fact, we were aware that she was a member of the Graduate Policy Committee, and thus had a hand in approving this reversal of policy. She was, in fact, one of "them." But in addition to being our supervisor, our professor, and a member of several of our dissertation committees, she also was our friend. Perhaps because of these ties, she did not do what one might expect. She did not offer sympathy as a way of smoothing over the differences suddenly yawning between us in that room. Even more significant, given our close work together all year, she did not try to construct herself as one of "us" by emphasizing her most significant role as our friend and attempting to downplay the real differences between us at the moment. Nor did she suggest that we talk about this some other time so we could address some rather pressing administrative concerns we had on the agenda that day. In short, she did not respond to this interruption by appealing to our "team" membership or to our "shared" collaborative work.

Rather, Alice took the riskier position of foregrounding our differences. She allowed us to be angry. She allowed us to express our rage over having a fifth year of funding disappear after working extremely hard to meet the difficult requirements. This anger was implicitly directed at her as a member of the Graduate Policy Committee. After she listened to us, she explained what had transpired in the committee meeting and identified herself as one who was in favor of the policy based on the information she had received from other committee members. After she spoke with us, she immediately went to the chair of the Graduate Policy Committee and insisted that the committee revisit the issue in light of the new information she had gathered. After weeks of further discussion, the possibility of fifth-year funding was reinstated, a decision that ultimately allowed both of us to finish our dissertations in a timely manner and to secure tenure-track positions.

We consider this action feminist because Alice chose to pay attention to the real differences in power between us—recognizing that, although we were all women and all acting administrators, she nonetheless possessed privileges that we did not share—and then chose to use her power in a productive way to remove a punitive regulation on our work. Although this incident interrupted our administrative work, she did not treat it as irrelevant to our work together. Taking this interruption seriously was not easy for her because it required confronting emotions and realities that friends often prefer not to confront. It also required her to confront her own peers on behalf of graduate students.

This model of feminist administrative collaboration is quite different from models that downplay differences in power between collaborators. In these models, having and using power tends to be coded as oppressive. However, Foucault persuades us that it is useful to think of power as productive. We can create oppressive contexts with our power or we can try to produce more libratory contexts for those positioned unequally in relation to us. In this case, we feel Alice did the latter: She sought to use her power to productively address an arbitrarily regulated labor situation.

This model of feminist collaboration—a model that values interruption and does not shy away from confronting the hierarchies that necessarily exist in writing programs—also challenges conventional wisdom about anger in the workplace. Peter Stearns, a historian of emotion, argues that the 20th century witnessed a shift from a Victorian to a Modern emotional style. Victorianism allowed for passionate emotions in some circumstances, whereas Modernism privileges a detached emotional style. Stearns situates this shift from passion to detachment in a material context, specifically the context of capitalist expansion and the rise of consumerism. Stearns argues that the scientific management movement in the workplace shifted the discourse surrounding anger dramatically: "the scientific management movement, maintained not only by engineers but also by the new breed of industrial psychologists, . . . first reconsidered the role of anger as part of an effort to make workers more machinelike and the workplace itself a smoothly running engine" (Stearns 121). Elton Mayo, one of these industrial psychologists who ran experiments for General Electric in the 1920s, "was simply disturbed by the angry atmosphere [in the factory] and he translated his disturbance into a sense that production must suffer from workers' irritability. From this, an emphasis on morale, defined as producing better cheer and less workplace anger, became a major focus in personnel psychology around the nation" (Stearns 122). The work of Mayo and others has created a mindset that still influences how we think of anger in the workplace: "in the new wisdom, anger had no place at work. The emotion was a sign of some personality flaw—'some disturbance in the equilibrium of an individual'—or of some relevant distraction, particularly in home life. This meant that control was all the more essential *lest the work flow be needlessly interrupted*" (Stearns 124; italics added). The message is simple: Anger is a problem because it threatens the level of productivity desired in capitalist working arrangements. Emotion brought on by status and material differences can interrupt the flow of work. To value interruption in the capitalist workplace, then, is a necessarily radical move.

Our experience demonstrates that interruption brought on by anger and other "outlaw emotions" can be productive (Jagger 160). Anger became a way for us to identify real material differences between members of our group and to suggest action to address inequality embedded in these differences. In contrast, other narratives of collaboration often focus on the satisfaction that group members get from their work—in other words, on morale. Material issues such as just compensation for one's work are often ignored or downplayed in such a context. We consider it crucial not to ignore such material issues and differences between group members.

INTERRUPTING THE BUREAUCRATIZING OF THE AFFECTIVE

College writing programs may seem a far cry from the workplaces Stearns talks about, but our second set of stories raises important questions about the ways in which our WPA work as graduate student course coordinators began our socialization into the role of emotional manager, a role we continue to be called on to play as tenure-track faculty in writing program administration and a role that risks replicating some of the disturbing conditions Stearns describes. Stearns argues that what he calls the modern emotional style requires managers to play a key role in managing worker anger in order to extract maximum productivity from them.

As graduate course coordinators—our specific roles on the administrative team—we were managers in a sense. Although the most rewarding part of our jobs was to help instructors with their teaching, the bulk of our time was actually spent preparing for and overseeing the process of group-grading final student portfolios—a decidedly bureaucratic enterprise. We held a number of staff meetings throughout the semester to discuss the criteria for passing portfolios and to practice reading and scoring model portfolios. We were indeed managers overseeing the production of a product—the final portfolios that instructors submitted to group grading. We found that in the process of extracting good products, we often thought about and constructed our fellow graduate students in problematic ways. For example, we found ourselves treating portfolios as evidence of the amount of work instructors were putting into their teaching, and we found ourselves judging them accordingly. When we made these types of judgments, we found we often ignored the material conditions these instructors worked in. Moreover, we found that our affective commitment to "good teaching," a commitment reinforced by our work together as overseers of teaching, was bureaucratized through our work. As Kenneth Burke employed the term *bureaucratization of the imaginative* to name "the vexing things that happen when [humans] . . . try to translate some pure aim or vision into terms of its corresponding material embodiment," so we name the *vexing* emotional responses we found evoked as we worked to put our pedagogical visions into practice a bureaucratizing of the affective (*Attitudes* 3). Collaborative teams can work to reinforce this process of bureaucratizing or they can be open to interruptions—moments when these affective commitments are put into question.

Our affective attachment to the work we were doing as graduate bureaucrats in training was interrupted by an e-mail message posted to our departmental graduate student listserv during the same year as our first story. A graduate student that Ilene had mentored during his first year of teaching posted a message that strongly and eloquently expressed his distaste for teaching composition and his anger at being required to teach composition courses instead of literature courses related to his areas of interest. His post reflected an astute awareness of his exploitation as a graduate student, who was required as a novice teacher to perform difficult work for little pay. He was angry that he was being taken advantage of and clearly felt deep alienation from his work as a composition teacher.

Our first feeling was one of betrayal. After working hard to create good courses for GTAs and show GTAs the rewards of composition teaching, this was the thanks we got? A public rejection of the writing program and of us? But after this post first appeared, we became more interested in the anger the writer expressed. His anger was a catalyst that allowed him to understand his situation from a materialist perspective. It reminded us of how our anger in our first story provided a way to initiate discussion and material change in our working conditions. We realized we needed to relearn how to see from the enraged perspective of graduate students like this one and seriously talk about the anger and alienation they might feel as part of our—or any—administrative agenda. If we brought the concerns of other graduate students to the table and worked to advocate on their behalf, this action could serve to interrupt the downplaying of difference that we felt undercut our effectiveness as feminist WPAs working collaboratively. We were not the same as other graduate students, but were we using our difference to make a difference?

Laura Bartlett recently argued that, as graduate students, compositionists identify with the position of managed teachers of writing and may overlook their growing secondary identification with management (271–276). Drawing from sociological research, Bartlett further suggests that the "movement from the feminized position of composition teaching to the . . . position of administration produces a subject whose self-understanding and managerial tactics function both to implement and to conceal . . . managerial practices" (273). In fact, we had at times discussed graduate student concerns in our collaborative meetings, but we now saw that our focus had mostly been on changing morale and creating a climate of good cheer—the very sort of strategies that Bartlett identifies as common to softer styles of contemporary management (274). We had worked to change the textbooks and design better assignment sequences so GTAs would enjoy teaching more. Although we certainly acknowledged that the teaching load was heavy, we did not really allow for a discussion of the anger GTAs felt. Consequently, we saw we had lost some opportunities to theorize the material conditions of the GTAs and adjuncts who taught in this program. We saw we needed to have more discussions about the alienation GTAs and adjuncts often felt and more discussions about *our* role in their alienation.

At the time, we already recognized that we needed to do more to make the material conditions of graduate student teachers and lecturers a focus of our administrative work. We needed to remind ourselves that we were asking new graduate students to do something extremely difficult. Most graduate students did not even have language for what we wanted them to do before they showed up at orientation. The field of rhetoric and composition has such a language, but it is a language and conceptual framework that takes time to develop. For example, new GTAs in our department often struggled with rhetorical concepts that were new to them, but which they needed nevertheless to teach immediately to their students. We placed them in a position where they were inexperienced, but still expected to produce a good product—passing student portfolios. Consequently, in our administrative meetings, our conversation could drift down the path of identifying "bad" behavior or identifying who was a "problem."

In Alice's own reflections on her collaborative work with us, she recognizes not only that she was fashioning a "dry run" for us materially, in that she was preparing us to go on the frontlines of our own writing programs some day as noncommissioned officers, but she also recognizes that as female noncommissioned officers there would be an explicitly gendered dimension to our work. In short, she was also fashioning a "dry run" for us emotionally during the time we worked together, in that our positions as graduate WPAs required us to practice the kind of emotional labor compelled of women administrators, noting that she "began to see a connection I had not heretofore seen between the 'emotional' labor I had expended in 'caring' [for the composition program and its policies] and the emotional labor and ethical costs entailed in being a graduate WPA collaborator" (Gillam, "Collaboration" 120). As Laura Micciche, another of our former team members, argues, "the gendered affective production involved in WPA work entails the production and reproduction of people (i.e., teachers) through processes akin to parenting. Engaging in this kind of domestic work in both private and public realms is a learned emotional habit for which women in capitalist culture are rigorously schooled" (441). Eileen

Schell similarly points out that "for women teachers caring is not merely a natural instinct or impulse" but rather "socially and historically mandated behavior" ("Costs" 78). Thus, we do not want to lose sight of the fact that economic paradigms enjoy a symbiotic relationship with specific affective stances that support and produce them. Our monitoring of our fellow graduate students' level of productivity and our attempts to manage their anger are examples of a kind of mothering that continues to construct faculty with lower status as children and ourselves as parents.

Teaching and administrative practices compelled by our socialization as women and justified by a cultural feminist-inspired ethic of care—practices labeled *feminist* by Schell, and perhaps *motheristic* by us—"make it difficult for feminists in composition to address gender inequities in academic work, particularly the preponderance of women in part-time and tenure-track positions" (Schell, "Costs" 78). As Gillam reminds us, "collaborative administration does not automatically or necessarily have anything to do with seeking a more just social order for women" ("Collaboration" 115). Women who are conditioned to nurture as teachers can continue to nurture as WPAs in ways that construct parent–child ties instead of collegial ties with fellow writing teachers, Schell argues. Marc Bousquet similarly notes the paternalism implicit in the pragmatist discourse of composition management, where assertions about "the value of 'getting ahead'" is "deploy[ed] . . . together with a set of assertions about 'the system as it is' in order to adopt a paternalistic standpoint of care within a general strategy of lowered expectations" ("Composition" 504).

We want to extend Schell and Micciche's critique of paternalistic, feminist or motheristic WPA practices to emphasize the colonizing relationship that such practices construct: to install oneself as (or to be installed in a position that positions one as) a parent to another colleague, as in the case of the (feminist) WPA and her composition faculty, is not only paternalistic, but it also reproduces the material and emotional relationship between colonizer and colonized. In her critical reading of the paternalism embedded in WPA listserv discourse, Jeanne Gunner similarly argues that "we can begin to see a version of the colonialist imperative at work—the attempt to expand the power of those who control the field, to expand control over its members, and to contend with other 'powers' in an effort to justify the field's existence, power, and methods" ("Among" 158). Although Bousquet does not foreground race or gender as part of his analysis of WPA work, we need to remember that the colonizer is not exclusively a White male figure: white women historically have served a vital function in maintaining systems of colonial oppression. As Vron Ware reminds us in *Beyond the Pale: White Women, Racism, and History*, white bourgeois women historically have acted as both symbols of civilization, as figures whose presence has been used to justify carefully managed relations (i.e., codified forms of legal and/or physical violence) between Whites and non-White colonized Others, and as agents through whom the socially stratifying colonial paradigms have been maintained via missionary-style charity work and bourgeois enculturation. We see motheristic attempts to dampen, deny, and manage anger, in particular, as an important way such class structures are maintained in writing programs.

Despite our recognition of this emotional management, we find the bureaucratizing of the affective to be tenacious. Now that we are both tenure-track faculty who share in the administration of large writing programs staffed by many graduate students (Donna) and part-time faculty (Ilene), we continue to be vexed by symptoms of our socialization into both the general context of the United States' modern emotional climate and also the specific emotional context of writing program administration and the role of WPA. Donna, for instance, has written elsewhere of her experience with GTAs at one institution, specifically of her realization that, although she had theorized this bureaucratizing of the imaginative as a graduate student, she nonetheless continued to be inattentive to habits that perpetuated this work (see Drew et al.). In an article cowritten with five graduate students, Donna recalls her first encounter with one of her coauthors as being marked by a dismissal of the new GTA's anxiety and a reinforcement of her own feelings of professional and personal correctness. She describes how, at a workshop for new GTAs,

> Steve expressed anxiety over his sense of inadequacy in being able to address grammatical errors in students' papers. My answer, which I at the time regarded as being politically astute, drew from my study of the history of composition teaching, a history that demonstrates the ongoing anxiety of the middle class when confronted with student "error." So when I answered Steve with what amounted to a dismissal of his concerns by explaining that there's nothing new about teacher anxiety over student error and that there are much more significant aspects of students' writing to worry about, I had no qualms about the work that my answer was doing. To my mind, I was simply educating an inexperienced teacher.
>
> What I was doing, as I would now describe it, was asserting my professional-managerial authority in a way that denied any potential challenges that negative GTA emotion might pose. (Drew et al. 174)

Moreover, the dismissal of Steve's concern, although (and perhaps because) it was supported by professional expertise, was a kind of motheristic response: a response that tells the other not to worry; everything will be fine. The mother/expert knows more than you do, so you should adjust your emotions accordingly.

Questioning our emotional investments and the economies they support needs to be a regular part of the work we do now as noncommissioned officers. Because our emotional landscapes have already shifted since we were graduate student WPAs, and we expect that they will shift again after we earn tenure and become even more materially secure, we recognize that our emotional shifts are important evidence of the material inequities between different faculty in our programs. Like Micciche, then, we believe "we need to address the ways in which our profession produces emotional dispositions for its workers" if we are to successfully interrupt our own narratives as WPAs (452).

TOWARD INTERRUPTION-RICH COLLABORATIONS

Simply recognizing our own emotional dispositions, however, is more often than not an individual performance that may segregate us from others with whom we might be able to form solidarity. Emotional performances that reinscribe us as solitary figures constrain our ability to be part of a collective in the ways that Bousquet argues has historically been the only viable way to effect material and social change for workers.

If attention to emotional interruptions is primarily an individual enterprise, "hope," according to Micciche, "is an act of mutuality—an act of collaboration between members of a community" (446). Hope is a performance of collective action; it is "an emotional investment we develop collaboratively" (454). We see value, then, in moving away from the figure of the solitary WPA and toward the figure of the hopeful/collectively identified colleague as WPA. Taking a proactive emotional stance of hope can lay an affective groundwork for "the abolition of the WPA qua manager" and "the rebirth of the WPA qua colleague among colleagues" (Bousquet, "Discipline" 924).

But surely those who benefited/benefit from colonialism, capitalism, and similar economically exploitative formations are working collectively as well. Bousquet's suggestion, then, that we simply need to act collectively needs to be tempered with a recognition that oppressive economic/social relations also are the product of collective action. How might a feminist materialist WPA act collectively, then, acting in a way that is attentive to interruptions and attentive to one's habitual emotional responses?

One hopeful possibility is to create alternative institutional locations from which to foster collegial relationships that still acknowledge different material conditions. This is the route Ilene has chosen. Several years ago, she worked with her then-chair to relocate herself from codirector of the composition program to composition faculty development coordinator. In that position, she chaired the committee that evaluates part-time faculty, and she funded and sponsored workshops, assessment projects, and collaborative course design that brought GTA, part-time, and full-time faculty together to create knowledge about writing pedagogy and to share in the work of building the composition program. She conceptualized the role of composition faculty development coordinator as a facilitator charged not only with putting faculty of different material locations in conversation with each other, but also with investing them with similar kinds of authority over each other. In portfolio assessment groups, on the part-time faculty evaluation committee, and in theory to practice workshops, all three constituencies created their agendas and revised their process together.

After earning tenure, Ilene and three of her tenured Composition colleagues formed a collaborative Composition Steering Committee to administer the Composition Program. As a Steering Committee member, she continues to lead the program's work in faculty development and assessment. The Steering Committee model is a unique one: Ilene believes it functions not only because its four members dedicate regular time to discussing the nature of their collaboration, but, perhaps more important because all four members are tenured. Their tenured status allows all four to have real influence in university-wide discussions about curriculum and staffing and real access to emerging resources for technology, student retention, and assessment.

Ilene uses the resources she has acquired as an individual tenured faculty member and a Composition Steering Committee member to address the material differences between faculty in her composition program—specifically, the fact that part-time faculty historically have been unable to receive monetary compensation for faculty development. To address this problem, Ilene has developed a set of practices for creating conditions where faculty of different ranks can interact with each other and have ownership of the composition program. She schedules multiple sessions for each workshop and assessment event to accommodate faculty. She buys back the time assessment group participants meet during the semester by allowing participating faculty to end their courses a week early. She schedules events at meal times and caters all events. Children are always welcome. She uses examples of faculty work and student writing that come from members of all three constituencies. Finally, events are product- as well as idea-driven: Participants leave with each others' practices, assignments, models, and so on. Most recently, she secured modest $100 stipends for part-time faculty attending pre-semester assessment workshops and $1,000 stipends for six part-time faculty to collaboratively develop and coordinate a large-scale portfolio assessment process with her. In her local context, there is money available for assessment; Ilene believes these resources are the best available means to address material differences between faculty at the moment.

There are times when Ilene feels vexed while doing this work. Some events have low attendance. Some faculty cannot attend any of the multiple sessions she has scheduled. There are always last-minute cancellations from people whose child has gotten sick, who have been called into a meeting at another school they teach at, or whose transportation has fallen through. Other faculty e-mail her with their regrets, expressing an interest in attending, but arguing that they cannot until they begin receiving monetary compensation. It is ongoing work to recognize these vexing moments as signals that she needs to interrupt herself and acknowledge that her strategies acknowledge and respond to, but do not erase, the material inequalities experienced by these different groups of faculty.

Strategies like Ilene's begin, but do not end, the process of collectively changing working conditions. To work collectively, a materialist feminist WPA must work for material change as part and parcel of her WPA work, which requires contributing to the creation of solidarity—a sense of shared purpose, project, and values—which includes difference and welcomes interruption as moments to recognize difference. Schell advocates that we become activists not out of a parental concern or care for contingent faculty, but because "the problem of contingent labor in composition studies is not just a professional issue that we can correct by eliminating contingent positions and hiring more full-time faculty members; it is a gender issue, and thus a feminist issue, tied to larger systems of exploitation" ("Costs" 90). Bousquet's call, then, to be activist is important, but his focus on more tenure-track positions will not necessarily transform the gender, race, and class structures that inform the economy of contingent labor in academe.

The "WPA as professorial colleague" is not a pipedream, Bousquet asserts, but "close to reality" on unionized campuses that have chosen to make the issue a priority ("Discipline" 924). In a September 27, 2004 letter to the Connecticut State University (CSU) AAUP, President David F. Walsh relates the national AAUP's call "to move from 'current to best practices' in the employment of part-time professionals." Walsh's letter uses the term *professional* rather than *professorial*, however, and does not cite gender, race, or class inequity as grounds for finally moving on these issues, choosing instead to argue in concert with the American Federation of Teachers that "part-time faculty working conditions equal students' learning conditions," and thus part-time faculty must have "suitable space to meet with students and phone and computer access to communicate with them, as well as to undertake online research" (Walsh). Interestingly, Walsh calls on full-time faculty, particularly chairs and senior faculty, to take the initiative to create mechanisms for orienting, evaluating, and assigning courses to part-time faculty because "supporting part-time faculty in their struggle for fair compensation, adequate support and professional personnel policies . . . make[s] a statement that they will accept nothing less than the highest standard of professional treatment for themselves" (Walsh). Ilene wonders whether this appeal reinforces a climate of disappointment and ultimately undercuts a climate of hopeful solidarity.

But a CSU AAUP Committee on Part-Time Faculty Issues also has formed. Its first action, akin to Schell's suggestion that faculty women's coalitions study and report on nontenure-track women's working conditions ("Costs" 91), is to collect data about the working conditions of part-time faculty. The English department at CSU has one of the largest concentrations of part-time faculty. Ilene believes, and her colleagues who are also on the committee believe, they are in a kairotic moment where they can create a local model that can gain popularity across the university. On the agenda thus far are attempts to secure health care for part-time faculty, primarily those who work the equivalent of full time at several CSU and/or Connecticut Community College campuses. It is interesting that the appeal is an emotional one: You are devalued if you let this happen to part-time faculty. With luck, this can be the kind of local action Schell and Bousquet feel will have an effect, although, to be clear, the conversion of part-time to full-time faculty lines is not on the table at this time.

Our current emotional investments in our programs and policies are necessarily different from those with whom we work. Consequently, we have had to constantly relearn and remind ourselves how to be *feminist*, rather than *feminist* administrators, undertaking feminist materialist administrative practices in ways that are distinct from what Marc Bousquet calls the *heroic* administrator. As Bousquet argues, it is easy for us to become enamored of the WPA figured as "hero" and "change agent" while losing sight of the fact that such noncommissioned officers have done virtually nothing historically to transform the material lives of exploited workers ("Composition" 496). Schell similarly suggests that the feminist WPA's investment in the good feelings that come from helping individual disenfranchised workers undercuts our ability as feminist WPAs to address the gendered structural equalities of women's work in the university ("Costs" 81). As we work collectively—even collaboratively—with contingent faculty, we consider it a feminist duty to be ever attentive to interruptions, to moments when status differences erupt, reminding us over and over again to reconsider the material effects and limitations of our practices.

7

THREE MODELS OF MENTORSHIP

Feminist Leadership and the Graduate Student WPA

Julie Nelson Christoph　　　*Rebecca S. Nowacek*

Mary Lou Odom　　　*Bonnie Kathryn Smith*

To consider the role of the graduate student WPA (GWPA) is to consider an institutional position that encapsulates the potential and peril of feminist administration. The existence of the GWPA can be seen as a valuable means of collaboration and a vital part of decentering writing program administration: GWPA positions can vest graduate students with authority to influence curriculum design and implementation and provide them with valuable administrative experience, and such positions can benefit the program and even the WPA by freeing the WPA from some of her many duties and by increasing investment from graduate students. In the ideal scenario, as described by Meeks and Hult, the relationships among the WPA, GWPA, and the instructors in the program they lead is one of co-mentoring, a relationship in which roles shift and everyone's expertise is equally valued and recognized.

But like any collaboration, GWPA work is rarely ideal. Becoming an administrator often places the GWPA in a tenuous relationship with her graduate student peers. GWPAs are, by definition, not the real WPAs; they carry less institutional authority, usually have less experience, and almost inevitably face a challenging series of negotiations with their peers. Johanna

Atwood Brown, for instance, laments that she "often careened back and forth between being a graduate student and an administrator" and felt she was "never in the right role at the right time" (121). Not only must GWPAs negotiate awkward social relationships with their not-quite-peers, but they must negotiate similarly awkward relationships with faculty and administrators much further up the academic food chain. They must do all of this as they learn the ropes of a preexisting program—usually one not of their own making.

We recognize, of course, that WPAs face the same challenges: administering programs to their faculty peers, needing to educate their chairs and deans, and walking into programs with long histories. Recognizing these parallels, we wish, in fact, to argue that the admittedly difficult and liminal position of GWPA is an excellent place to try on and develop models of feminist leadership even in places and programs where masculinist assumptions and conventions may be alive and well.

As GWPAs, we were expected to lead—but our authority often was tempered by issues of gender, institutional position, and experience. To lead within these constraints, we unconsciously adopted a variety of mentoring approaches that suited the situations in which we were leading. These approaches were not explicitly described or taught to us by the WPAs we worked with; they were models we were drawn to via our institutional positions as graduate students administering a variety of writing programs.

In this chapter, we explore three models of feminist mentorship, models that derive from our experiences as GWPAs, but that we believe can inform the work of WPAs, as well as GWPAs. These models are grounded in our diverse experiences with GWPA work at the University of Wisconsin, Madison. During a 5-year period (from 1996–2001), we served at various times as the Assistant Director of First Year English (Mary Lou), Assistant Director of the Writing Fellows Program (Julie), Assistant Director of Writing Across the Curriculum (Rebecca and Bonnie), and Director of the First Year English Tutorial Program (Rebecca and Mary Lou). In these capacities, we worked with fellow graduate students (inside the English Department and out), faculty members throughout the university, and undergraduate students.

We begin by describing our three approaches to mentorship—friendship, guidance, and diplomacy—with a special focus on how the institutional position of GWPA made these approaches more attractive than traditional masculinist ones. Specifically, rather than functioning within a strict hierarchy, dependent on ideas and goals radiating out from a center, we intentionally, although not always consciously, developed feminist, decentralized approaches to program administration. What these three approaches share is the assumption that as WPAs and GWPAs we can best facilitate decentralized administration by actively listening to program members, by being well-informed members of a larger community of WPAs, and by not being rigidly committed to any one particular method of administration: Furthermore, we recognize that a decentralized writing program must be flexible enough to accommodate the unique situations that arise in particular classrooms and between particular instructors and students. We conclude by exploring the implications such GWPA work might have, both within the program and in other programs when the GWPA goes on to be a WPA elsewhere.

MENTOR AS FRIEND

Because we were often in a position of mentoring peers—some of whom we had previous acquaintance or relationships with—we often found ourselves approaching such interactions as friends. To lead by mentoring as a friend was a powerful and satisfying approach. After all, we could not and did not want to forfeit all current and future social relationships with our peers to do our job. At its best, friendship allowed us to negotiate everyday life in both its banality and chaos, and, as GWPAs, we found that friendships informed us in very practical ways as we engaged in the learning and decision making accompanying administrative work. But the parameters of such friendships were shifting and often ill-defined. As we have already mentioned, GWPAs writing about their experiences often represent friendship as problematic. For instance, Johanna Brown and Jukuri and Williamson describe their social and personal connections with their peers as complications, tacitly suggesting friendship would best be avoided. We disagree, but recognize the need to interrogate what friendship might mean in the context of GWPA work.

Friendship as a model of feminist leadership might be understood through the lens of an ethic of care. But an approach grounded in care does not adequately account for the implications friendship might have for feminist leadership. Although it may support the compassionate wielding of power and authority, it does not eliminate the tensions that can occur between peers in relationships where there exists an authority differential. Here, like Eileen Schell in "The Costs of Caring," we see concerns over the potentially limiting and problematic nature of an ethic of care.

Therefore, in our model of friendship, we find it helpful to think about Aristotle's understanding of friendship and the common good. Although Aristotle did not always take what we would now deem to be the most ethical stances on women, we believe that his classifications of friendship can enrich current understandings of feminist leadership principles and the

GWPA. In Books VIII and IX of *Nicomachean Ethics*, Aristotle character-
izes friendship as having three components: Friends must take pleasure in
each other's company, friends must be useful to one another, and friends
must share a common commitment to the good. Often the administrative
model of friendship that sustained us as GWPAs was characterized less by
utility or pleasure and more by the camaraderie and solidarity that comes
when friends share a common commitment to goals they identify as good.
Furthermore, we found that friendship often forced us to recognize that the
common good may be amorphous and situational.

As successive assistant directors of the WAC program, Rebecca and
Bonnie found themselves working with teaching assistants in all disciplines
who were teaching with writing (and, often, teaching) for the first time.
Frequently, our initial encounters with the new TAs would take place over
coffee the first morning of mandatory TA training sessions. As graduate
student peers, Rebecca, Bonnie, and the TAs from various disciplines could
have easily met one another in a casual social setting, but the training session invited a more professional and hierarchical relationship. In these settings, our expertise as teachers of writing was almost always and immediately recognized and valued by our TA peers, but as assistant directors we
aimed for more than acknowledgment of our relative expertise: We hoped
to cultivate long-term relationships with individuals in order to foster
thoughtful conversations about the teaching of writing in departments
across the university. Plus, we frequently took pleasure in the company of
those peers we met through our administrative work. Thus, we found ourselves relying on a model of mentorship that focused less on our expertise
and more on our shared goals—a model of mentor as friend that drew us to
both enjoy and capitalize on our peer relationships with other TAs, a relationship that the WPA could not develop in the same way. After all, the
GWPA may have a richer understanding of a peer's particular situational,
disciplinary, or even rhetorical context. As a result, identifying the shared
goals of the program in which they work may be more easily achievable.

When we mentored as friends, these relationships did prove both useful and pleasurable. However, the good will and friendship that accompa-
nied such WAC work was grounded most fundamentally in the third component that Aristotle describes: seeking the common good, which we
accomplished by the identification of shared goals. These shared goals
included meeting the criteria of the general education requirement, teaching
writing in such a way that satisfied disciplinary expectations, and identifying ways that teaching with writing enlivened and pushed our undergraduates as they waded into new disciplinary waters.

Mentoring friends is not always smooth sailing. Perhaps more than any
other model we explore, considering the role of friendship in mentoring
reveals how individual and situational mentoring actually is. When friend-

ships deepen, becoming as personal as they are professional, the complicated nuances of individual relationships can press on the already operative factors of gender, age, class, and race and create a palpable tension for GWPAs. Negotiating this tension can then become an obstacle, rather than an aide, in the mentoring done by GWPAs. In such scenarios, we benefited from recognizing that mentoring friends hinges on that shared vision of what common good means; like Hildy Miller, and like Amy Goodburn and Carrie Leverenz, we learned that friendship means constantly reconsidering what is the common good. When GWPAs and the friends they mentor begin to identify different visions of the good, this model becomes problematic.

Consider, for example, the TA who sits in the GWPA's office for close to an hour one morning, chatting about everything from politics to the weather. This same TA, with whom the GWPA believes she has forged a friendship based on shared goals, might then announce that he would appreciate permission not to attend a mandatory staff meeting. What does the GWPA do when shared goals and a vision of the good are breached? Her authority provides her several choices—namely, the right to say yes or no to this not-so-subtle request. But on what factor does this decision hinge? A concern that her authority is being dismissed by a friend? Some sense of her continued relationship with the friend? Fairness to all involved in the program? What of other, less evident concerns that might come into play only because of the knowledge she possesses due to her role as a friend? For example, might she know that her friend is struggling in other academic, emotional, or physical arenas? Might sustaining the good health of the friend and the well-being of the friendship trump her goals in her role as GWPA? Here again, we reiterate the problems with relying exclusively on the care ethic when conceptualizing friendship. In this situation, we believe it is more useful for the GWPA friend to ask both herself and her mentee questions about the common good instead of questions about care.

Ultimately, this model of friendship challenges one prevalent model of feminist collaboration in that it is informed but not anchored by Noddings' ethic of care. Friendship is subject to all sorts of pressures and constraints, and how we encounter, define, and handle such pressures contributes to the ways friendship helps us understand the changing nature of our identities. At its best, mentoring friends and being mentored by friends is supported by a vision that is established when friends establish working definitions of good outcomes. When a common definition of the good is reached *and* when those working toward the good are friends, those involved then wish "the good" for each other and are more apt to work toward that good. When, as Aristotle suggested, you want to please your friends with your conduct and virtue, the highest form of friendship is reached.

MENTOR AS GUIDE

Perhaps because of the pressures and constraints that friendship can exert on individuals and their identities, this model of mentor as friend is not always a viable option for GWPAs. A shared vision supports and creates a place for friendship in mentoring relationships, but what if there is no such shared vision? In writing programs with a diverse assembly of instructors across a continuum of experiential, disciplinary, and commitment levels, such a disconnect is possible, even probable. In such a situation, an alternate model of mentorship emerges: a model that goes and is necessitated by what lies beyond the bonds of friendship, instead calling upon the mentor's commitment to providing guidance to those she must lead.

The notion of a guide as a model for mentorship might initially evoke images of leaders and followers. We might picture an ensemble of mountain climbers: a leader setting the pace at the forefront, guiding and directing other, less experienced hikers through unfamiliar, rocky terrain. Although difficult, even perilous, the journey culminates ideally in a safe, successful venture for all—thanks to the guide's leadership. This expedition is metaphorically akin to that which GWPAs make with those they mentor and who mentor them.

Rather than advocating this leaders-and-followers version of guidance, we would like to suggest a notion of mentor as guide that builds quite naturally off the notion of mentor as friend. Friendship involves commitment to working toward a common good and a shared goal, just as the guide and the guided on the mountain do. Furthermore, guidance is generally perceived as a kinder, gentler sort of leadership. The mentor who guides does not direct or dictate, but facilitates, shows, and encourages. Rather than administering in a top-down fashion, the mentor-as-guide model suggests a side-by-side relationship. Our mountain climbing guide does lead, but leads while also making the journey *with* those depending on her.

So what might this kind of guidance look like in a WPA setting? Being a mentor who guides might be as uncomplicated as the GWPA who sits in her office with a new instructor and discusses course language, possibilities for lesson plans, or syllabus design. Perhaps the GWPA's mentoring takes the form of commiseration with fellow TAs about managing heavy teaching and course loads as well as practical suggestions for handling such challenges. Even a casual recounting of some of her own experiences can benefit the GWPA's peer-mentees who seek guidance. No matter the task, mentorship that takes the form of guidance often replicates the elements of camaraderie that characterize the mentor-as-friend approach. However, these friendly qualities do not exclusively characterize the mentor who guides. In our experience, this seemingly gentle model of leadership is far more complex—in both its genesis and execution—than it first appears. In particular, the sometimes ambiguous nature of guidance (gentle, yet, after all, still guiding) compounds another ambiguity—that of the GWPA's institutional position. Occupying a new, often unfamiliar role as an emerging teacher/scholar/administrator, the female GWPA feels the implications of her position as a graduate student, much like her gender, quite deeply.

Like Bonnie and Rebecca's mentoring of teachers in the WAC program, Mary Lou's primary duties as assistant director of the First-Year Composition (FYC) program dealt with the training and mentoring of TAs. The FYC program, however, was comprised of only a single course. Furthermore, this course—and, thus, much of the training of the program's TAs—was based on a specific model syllabus already developed by the WPA and previous GWPA. This syllabus and its approach to teaching composition was required use for all new teachers in the program and strongly encouraged for returning instructors. As a result, graduate students serving in the assistant director role had a fairly specific and predetermined set of goals and structures through which to guide their mentees.

But why in such a structured situation would a GWPA guide as a mentor rather than leading in a more directive way? Some possible answers can be found by examining the unique but often unclear institutional position of graduate students, who, although clearly more than just students, still have a way to go before achieving the status of the tenured or tenure-track faculty with whom they work so closely. It is here, where issues of experience and institutional hierarchies intersect, that the feminist aspects of the guide model come most fully into play. For the GWPA who desires a feminist form of leadership, the guide model may well seem a natural fit. By positioning herself alongside her mentees (and even her mentor, for that matter), the GWPA avoids participating in a leadership style that seems too authoritarian and top-down. In actions that call to mind models described by Gunner ("Decentering"), Meeks and Hult, and others, the feminist GWPA may thus work to decenter WPA work, mentoring her peers in ways that redistribute expertise and responsibility among the many participants in the writing program. In addition to the advantages for writing programs described in previous scholarship, this decentered guide approach can have real benefits for the GWPA as well.

In Mary Lou's case, for example, much of her work involved facilitating a program and curriculum she had little hand in shaping; thus, she was in a real sense truly learning alongside her mentees. Although her experience in the program and as a teacher lent her a certain authority—both with her mentees and in her own mind—she still lacked true ownership regarding the program's curriculum and pedagogical theories. Without a sense of ownership and because the material was also new to her, she felt at times as if she were only a small step ahead of her mentees. Mary Lou's office hours were frequented by TAs frustrated by their inability to understand the program's model syllabus. Having herself struggled to master this material, Mary Lou could speak from experience as she mentored her fellow TAs not only in learning the ins and outs of the syllabus, but also in concurrently teaching it to others. When her own experiences echo so closely those of her peers, the GWPA can empathize with their confusion over programmatic content while also using her experience to suggest strategies she found useful in her own process of understanding how to approach the material.

Yet for all the positive attributes of the guide model of mentorship, it is hardly problem-free. Adopting the mentor-as-guide model might complicate and even call into question the efficacy of the GWPA's leadership. Because female GWPAs—like female graduate students—may already have to contend with the undermining of their authority based on gender, the way in which the mentor as guide positions herself as a learner alongside her mentees might further lessen perceptions of her authority. By virtue of the mentor as guide's feminist approach to leading—reducing in many senses the figurative (and often literal) distances between mentor and mentee—the GWPA may find that her authority also seems reduced. This fact does not, in our minds, diminish the value of the mentor-as-guide model; it does highlight the inevitable challenges of inhabiting the institutional position of GWPA.

This model of mentorship as guidance—and its consequent decentering of the GWPA's institutional position—also can have far-reaching effects on writing programs. Our examples so far illustrate how multifaceted and multidirectional mentorship can be: When successful, the mentor-as-guide model can come full circle as a means to develop and teach the GWPA to in turn develop and teach her own mentees. But as institutional labels and boundaries are blurred, other important changes can occur in the fabric of a writing program. Mary Lou found that, ultimately, her lack of a role in designing the program's new curriculum made both her and her mentees much more comfortable discussing difficulties with that curriculum. Eventually, Mary Lou was able to take these shared concerns to her WPA, and together they made changes to the program's model syllabus. Keller and her colleagues concluded that their own efforts to decenter authority in their writing program brought about similarly positive results, pointing to this decentering as the cause of vastly improved dialogue between teachers and administrators. This communication, they contend, in turn produced a more holistic view of the program and enabled them to address more practically and with greater efficacy any challenges that arose. Such an end result of GWPA mentorship as guidance seems fitting for, like our guide on the mountain, the GWPA may find that the communication she can facilitate among traditional hierarchies of the writing program is key to negotiating the challenges and problems that appear along her journey.

MENTOR AS DIPLOMAT

Sometimes WPA work can feel less like guiding and more like navigating a minefield. Universities are full of strong personalities, and academic programs and departments are all too often characterized by strong territoriality. When the GWPA steps into her job—particularly one involving WAC—she is likely to be in the politically dangerous position of having relatively little institutional authority, while being expected to administer a program that is comprised of individuals both above and below her in the institutional hierarchy, each likely committed to defending a particular area of turf within the university.

A third model of feminist mentoring—international diplomacy—can be helpful for mentoring people who have more institutional power and/or have vested interests in protecting a particular area of knowledge or mode of teaching. Diplomats facilitate relations between nations, working on ongoing issues in the midst of changing personnel and within often-tense power dynamics. *How* diplomats approach this work varies considerably, however—especially when conflicts emerge. As Roger Fisher and William Ury of the Harvard Negotiation Project observe, negotiators often see two approaches to diplomacy: the "hard" approach, in which the negotiator perceives any conflict between sides as a battle of wills in which both sides defend extreme positions to avoid giving in to the other side, and the "soft" approach, in which the negotiator avoids conflict and potential damage to personal relationships through making concessions to the other side.

These hard and soft extremes almost caricature the masculinist and feminist leadership styles that Hildy Miller and others have critiqued, but they are nonetheless negotiating strategies that can seem like viable options to GWPAs, particularly when "mentoring up" to faculty. Because the writing program the GWPA represents has existing policies that might seem to have more institutional weight than the GWPA does, one ready approach is to stand behind the policies and enforce them, ceding one's personal authority to the policies. Soft negotiating, too, can be an appealing approach because it would seem that the best way to keep faculty happy and to avoid creating enemies would be to give in to faculty demands wherever conflicts arise.

Although these extreme models of diplomatic administration are readily available options, GWPAs are ideally positioned to explore a more situational kind of diplomacy based on mutual gain, rather than on binary conditions that must be either met or rejected. Because they are not expected to know everything already about the programs they help administer, GWPAs have license to talk to members of the program and to ask questions and to listen to what is going on in individual classrooms. This kind of listening is a wonderful way to benefit from others' experience and is also a way to learn about problems and conflicts within a program that might not otherwise surface. Like friendship, this style of mentoring is based on seeking the common good of mutually acceptable solutions. Unlike the models of either mentor as friend or mentor as guide, however, this style of diplomacy uses the one-to-one communication with members of a program as a preliminary step toward decentralization—putting people in contact with each other, to mentor each other.

Thinking about mentoring in terms of diplomacy was helpful to Julie as she worked in the Writing Fellows program, which has multiple programmatic layers. As a GWPA, Julie mentored down in the institutional hierarchy when she worked with the undergraduate writing fellows who were just beginning to teach writing through one-to-one tutorial work with peers, in the writing-intensive classes in which they were placed. Julie also mentored up to the faculty teaching these writing-intensive courses, because these faculty typically considered themselves new to teaching writing and had joined the program to learn a wider repertoire of techniques for teaching writing in their respective disciplines. The undergraduate writing fellows enrolled in a semester-long three-credit course, in which they read composition theory and learned strategies for helping their peers first with global concerns like focus, purpose, and audience before moving on to help with local concerns like grammar and mechanics. In agreeing to participate in the program, faculty accepted the writing fellows' status as skilled readers, and they agreed to meet with their writing fellows regularly to discuss the pedagogic goals for the course writing assignments, as well as the comments fellows wrote on student drafts.

Mentoring these two different groups of novice writing teachers presented many challenges. Although for the most part faculty and fellows alike found the program tremendously rewarding, there were perennial tensions around the clarity of professors' writing assignments, the extent to which fellows should focus on proofreading, the extent to which fellows were responsible for advising students on disciplinary content in their papers, and the extent to which fellows had internalized professional norms for such things as punctuality and dress. Fellows and faculty came to the Writing Fellows program from different places. Although it would be a stretch to say that any of these conflicts merited international diplomatic efforts, the constituencies Julie mentored could be, at times, quite committed to defending such practices as the use of passive voice or the right to sport facial piercings in professional settings!

Complicating the possibility for mentoring, the program was a new program with temporary funding, and for that reason it was especially important to keep everyone in the program happy so that the word of mouth would help gain both monetary and institutional support for the program. When Julie was aware of conflicts within the program, it would not have been effective to take a hard approach to negotiation and inform the faculty member, for instance, that the program position is that writing fellows do not proofread. To do that would be to force the faculty member to lose face to a graduate student and to place the writing fellow in the uncomfortable position of having to continue through the end of the semester, after being identified as a "spy" for the program who had exposed the faculty member's "incompetence" as a writing instructor. Similarly, it would not work to acquiesce to faculty desires for a proofreader and to signal to the writing fellow that their training and ideas were worthless. Either approach would undermine the pedagogic aims of the program and would jeopardize the program's future relationships with faculty or students.

What worked best was to mentor faculty and students through a process of seeking out the underlying interests and concerns of the many members of the program and creating opportunities and conditions in which members of the program could be mentored by whomever was most able to help. Although this mentoring was, in a way, quite centralized, the end goal was to decentralize so that the people in the program could do what the program was designed to help them do: learn from each other about teaching writing.

An example of how Julie and her WPA accomplished this mentor-as-diplomat work was through the brown-bag lunch session, the most unexceptional and seemingly innocuous form of campus meeting. Each semester, after meeting with writing fellows to discuss commenting on paper assignments and e-mailing with faculty to touch base about how the semester was going, Julie and the program director held brown-bag sessions, which program faculty were expected to attend. At the meetings, the agenda was minimal; faculty were asked to tell a little about the topic of the course they were teaching and to reflect on how the experience of working with writing fellows was going.

Under ideal conditions, problems and frictions about paper assignments and pedagogy came up naturally during these conversations, and faculty could talk with each other about how they had resolved problems in past semesters. Sometimes, if it seemed unlikely that the conditions would be ideal, Julie or the director would invite a sympathetic faculty member within the program to attend the meeting as an experienced faculty member: Experienced faculty would offer insight on a particular topic, such as how to use writing fellows to help students use evidence more effectively in subjects outside their major field of study. Sometimes Julie or the director would offer advice. Sometimes Julie or the director would ask a seemingly open-ended question like, "One thing new writing fellows tend to find difficult is prioritizing what elements of a student's paper to comment on first. Is there anything we can do to help your fellows in the next paper cycle?"

The reconnaissance work Julie did with fellows and faculty members was essential, not in the sense of espionage, but of finding out strengths and weaknesses—of which the faculty and fellows were not always mutually aware—and bringing these elements to light in ways that were friendly and constructive. The cyclical nature of semesters and the ability to plan brown-bag sessions in advance helped, too, to prevent crises. In most cases, crises were averted through regular maintenance of ties—between fellows and faculty, between faculty and the program, between fellows and the program. These multiple layers of mentoring—in which faculty from across the disciplines could mentor each other and even undergraduate fellows could mentor faculty—embodied feminist ideals of enabling collaboration outside of traditional hierarchies.

One drawback of this kind of mentoring is that it works best when it is most invisible, and it is thus open to the kinds of critiques leveled at many feminist modes of leadership (see e.g., Schell, "Costs"). Although Julie knew a great deal about what was happening among the various constituencies in the program and was strategic about bringing problems to light and creating conditions for solving those problems, it is possible that, because Julie did not overtly solve the problems, it could seem as if she did not wield sufficient control as an administrator. Another drawback is the time and emotional energy it takes to do the behind-the-scenes work and planning necessary to make this kind of mentoring work (Schell, "Costs"; Hesse, "WPA as Father"). Ironically, when so much of the difficult interpersonal and pedagogic negotiation is filtered through a proactive and engaged GWPA, the individual constituencies in a program can come to depend on the GWPA to help create conditions for solving problems.

Although these problems are real, they are not insurmountable. A program in which writing instructors have a good experience is likely to be perceived as a good program—and the WPA to be a good director. The trick, then, is to decentralize sufficiently and get enough people involved that the process of creating a good experience and a good program does not wear out the WPA. The end goal of the centralized reconnaissance here is ultimately to facilitate problem solving among participants in the program. Remembering that, and keeping in mind that decentralization is essential to the success of the program as well as the long-term well-being of the WPA, can help ensure that decentralized diplomacy, rather than centralized espionage, is what happens.

CONCLUSIONS

These three models represent roles and relationships that we stumbled into as we sought to reconcile our leadership styles with our institutional positions and the particulars of our programs. We recognize that the needs of other GWPAs and WPAs differ in significant ways from our own. By way of conclusion, then, we would like to explore the qualities that made our GWPA experiences successful opportunities for learning and performing feminist administration and that might extend to the work of other GWPAs—as well as to WPAs, to faculty WPAs working with GWPAs, and to assistant professors in Composition and Rhetoric.

Although we definitely developed our mentorship styles with the help and support of our WPAs, we did not learn any of these models explicitly, nor were any of the programs in which we worked characterized by explicitly feminist theoretical frameworks. However, we were throughout our work as GWPAs quite conscious of what we wanted to accomplish and how. This intentionality of approach to WPA work is the most lasting benefit that we have derived from our work; it is also what helped us most to develop our commitment to performing feminist administration. Our respective WPAs encouraged this kind of self-reflexivity by assigning us to do work that we were capable of doing well, by asking us how we wanted to approach particular situations we encountered, and by expecting us to be intentional about how we approached our work. Our WPAs modeled decentralized administration to us in their approach to mentoring: Rather than telling us what we should do or letting us feel as if we were careening between our roles as graduate students and as administrators (although we certainly experienced some days that felt like that), they helped us learn for ourselves some possible approaches that worked for us as individuals within particular administrative situations.

Embracing the possibilities that go with the territory for GWPAs can, we believe, enable even GWPAs in decidedly unfeminist writing programs to develop feminist administrative habits of mind. Being intentional about asking questions and searching collaboratively for solutions can help one develop feminist mentoring abilities even when the official model in a program is more hierarchical. Sometimes a situation will dictate a more masculinist approach to administration, as in the initial WAC training sessions that Rebecca and Bonnie led, but not *all* contexts within any program dictate a particular approach. As Hildy Miller notes, "in the bi-epistemological institution," which includes both masculinist and feminist epistemologies, "personas have to change with context" (53). Being intentional about how we mentor from situation to situation in our WPA work can help us name and, thus, use consciously a range of approaches to mentoring, including a range of feminist approaches.

A good part of what we learned about administration through our work as GWPAs came, as well, from just being in the somewhat awkward position between graduate student and administrator, and we want to suggest that this liminality can have distinct advantages. As a GWPA, one is in many ways ideally situated to learn feminist administrative practices. Graduate students have license to collaborate, ask questions, and learn from others—license that can *seem* to have been revoked for those who have moved on into full-time positions and who can sometimes feel pressure to be experts already, to be able to lead without collaborating. But faculty WPAs experience versions of the same difficulties that GWPAs encounter, working in programs and institutional structures they have not created and working with people who may not always respect or appreciate the WPA's position. The long-term value of our GWPA experiences, then, has included more than experience forming a budget or coordinating a large training workshop; it extends to the habits of mind and of collaboration that continue to characterize our post-GWPA administrative work.

Finally, feminist mentoring is ultimately an individual and situational activity. Because it depends on decentralization and a leveling of hierarchy, it cannot exist without the strong support of a community. We believe that, although not perfect, GWPA positions can foster feminist WPA work by training feminist WPAs, but also by training people who understand and support this kind of leadership. Feminist WPAs (especially those who are untenured or in year-to-year positions) need the support of people within their programs and departments, and all of us (whether GWPA, WPA, faculty, or instructor) can help support their work.

PART III

Performing WPA Work

Challenging Institutional Assumptions About Gender and Agency

. . . can we, take what we do best as a discipline—
reflect, rethink, revisit, and revise the stories
that create who we are?

–Malea Powell
"Rhetorics of Survivance" (428)

8

A TALE OF TWO TECH CHICKS

Negotiating Gendered Assumptions About Program Administration and Technology

Amy C. Kimme Hea

Melinda Turnley

The impact of gendered institutional structures on WPAs' work has received much attention in our scholarly conversations. In particular, researchers have critiqued the ways in which masculinist academic hierarchies influence definitions of administrative authority. In response to such patriarchal, individualistic constructions of power, WPAs have sought alternative strategies for effectively leading programs. Most significantly, they have explored feminist and collaborative models that blur lines of authority, foster experimentation, encourage flexible decision making, and share responsibility. Similarly, critical technology scholars have critiqued dominant narratives that frame technology in relation to masculinist, deterministic values such as control, transparency, and linear progress. Because technologies are increasingly integrated into writing classrooms, program administrators should consider ways in which these institutional and technological assumptions interrelate and impact our work. We assert that WPAs should complicate notions of technological mastery, which support deterministic, essentialist framings of agency and thus run counter to rhetorical, critical engagement with technology. Feminist and collaborative administrators, especially those directly involved in teacher technology development, should challenge notions of mastery to facilitate teacher effectiveness and productive student outcomes.

Drawing on the gender theories of Judith Butler and Donna Haraway, we argue for approaching mastery as gendered performance, rather than a reified element that can be possessed. Technology learning, like gender, is a doing—an iterative process. Framing this process teleologically in terms of control merely reinscribes hegemonic cultural norms. Critical approaches to technology, however, complicate these assumptions by articulating learning as a dynamic set of practices. As Donna Haraway suggests, "The machine is not an *it* to be animated, worshiped, and dominated. The machine is us, our processes, an aspect of our embodiment. We can be responsible for our machines; *they* do not dominate or threaten us. We are responsible for boundaries; we are they" ("A Cyborg Manifesto" 180). In pursuit of such responsibility, we explore the problematic role of mastery in teacher technology learning. Our discussion begins with an overview of the principles informing our approaches to gender, administration, and technology. We review relevant WPA scholarship on feminism and collaboration and research on gender in computers and composition. In conjunction with these sources, we also engage the theories of Butler and Haraway as potentially productive approaches to performing feminist administration.

After developing this framework, we turn to examples from our experiences as co-administrators charged with mentoring instructors to teach first-year composition in technology-rich environments at Purdue University. In this role, we sought to instantiate a non-deterministic, contextualized approach that emphasized pedagogical goals rather than technological imperatives. Despite our efforts to engage participants in an open-ended, recursive process, we were challenged by dominant assumptions about technological ease, efficiency, and mastery. After continued reflection on our experiences as graduate student administrators, we better understand the complex role that gender played in these technology mentoring groups. To explore this complexity, we examine two examples from the four computer composition practica courses that we facilitated. No example, of course, can fully represent the diverse dynamics of an administrative context. These situations, however, provide useful figurations of how masculinized notions of technical mastery can subvert collaborative, rhetorical frameworks for technology learning. Following our analysis of these examples, we conclude by offering recommendations for ways in which administrators can complicate assumptions about mastery in teacher development and facilitate alternative, feminist performances of technical agency.

FEMINIST AND COLLABORATIVE
APPROACHES TO ADMINISTRATION

WPA literature has highlighted the significance of institutional positionings to administrative work. Whatever our theoretical commitments, our administrative practices are always located within complex power dynamics. Therefore, scholars such as Chris M. Anson and Carol Rutz argue that administrators, including graduate students who are new to administrative roles, should be critically aware of the ideological underpinnings of institutions. Pursuing such critiques, researchers have problematized masculinist academic conventions which valorize individuality, rationality, and hierarchy. For example, Marcia Dickson, describes traditional administrative structures as based on individual power and patriarchy. Within this model unilateral control is privileged over dialogue and cooperation. Hildy Miller also examines the ways in which the positioning of the administrative domain within the masculinist traditions of the department and academy creates tensions between nonauthoritarian forms of leadership and institutional conventions.

In response to such masculinist frameworks, researchers have offered feminist approaches to writing program administration. Feminist models seek to blur lines of authority, flatten hierarchies, encourage experimentation, reward excellence, and support members of a program (Dickson). They also encourage a both/and, rather than an either/or, leadership stance, which fosters community, interrelational authority, flexible decision making, and a collaborative sense of community (H. Miller). Discussions of feminist administration also complicate male/female dualisms and essentialized notions of gender. For instance, Judith Glazer argues for destabilizing masculinized bureaucratic models not only pedagogically but also administratively, in the feminist professionalization of teachers. Likewise, Louise Wetherbee Phelps analyzes the problem of empowerment in relation to characterizations of feminization. She asserts that, rather than approaching femininity as essentialized identity or coterminous with feminism, we strategically should approach it as a dynamic concept that makes possible any number of stances ("Becoming" 314).

As a complement to feminist approaches, WPA scholarship has explored collaboration as a means to subvert masculinist practices and structures. For example, in their discussion of collaborative leadership, Anne Aronson and Craig Hansen suggest that feminist approaches to writing program administration can counter masculinist models by encouraging interdependence, relationality, and mutual empowerment. Similarly, Lynn Meeks and Christine Hult advocate co-mentoring—a practice that decenters a WPA's power and asserts a postmasculinist stance on administrative work. Although these frameworks encourage WPAs to see their roles as contingent and situated, they also acknowledge that institutionalized definitions of authority cannot simply be erased or ignored. Trudy Smoke aptly argues that power is unpredictable and dynamic, and thus power in collaborative administration involves both loss and gain. WPAs cannot be guaranteed that collaboration always leads to equitable relationships among administrators, staff, teachers, and students in their programs. This struggle to enact more equitable collaborative practice also is part of Susanmarie Harrington, Steve Fox, and Tere Molinder Hogue's work. They note that professional rank and lack of value for administrative work also conspire to undermine collaborative relationships. To foster better understandings of the ways in which collaboration is enacted, Eileen E. Schell in "Who's the Boss" urges collaborative administrators to construct case studies that address both the possibilities and constraints of collaborative leadership.

COMPUTERS AND COMPOSITION RESEARCH ON GENDER AND TECHNOLOGY

Like feminist and collaborative approaches to administration, critical approaches to technology highlight the importance of larger cultural and institutional contexts (Feenberg; Haraway; Johnson-Eilola; Selber). Such theories seek to complicate determinisms that position technologies as either neutral tools or autonomous forces of social change. Critical frameworks, therefore, critique social biases that inform the design, distribution, and use of technologies. In pursuit of critical, contextualized approaches, researchers in the field of computers and composition have examined the ways in which technology is masculinized and plays a role in unequal power relations (Hocks). Scholarship has explored gender and technology in relation to topics such as the technology industry as a workplace (Brady-Aschauer), rhetoric in online public spaces (Eble and Breault), the rhetoric of resistance in female-authored websites (Gerrard), the politics of textual production (Barnes and LeCourt), feminist activist hypertexts (Sullivan), feminist web spaces for girls (Takayoshi et al., "No Boys"), power in online conversations (Wolfe), and gender identity in online pedagogies (Pagnucci and Mauriello).

As part of these scholarly conversations, computer compositionists complicate reductive cultural assumptions about gender and technology that position women as nurturers and men as conquerors. They seek to deconstruct dualistic definitions of male/female and masculine/feminine that are imbricated in popular technological narratives (Takayoshi et al., "No Boys"). As Rebecca Rickly asserts in her empirical research on computer-mediated conversations, we should focus not just on biological sex but also on socially constructed gender roles. We must look at ways in which technology is gendered as masculine and development often is associated with mastery ("Gender Gap"). Angela Haas, Christine Tully, and Kristine Blair discuss these issues in their collaborative work on gender negotiation in web-based writing spaces. They suggest that traditional gender–power dynamics often define technological literacy as a product to be mastered, rather than a process to be nurtured. To counter these structures, Haas, Tully, and Blair offer narrative as a methodology and pedagogy that allows women and girls to voice their technological literacy histories. Their discussion of technology learning provides a generative framework for thinking about technology education as a complex, recursive process. Although women's anxieties were highlighted in Haas, Tully, and Blair's development experiences, mastery was a problematic issue for both men and women in our mentoring groups, which often included new computer composition instructors of both sexes. Thus, to account for this distinction in our own analysis of examples, we engage theories of gender performativity.

GENDER PERFORMANCE
AND TECHNOLOGICAL ARTICULATION

As a complement to conversations in WPA and computer and composition scholarship, we now turn to the antifoundational theories of Judith Butler and Donna Haraway. Their concepts of performativity and articulation provide productive critical lenses for connecting issues of administration, power, agency, gender, and technology. Butler's work challenges essentialized definitions of gender. Rather than viewing gender as correlating with or being caused by biological sex, she positions gender as a social temporality, a recitative performance of contingent norms and relationships. Butler argues that, "[g]ender ought not to be constructed as a stable identity or locus of agency from which various acts follow; rather gender is an identity tenuously constituted in time, instituted in an exterior space through a stylized repetition of acts" (*GT* 140). Thus, according to this framework, masculinized qualities such as mastery are not inherent or exclusive to men.

The instability and contingency of gender, however, does not render it autonomous or voluntary. In other words, gender is not simply a matter of choosing to be masculine or feminine from one moment to the next. Instead, gender performance is deeply imbricated with issues of power and the positioning of subjects within hegemonic social structures. Cultural definitions of gender, then, impact gender performance. To emphasize this point, Butler stresses that "gender is performatively produced and compelled by the regulatory practices of gender coherence" (*GT* 24). Certain expressions of gender are privileged over others, and thus we are compelled to reiterate these existing norms as we perform in relation to other subjects. Although repetition of certain gender constructions is ritualized, it is not wholly determinative. In both *Gender Trouble* and *Bodies That Matter*, Butler suggests that gender norms are never fully internalized. If gender is a provisional set of categories that must be sustained through repetition, subjects have the potential to disrupt hegemonic patterns and perform their gender differently and in potentially subversive ways.

Like Butler, Donna Haraway is wary of totalizing theories and strives to destabilize binaries such as male/female, active/passive, and culture/nature. She argues that contemporary feminists should seek pleasure in the confusion of boundaries and take responsibility for their construction ("A Cyborg Manifesto" 150). To this end, she embraces partial, contradictory, permanently dynamic constructions of collective selves and political identities. Thus, Haraway views gender as an articulation, a contingent, non-necessary set of culturally situated connections. Haraway argues that "[g]ender is always a relationship, not a . . . possession that one can have. Gender does not pertain more to women than to men. Gender is the relation between variously constituted categories of men and women (and variously arrayed), differentiated by nation, generation, class, lineage, color, and much else" (*Modest* 28).

As Haraway discusses throughout *Simians, Cyborgs, and Women*, technology is also a permanently partial set of relationships formed in combination with other social forces, practices, identities, and ideologies. Although technologies traditionally have been positioned as masculinized and deterministic, such characterizations are ideologically and culturally constructed rather than inherent. Thus, she argues that feminists should reexamine their traditionally agonistic relationship with technology. Like gender, technology is contingent and thus can be rearticulated: Productively engaging in and disrupting technological processes, therefore, can offer new sources of feminist agency.

Combining notions of gender performativity and technological rearticulation with the research discussed in the previous sections offers us a complex interpretive framework for analyzing our mentoring experiences. Nonessentialized notions of gender allow us to consider the complex relationships that both male and female mentees have to masculinized constructions of mastery. Additionally, understanding gender and technology as contingent cultural constructions allows us to engage not only the positions of individual instructors but also the larger ideological categories that inform their experiences. Lastly, these critical, nondeterministic theories encourage both critique and situated action. These approaches provide the potential for agency in relation to the frustrations and complications of technological mastery. Although dominant narratives about technology may encourage users to perform masculinized dominance and control, other forms of agency are always possible.

OUR MENTORING NARRATIVES

To explore how the determinism of mastery influences computer composition teachers, we now discuss our own co-mentoring in more detail. Throughout our 4 years of mentoring new computer compositionists, we worked to create a collaborative environment—one that valued pedagogical exchange and encouraged a range of peer interactions. Just as Peter Blakemore argues that administrators must reject a model of teacher development that positions instructors as "empty vessels" ready to be filled with an administrator's knowledge, we sought to establish relationships that acknowledged and drew on mentee experiences (140).

Instead of taking the position that we, as administrators, held all the expertise and power, we hoped that a collaborative, praxis-based model of mentoring would work against technological determinism and highlight multiple ways of teaching and learning with technology in the composition classroom. Rather than privileging the newest, most elaborate technologies, we encouraged instructors to consider ways in which more familiar technologies, like word processing and e-mail, also could be productive components of their computer composition teaching. Through course evaluations, continued communication with former mentor group participants, and assessments from the Director of Composition, we continually evaluated the effectiveness of the mentoring and worked to emphasize the aspects most valued by members of the writing program. Though our feminist, collaborative framework for the practicum generally garnered positive feedback, we also experienced some moments of tension. Both men and women in our mentoring group at times were hailed into the masculinized role of technological mastery. When learning new technologies, users typically face moments in which they feel frustrated and disempowered. Finding themselves in traditionally feminized positions, members of the mentoring sometimes would respond by aligning themselves with dominant narratives of technology that deny tentative answers, in-process learning, and collaboration. Such attempts to perform masculinized control and dominance are reflected in particular moments from our technology mentoring. These instances illustrate the friction that can occur between theory and practice—between instructors' understandable desires to assert control over instructional technologies and collaborative, feminist approaches, like the one valued in our mentoring group. Returning to these points of tension, we seek to re-articulate hegemonic notions of gender, technology, and power that come into play even in collaborative, feminist models of technology learning.

We designed English 502I: Computer Composition Mentoring—a required graduate-level, one-credit hour course—to have several key requirements: (a) instructor development and publishing of a web-based syllabus, (b) participation in resource-sharing presentations to the group, (c) peer and instructor classroom visits, and (d) regular attendance at meetings. Course requirements offered instructors opportunities to share their own perspectives on composition teaching and collaborate with other course participants. Seeking to share authority, encourage experimentation, and foster a collaborative sense of community, we hoped that this pedagogical approach would enable us to perform feminist administration. The mentoring groups enrolled a range of self-selecting instructors who wanted to teach in computer classrooms. They represented diverse scholarly interests within English studies and expressed varying degrees of technological experience, including both expertise and technophobia. To support this wide-ranging population, our course structure provided all instructors with the chance to define their own goals and share their computer teaching strategies with the group. We knew then—as we know now—that the integration of technology was not a neutral task—not simply a matter of adding new resources to formerly taught courses. In fact, we viewed collaborative learning and critical constructions of technology as two of the mentoring's greatest strengths. Therefore, we sought to create space in our weekly meetings where computer composition teaching roles could be explored rather than imposed. In pursuing critical, collaborative methods, however, we could not simply erase dominant assumptions about technology or nullify their impact on instructors' learning. Although mentoring participants valued nondeterministic approaches to technology and pedagogy, instructors still encountered moments in which they were hailed into performing masculinized technological roles. Even if we as technology learners intellectually understand the impossibility of mastery, we still sometimes have the desire to assert individual control and maintain some sense of hierarchy and authority over technology. Anna and Keith are two former mentees who were enrolled in different sections of the mentoring group. The narratives we share here about their particular moments of struggle with technological mastery illustrate the masculinized pull of technology learning we have suggested. Before articulating these tensions, we want to emphasize that both Anna and Keith were dedicated, experienced teachers who contributed a great deal to the mentoring group and their own first-year writing courses.

ANNA

Anna was a second-year PhD student in Purdue's literature program. She had taught the required first-year composition sequence and enrolled in the mentoring, expressing both moderate comfort and experience using technology. Anna often shared her perspectives on teaching and was at ease working with her colleagues in the mentoring group. She took copious notes at our meetings and engaged the optional readings on technology theory and practice. Anna's diligence and interest in teaching with technology were evident in her contributions. Her point of struggle, however, was to become as expert with the technology as she was with her own pedagogy. In other words, Anna's new role as a computer compositionist complicated her sense of agency as a teacher. The institutionalized role of teacher traditionally is situated within academic hierarchies that privilege individual authority. Therefore, even the most experienced of teachers can feel uncertain about learning new skills and potentially stumbling in front of students.

The reiterative power of mastery presented itself in Anna's work with web design. As she was learning HTML and making her first web-authoring choices, she wanted encouragement, or proof, that her decisions were sound. This need to know that her choices were valid is not unique. Most of us want assurances that our pedagogical materials, web or otherwise, are appropriate and useful to students. Anna's experience, however, was complicated further by culturally dominant narratives about individual authorship and transparent technological design. In Anna's case, her need to validate her web choices allows a glimpse into the power of the concept of technological mastery and the ways it can undermine collaborative and in-process views of technology learning.

Anna was pleased that one of the requirements of the mentoring was publishing web versions of her syllabus. One of her goals was to become skilled at web development, and so she was eager to participate in workshops on HTML and Dreamweaver. Because instructors in the mentoring had a range of web-authoring skills, we provided web templates as a means for mentees to learn HTML code and begin their first versions of web syllabi. We encouraged instructors to consider their own pedagogical and rhetorical needs as they worked with one another to make changes and coordinate the templates with their pedagogical practices. The templates, then, were collaborative documents that functioned as heuristics for exploring web development.

Another required element of our mentoring was resource-sharing presentations. These presentations provided group members with an opportunity to not only support their peers but also explore theoretical, technical, and pedagogical issues relevant to their own teaching. The topics and structures of these presentations were diverse—workshops on course technologies like Adobe Page Maker and Microsoft PowerPoint, analyses of scholarly articles covering topics such as critical theories of technology and the evaluation of student writing, reflections on assignments related to web research, and electronic peer response, among others. In general, teachers used the resource sharing presentations as ways to both teach and learn from their peers. Typically, mentees would share practices that they had successfully integrated into their classes, ask us to participate in "trial runs" for upcoming technological activities, or facilitate discussions of pedagogical issues related to their new roles as computer compositionists.

Anna highlighted her development of web materials in the resource presentation assignment. As a way to engage the mentoring group in a discussion of web design, Anna described a survey she had conducted in the first week of the semester. Her survey asked students in her course to provide feedback on revisions that she had made to the original web templates. Anna had taken the content of the pages and translated it into a format with similar architecture, but different colors and graphics. Anna's survey asked students to compare her versions of course web materials with the original templates she had modified with her colleagues in our mentoring group. She asked students to comment on which design they preferred—the original template or her revisions.

In her presentation, Anna explained that her visual design had gone through many iterations. As she narrated her revision process, she remarked that she was not accustomed to devoting this much attention to the structure of her teaching documents. Her motivation for administering a survey was to "prove" that her efforts had been fruitful in generating an effective redesign. In her reflection on this activity, Anna noted that her students were not likely to evaluate her new template negatively especially because it was the design that she ended up using. Despite her reflection on this bias, Anna turned her discussion to how the survey's results provided her with the much-needed assurance that her new pages were well designed.

Customizing her web pages to better reflect her own pedagogical perspective was indeed one of the mentoring group's goals. We were impressed with the initiative that Anna and other instructors took to individually and collaboratively troubleshoot their HTML code and offer feedback on design choices. Reflecting on Anna's presentation, we thus were struck by her unease with her own abilities. Feeling feminized in relationship to technology, Anna assumed a masculinized stance by attempting to prove her work to herself, students, and those of us in the mentoring group. Working through a collaborative design process in the mentoring group had not given her an absolute sense of authority either in relation to her web teaching materials or her role as a new computer composition instructor. Dominant assumptions about technological mastery emphasize making universally "right" choices rather than exploring multiple design possibilities. Thus, Anna felt the need to demonstrate and even evidence her expertise in a verifiable way.

KEITH

Anna's attempts to master the technology, demonstrate her expertise, and assert her individualism are not foreign to those of us working with and researching technology. In fact, such masculinized gender performances in relationship to technology can be noted in another experience that occurred in our mentoring group. Keith, a fourth-year PhD student in literature, also experienced the pull of reiterative constructions of technological mastery during his participation in the mentoring group. Keith's teaching experience included Purdue's first-year writing courses and composition courses at one of the local community colleges. He began the semester by self-identifying as a novice in relation to technology. Part of his rationale for enrolling in the mentoring group was the value that technical skills could have for his marketability. Keith's struggle shares a commonality with Anna's: Keith also was invested in gaining and proving his computer composition expertise. He understood that his own technological mastery might not only enhance his teaching but also lead him to better employment options. Keith was hopeful that he could use what he was learning in the mentoring as a means to retain his local summer teaching position. For Keith, mastery was less about validating a particular skill, such as web design in Anna's case, and more about gaining as much knowledge and expertise as possible to improve his teaching and compete in the marketplace. Dominant frameworks often link technology to increased professional and fiscal opportunities. As Haas, Tully, and Blair suggest, technological literacy often is reified as a product to be mastered rather than a process to be nurtured. Such approaches present technology learning as a clearly defined process that results in discrete, commodifiable results. Keith's response to peer and instructor visits demonstrates his struggle to negotiate these deterministic narratives about technology, economics, and mastery.

Instructors in the mentoring group were required to participate in peer and mentor visits. Rather than being conducted as evaluative observations, the visits were framed as another opportunity to share and collaborate with other computer composition teachers. Understanding that observations of any sort can create anxiety for instructors, we wanted to ensure that the visits were framed as supportive rather than judgmental or corrective. Peers would invite another mentoring group member to one day of their classes.

Colleagues would use a prompt that we provided to discuss the agenda for the visit and identify issues about which they wanted specific feedback. For example, an instructor might ask a peer to pay particular attention to students' responses to a web research workshop. These visits emphasized multiple perspectives on technology teaching. Rather than assuming a right or universal way to teach an aspect of technology, peers were able to see other interpretations of technology integration and discuss their views on and experiences with technology teaching. As mentors, we also visited each instructor, following the same process of collaboratively scheduling and setting the agenda for the class day when one of us would attend.

Although Keith had engaged other mentoring activities, he seemed to distance himself from our mentoring group's conversations about planning the peer visits. After Keith's partner mentioned that he had tried unsuccessfully to make arrangements, we decided to schedule a conference with Keith to talk about the assignment. We were surprised by Keith's explanation about his reluctance to participate in the peer visits. He noted that incorporating technology into his pedagogy already was taking more time than he anticipated. Therefore, he wanted to optimize his learning. Keith explained that, although our visit would be welcome, having another member of the group come to his class would not be productive. He viewed our comments on his computer teaching as beneficial because we were the experts, the "tech chicks," responsible for preparing him and the other instructors. Having an equally inexperienced peer visit, however, was much less likely to enhance his teaching.

Like Anna, Keith wanted the effort he put into technology to be productive for his teaching. In fact, the mentoring pedagogy supported this prioritization; discussions often focused on the importance of emphasizing pedagogical goals when making technological decisions. Dominant cultural constructions of technology often highlight ease and efficiency; they suggest that, if you individually master the "right" ways to use technology, your work automatically will be streamlined and more effective. Teaching in a computer classroom, however, generally does not simplify teachers' roles or lighten their workloads. Therefore, Keith experienced a clash between his technology learning experiences and his desire to efficiently increase his teaching effectiveness and professional status. Keith's response to this tension understandably was to reiterate masculinized hegemonic norms related to individual mastery and institutional hierarchy. He resisted being observed by his peer because the activity violated the lines of authority traditionally associated with technological expertise.

Similarly, our feminist performance of administration also ran counter to traditional constructions of power and mastery. Hildy Miller describes the misperceptions of administrative leadership when viewed through such a masculinist lens, arguing, "leadership can appear weak if receptivity is mistaken for passivity; affective responses for lack of seriousness; and the sharing of power for looking to others for direction" (54). Our goal to share authority with members of the group controverted our position as strong leaders. Keith negatively assessed the value of the required peer visits and initially chose not to participate, although it was a course requirement. Further, our desire to create a collaborative environment where instructors provided insights into one another's teaching and learning complicated the assumption that technology mastery is an achievable, productive goal. Keith was feeling frustrated about the indeterminacy of technology learning. He was putting in a great deal of effort, yet achieving no closure. Rather than experiencing this process as a productive *becoming*—to use Haraway's term ("Promises" 299)—Keith saw himself as failing, as using his time unwisely. Keith ultimately agreed to the peer observation, but he seemed unconvinced of the value in the process. He continued to measure his work with technology in relation to masculinized notions of mastery.

Such hierarchical interpretations, again, are not unique to Keith. These assumptions about technological expertise are even more complicated than our telling reveals. Feminized and masculinized gender performance in relationship to technology is not reserved for only women or only men. The cultural determinism of mastery can influence any teacher to believe that, to be technically proficient, one must assert his or her individual dominance over technology (Kimme Hea). Here we also want to stress that these two mentees, Anna and Keith, were valuable members of our mentoring groups. Despite the issues that our articulation raises, they both worked to make the weekly meetings meaningful to their own teaching experiences and successfully transitioned from traditional classroom teaching to networked classrooms. Yet we still wonder about the ways Anna's and Keith's moments of technology mastery are connected to gendered assumptions about technology. Looking back on our experiences, we are interested in reframing these narratives to think about the teachable moments we may have missed as mentors. Without trying to resolve all contradiction and conflict from our mentoring experiences, we want to discuss strategies for rearticulating gendered performances of technological mastery.

TACTICS FOR FEMINIST TECHNOLOGY
TEACHER DEVELOPMENT

When the position of computer composition mentor became vacant while we were at Purdue, we immediately decided to apply jointly, although the opening advertised a single job. We made this choice because of our shared commitment to critical approaches to technology. We believed that collaboratively facilitating the mentoring group would help us to enact a feminist, participatory model of administration and technology learning. Although critical commitments influenced our work from the outset, we still found that our design for the mentoring course was not impervious to deterministic constructions of technology. As part of their technology development, instructors experienced moments of contradiction and frustration. Dominant assumptions about the gendered performance of mastery complicated mentees' sense of authority, expertise, and productivity. Reflecting on these experiences, we want to find ways to learn from these tensions and foreground issues of technological mastery as a more explicit aspect of mentoring. Rather than framing technological agency in terms of individualized control and dominance, we seek to facilitate a more critical, feminist form of agency. As Butler suggests, hegemonic norms never are fully internalized or stable. We can rearticulate hierarchical models of administration and masculinized models of technology development.

To challenge the deterministic notions of technological mastery, we want to revisit our own mentoring practices and explore ways that we may have been better able to support feminist teacher agency. We also want to stress that local situations and teacher technology development practices are intimately connected. The administrative structures, positions of administrators (tenured, nontenured, compensated, uncompensated, among others), and positions of the instructors (tenured, nontenured, full-time, part-time, faculty, lecturers, graduate students, among others) all play roles in shaping teacher technology development practices. A feminist perspective seeks to rearticulate technology teacher development along multiple lines, making certain that the local student–teacher–administrator context is central to pedagogical practices. This stance emphasizes partiality, contingencies, collaboration, and self-reflection. Our own rearticulation, then, draws on our roles as administrators and tries to reconceive a feminist teacher technology development approach—one that directly challenges mastery models and offers teachers ways of intervening in the constructedness of technology.

One well-researched and often discussed method for facilitating teacher agency is the use of narrative and autobiography. Haas, Tully, and Blair argue that, for a mentoring method to be empowering, it should not assume that all students and teachers approach technology in the same way at the same time (241). To foreground the situatedness of technology, they offer the strategy of computer literacy autobiographies. They suggest that, by narrativizing their histories, technology learners can begin framing technology literacy as a life-long process; users can theorize their experiences and better understand the way socio-economic and cultural conditions have contributed to their everyday routines. Likewise, Cindy Selfe and Gail Hawisher's technological literacy project is an excellent model of historicizing and contextualizing technology learning through political, social, personal, and cultural factors. Through a personal technology literacy narrative (Duffelmeyer; DeVoss et al.), instructors can begin to challenge the idea that technology is an autonomous, self-perpetuating force. Seeing how, and even why they have learned technologies as they have (or have not), teachers can claim their own stakes in their technology teacher development. Instructors can share their narratives, helping one another question otherwise taken-for-granted assumptions about themselves and their technology learning.

Such collaborative, situated practices also can include mapping of technology learning. Instructors can create multiple maps that articulate their interactions with technology. This mapping practice can help to visualize the tension and ambiguities of technology learning, making clearer the "gaps" that each of us has in our own technological literacy (Peeples). Technology is depicted in more contradictory ways, and teachers can envision new methods to assert their own agency in relationship to normalized, gendered assumptions about teaching and learning with technology. Just as with the technological literacy narratives, these visual maps must be shared and discussed in the community of teachers. These different interpretations can reassert the ways technology has been constructed in our lives. The literacy narratives and visual maps are both ways of historicizing our experiences in relation to the larger cultural milieu.

Historicizing personal, professional, social, and cultural aspects of technology also can be complemented by ideological critiques of mastery. Ideological inquiry as a part of mentoring can raise questions about how and why certain pedagogical and technological experiences occur as they do and what the consequences of such experiences are for those involved. Rather than assuming that the technological and pedagogical circumstances are always in line with one another, instructors consider the larger cultural meanings imbricated in their use of technologies and how those technologies, in turn, influence pedagogical possibilities. Getting at the ideological implications of technology in a mentoring group can allow for more complex incorporations of technologies in the classroom and raise issues that may remain underexplored. Drawing on Bryan Pfaffenberger, Stuart Selber discusses how we must work to reveal and interrogate areas of inconsistency and outright contradiction with technology. Among his many salient points regarding technology teacher development, Selber discusses how sites like Girlhoo may be lauded for including women on the World Wide Women, yet simultaneously critiqued for using this inclusiveness as a means to reinforce traditional gender roles ("Technological" 175–76). Critiques of educational websites, institutional policies on technology, and other media articulations of technology may allow instructors in a practicum to assert more complicated technology teacher subjectivities— positions that acknowledge the potentials and constraints of technology teaching and learning.

To further contextualize teaching practices, historical and ideological inquiries can be complemented by rearticulating other technological practices. Rearticulation asserts that context is primary in determining possible uses for that technology. In other words, rather than emphasizing only the technological artifact, rearticulation illuminates how environment, persons, language, and situations affect technological integration. Although rearticulated acts may be small in scope, their impact can be far reaching in terms of the learning opportunities offered to an instructor (Johnson-Eilola and Kimme Hea). Thus, in the move to develop critical feminist agency, a practicum can help an instructor gain a better awareness of the underlying technical and cultural logics of technology. Redesign projects can help technology users map existing relationships and imagine alternative ways for articulating them; they foreground the potential for change and thus can encourage critical, rhetorical agency (Turnley). A practicum redesign project could include critiquing and revising course-in-a-box software interfaces, educational and corporation websites, even institutional technology policies on campus, in a department, or in a particular program. This rearticulation would include a rhetorical analysis of the technological practice in relationship to issues of power and its associations with gender, race, class, and other cultural constructs.

Situated performances are yet another method of reenvisioning technology learning in a mentoring group. Shirley K. Rose and Margaret J. Finders envision situated performance as a postmodern revision of role-play, which sees "teachers as simultaneously occupying multiple roles, which are fluid, fragmented, and transient, positions that are complex, conflicted, and constrained by context" (207–8). They support situated performance as a way to encourage teacher agency, contextualize teacher practices, and create a space for critical reflection (Rose and Finders). Having teachers engage in problem-posing scenarios can allow members of a course to intervene in technological processes and act out possible alternative strategies for dealing with gendered performances of mastery as part of technology learning. As Augusto Boal argues, these scenarios are defined by the stakeholders and allow even the audience to move from passive receptors to active agents.

As Haraway suggests throughout *Simians, Cyborgs, and Women*, the productive rearticulation of technological processes can offer new sources of feminist agency. As we continue to work with issues of technology administration and teacher development, we hope to use these and other strategies to foreground masculinized notions of mastery and subvert the negative influence that they can have on technology learning. In particular, we encourage technology mentoring as an opportunity to continue the work of feminist administration. Through situated, collaborative approaches to teacher technology development, administrators can model critical pedagogical practices and facilitate alternative forms of feminist agency.

9

MANAGED CARE

All-Terrain Mentoring and the "Good Enough" Feminist WPA

E. Shelley Reid

Lacie sits down in the chair alongside my desk, trying not to look defeated. "As I said in my e-mail," she begins, "I just wanted your feedback. I guess I knew that improvement wouldn't be an overnight thing, but when the Review Committee rated me just 'adequate' again, I was stunned. We'd been working well this semester, you and I, and the committee member's report on my teaching called me 'well prepared and energetic.' " She shifts her multiple book bags, which are more substantially her "office" than is the desk she shares with five other adjunct instructors, to a new formation near the chair.

> All the review letter says is "try to work on engaging more students in your class" and "see your program director for more advice." But I've been working with you all semester. How can they judge so much based on one class observation anyway? I don't have any problems at the other school I teach at. They've taken away one of my comp sections here for the spring and given it to someone else, because of the rating, so I'll have to find something else somehow to pay the bills.

Lacie, an imagined adjunct faculty member who stands in for half a
dozen composition instructors I have worked with recently, and many
more I expect to work with in the future, clearly needs a feminist WPA.
(Doesn't everybody?) But as I consider her story, I find that figuring out
how to be(come) the feminist WPA Lacie needs, or even how to adequately
perform that role, is a complex project. I am at once a teacher-mentor and a
program director, needing to provide both personalized care and procedural justice. Moreover, Lacie's story is not easily separable from layers of
other stories, programmatic and institutional, in which my own actions are
implicated. Because I am also listening as a fellow teacher and pretenure
administrator—institutional positions that complicate if not lessen my own
agency—I am having a significant "personal is professional is political"
moment. Certainly my professional situation is more stable than Lacie's
and more respected by the academy, but I empathize in sometimes conflicting ways with the frustrations she feels toward the institution(s) I embody.
Listening as both the boss compositionist and a feminist woman, I can
hardly keep up with my own recognitions of contradictory pressures and
impulses. I am a "both/and" woman by inclination and education, but I can
take only one administrative action at a time.

In the pages that follow, I use the previous scenario as a stepping-off
point to explore some of the challenges facing a pretenure WPA who is
also a woman (in my case) and a feminist. Marlene Fine and Patrice
Buzzanell argue that feminist leaders should articulate tensions and conflicts in order to use them to "confront the 'dark' places of our souls and
think through possibilities in our lives"; they also suggest that finding
answers to dilemmas and paradoxes is "less important than the self-aware-
ness of the internal conflict" (149, 155). Intellectually, I agree: Who would
want to be non-self-aware, to ignore conflicts or challenging data? The last
italicized journal entry they include in their article, however—tucked in
between these two rational conclusions—is something of a wail: "We feel
like such hypocrites. . . . [W]e both feel as though we fall so short of these
ideals. We can't be everything to everyone. . . . We both feel all-too-human
tensions, ambivalences, and resentments about our roles" (Fine and
Buzzanell 155). Clearly the theoretical oxymorons that delight us as scholars can stalk and even injure us when we try to perform as leaders in institutional settings. Fine and Buzzanell's journal entry circles valiantly back
to acknowledge that "it is worth the struggle," but that assertion's calm
assurance is undercut by the next line: "How else could we be at peace
with our decisions. . . . ?" (155). I read and I sympathize, and I cannot help
but wonder further: Is this what awaits me as a feminist WPA? Have we
vanquished the Angel in the House or has she just morphed to become the
Feminist in the Conference Room, silenced this time by her own fears of
not measuring up, of being "all too human"? Didn't we weed out the

superwoman myth decades ago? If so, why does it keep popping back up to interrupt what little peace we can find?

So here is my opening confession: As a pretenure compositionist woman and newly hired WPA, I have plenty of self-doubt on my plate already, thank you very much, without having to worry every moment if I am being properly feminist, caring enough or too much, or "fall[ing] so short of [the] ideals." I would love to be the warrior feminist that Louise Wetherbee Phelps describes in "Becoming a Warrior: Lessons of the Feminist Workplace." Yet then again, reading Phelps' powerful story, among others that embody the familiar success narrative of an academic article, it does not take long for me to succumb to my own case of "I'm not worthy." Certainly one goal I have for this chapter is to articulate some of the conflicts and complications that WPAing brings up for me as a feminist and to lay out some possible strategies for releasing my own and other feminist WPAs' inner warrior. But a second goal is to clear some room for thinking about the various ways we each need to define, locally, and perform the role of a "good enough" feminist WPA. Feminist principles of all sorts, of course, support a good enough approach to living and working, but in a difficult world of women and institutions and stories of administrative heroics, it can be easy to lose sight of that crucial element.[1] I believe that one good enough path can be constructed from a revisioning of what *mentoring*—with its implied feminine undertones and care-full overtones— can be and can accomplish. Learning to construct that more complex map can help a feminist WPA learn to manage care in the writing program.

MENTORING AND THE WPA

I begin with Lacie, rather than with any of a myriad of other conflicted situations, because the scene I described is, ostensibly, about mentoring. This is an important site for me and an important site for a discussion of performing the work of a pretenure, female, feminist WPA. It is important for me because, in my previous job as an associate composition director at a different university, my role was defined almost entirely as a mentoring role. In professional terms, I was granted the relatively safe space provided by working primarily with

COUNTERNARRATIVES: LOCATION

In my department, the chair, associate chair, and writing center director are feminist women; the associate dean is also a feminist woman. Out of 50 tenure-track faculty in the department, 7 are tenured or tenure-track in composition or a related field. Tenure-line faculty in other subfields regularly teach in the composition program (at the advanced composition level). My position was created with adequate released time and with a promise that my administrative work would "count," separately from and equivalent to teaching, graduate student TAs and composition curriculum issues while I learned the ropes, established my research agenda, and earned academic capital. In more gendered terms, one could say I "stayed home" and "minded the kids" (and, as Debra Dew has pointed out, tried to fulfill the common, but antirhetorical, pretenure dictum of "shut up and write") while the tenured director (also a woman) sat on departmental and university committees, hired and fired instructors, handled most student complaints, and interacted with other faculty, staff, and advisors across the university. To be fair, I enjoyed my work in the more "domestic" sphere, and indeed I felt sheltered from a range of slings and arrows. I also consistently turned this "soft" work into "hard" research and formal program development projects, thus dismantling some of the gender divide. I have wondered whether this experience was too limited a performance, resulting in my not being fully prepared for the additional tasks and approaches common in the "masculine" sphere that my current position includes. However, I believe that my inclination to see many program issues as being first of all local issues that can best be addressed via mentoring may also be a core value on which I can build an administrative philosophy.

Mentoring is also an important and conflicted site more generally for a female feminist WPA. In many ways, mentoring is gendered masculine by its traditional institutional appearances and effects. I think here of old boys' clubs, the protégé as a status-enhancing replication of the mentor, and the initiation/indoctrination of a newcomer into

service, and scholarship, toward tenure (although it has never been done that way here before). We have a thriving WAC program, a composition curriculum that assumes all teachers will choose their own texts with care and helps them do so, and composition education for GTAs. There's a general spirit of collaboration and experimentation, and a number of tenured faculty are intensely interested in the project of teaching. It's pretty fertile ground for a feminist WPA.

In my department, in addition to the tenure-track faculty, we rely heavily on the back-breaking work of some 25 "term assistant professors" (long-term adjuncts on yearly or biannual salaried contracts who teach eight writing-intensive courses a year), about 20 GTAs, and over 50 adjuncts—this group earning, for many years now, a per-course salary that is embarrassingly inadequate given their work and given the local cost of living. Many of the non-tenure-line faculty are women, about half of them young women just entering their first career, and about half women in their 40s and 50s newly or still teaching composition as an adjunct. Morale can be low; skyrocketing housing costs in the nearby counties eat up meager paychecks and turn people into freeway-creepers who may spend more time on the road each day than on a campus; community operates mostly below the radar. Two different people told me, as I started this job, that what they knew of this university was how badly the adjuncts had it here. It's difficult territory for a feminist WPA.

the institutional status quo.[2] It can also be—sometimes simultaneously—gendered professionally feminine in its workload and (lack of) potential for institutional recognition. Female faculty members, as Theresa Enos notes, can be so swamped by mentoring activities, particularly when mentoring is gendered feminine in a way that constructs it as "unlimited caregiving," that they do not accomplish other, more rewarded tasks ("Mentoring" 141). At its poles, mentoring can be read as the ultimate in egocentric self-promotion or just as easily seen as a selfless and even self-abnegating kind of emotional support.

Yet mentoring remains a flexible enough paradigm to be defined as and used to create space for feminist action within the academy and within the writing program. Gail McGuire and Jo Reger argue that mentoring can be undertaken so as to implement several common feminist understandings: that hierarchies and power imbalances should be questioned if not always attacked or dismantled, that building interpersonal relationships should be at least as high a priority as establishing structures and rules, and that emotion should be valued as highly as intellect (54-55). I can mentor people in ways that help me foreground not just caregiving, but an ethic of care—an approach to problem solving that (as writers such as Carol Gilligan and Nel Noddings explain) emphasizes relationships and individual circumstances more than abstract principles or rules. Moreover, mentoring in a composition program certainly allows me to pay particular attention to the needs of women and all those whose position has been feminized or disempowered within the academy. Yet it is problematic to see mentoring as a feminist administrative cure-all. Simply shifting one's administrative standpoint to a mentoring center does not guarantee that one's actions will be feminist, will be administratively successful, or will feel good enough. Making mentoring into manageable caring is, I have been discovering, a significant challenge.

MENTORING AS UNMANAGEABLE CARE

In a recent *Sally Forth* cartoon, Sally imagines her possible first day if she were promoted to Human Resources Director. After a few ordinary complaints about upcoming meetings and project deadlines, staff members' crises become unmanageable: They expand in urgency, moving swiftly to, "Sal, the world's economies are collapsing!

COUNTERNARRATIVES: IDENTITY

I need feminism for the world I live in. Sexism and classism; the systemic and often conscious oppression of the marginalized; the multiple levels of outsidering faced still by women, compositionists, adjuncts, and other minorities. I need feminist standpoints, need to blur boundaries between personal and political, to add caring to judgment. I've written a dissertation on non-white women novelists, arti-

We have only ten minutes for a solution. . . . !", and finally to, "Sal! The
dead have risen, robots are turning
against us and apes are our new masters! What do we do?!?" (Marciluiano
and Macintosh). A WPA's job may not
always match Sally's "worst-case scenario," but the tendency is already
there—and reading feminism or mentoring in either too limited or too ideal-
istic a way can speed the journey
toward an unmanageable situation.

For example, we can imagine for a
minute how my encounter with Lacie
might be extrapolated á là Sally Forth.
Say that, to begin with, I use a common,
but too-limited, definition of *mentoring*
as individualized caring—a version that
paints the caregiver, often a woman, as
selflessly pouring energies into the
cared-for—as the basis for my response
to Lacie's situation and mentoring tasks
in general. Say I use a couple of basic
indicators to measure the feminisms in
my actions: resisting destructive hierarchies, particularly those built on gender,
for instance, and emphasizing the personal work of relationship-building and
cooperation as ways of engaging with
my colleagues.

Given those starting points, I can
see that working one on one with Lacie
could allow me to value and build on
her own talents, to "foster a [more]
equal balance of power" between us,
and to open a space for "mutual . . .
learning," all elements of feminist mentoring identified by McGuire and Reger
(54-55). Yet my caring for or about
Lacie, however intensively one on one,
is not enough to improve Lacie's classroom teaching, our current focal point.
Margaret Vaughn has demonstrated that

cles calling for better support for
undercompensated teachers, love
letters to *Ms. Magazine*. My feminist relatives and friends have
endured second-class status in
many settings for as long as I've
known them. I've nearly been fired
for not "measuring up" as a pretenure spousal-hire WPA. I wince at
the concept of "postfeminism" (like
postoxygen?). I deliberately clear
space for my women students, and
I've asked whole classes to chant, "I
might be a feminist," just to have
them see if it could be true. This is
what a feminist WPA looks like.

I'm also a good girl—and both
very good and very comfortable at
it—who got this far, in no small
part, by working to tune out the
"static" and follow the rules. I'm
very much drawn to rules, even
unfeminist ones. I'm a privileged
White girl, a third-generation writing professor proud of my "mastery." I still don't have much trouble identifying with Rip van Winkle
against his wife, regardless of what
Judith Fetterly says. I'm INTX in the
Meyers-Briggs alphabet, that intro-
vert "I" representing a tendency to
squirm at the thought that an ethic
of caring might require repeated
public displays of affection, that
waffly "X" a notation of my deep-
seated impulses to judge people by
my own single high standard—"off
with their heads!"—even when I
firmly believe in the need for and
benefit of individual variation and
agency. I interrupt and problem-
solve more readily than I listen and
sympathize. I know there are many
kinds of feminisms, but still I wonder daily: Is this what a feminist
(WPA) looks like?

teachers, like everyone, resist changing their classroom pedagogies. In her study of over 100 teachers, she found that 13% changed their teaching after experiencing a low-intensity interaction in which new rules or actions were described and suggested to them. Another 24% demonstrated pedagogical change when they received individualized instruction. An additional 28% demonstrated significant change only in response to artificial, external motivators, such as required checklists and repeated cues from classroom observers, and nearly a third of the teachers resisted even that (Vaughn 117-120). If it were only Lacie who needed my caring, I could still expend enormous amounts of well-intentioned time and energy without a guarantee that she would, by whatever standards were set, improve her teaching. Moreover, whatever changes she might make would likely become visible only over several semesters. Multiply Lacie by five, a dozen, or fifty, and my other professional obligations as an untenured faculty member would suffer. I might not be around to see Lacie teaching in a more successful mode, and Lacie might have long since lost patience as well.

Besides, as I expand it to cover multiple teachers, that one-on-one "rescue mentoring" starts to sound like a paternalistic patron–novice relationship, in which it would be easy to focus on "fixing" others. Such a strategy is not only unmanageable, because of the sheer numbers, but also much less feminist than I would hope to be. Moreover, my position as director creates an uneraseable hierarchy in that kind of one-on-one mentoring: Despite any of my good intentions, I may be working against my own goals. To take a more collaborative approach to mentoring, I will thus need to open up more spaces for teachers to mentor one another. Professional development activities, such as brown bag lunches and presemester workshops, can spark informal co-mentoring among faculty. To support more formal mentoring activities—identifying a few "senior" TAs specifically to help mentor their more "junior" peers—I can also invest time in workshops to help others develop their mentoring skills. Through this kind of expanded network of mentoring, I can shift my role to become the kind of feminist leader Janice Lauer talks about, "helping to release in others unexplored resources and transformative power" ("Feminization" 547).

Unfortunately, as I watch this project ripple outward, it starts to escape the boundaries of even a wide web of one-on-one care. I note that many of our adjunct faculty cannot or choose not to attend special professional development events, and my department administrators are understandably reluctant to require professional development participation of faculty whose salaries are so low. If mentoring is fully available only to those who have resources to participate, then it is elitist and serves to exacerbate the inequities I am trying to lessen. Similarly, if I begin to design strategies and recruit participants for a peer-mentoring program, here, too, I will need to rely on volunteers who would participate in their "spare time" because

there is currently no money to support stipends or released time for participants in such a program.

Indeed, as I listen to Lacie and her colleagues, it is not difficult for me
to see the wealth of system-level problems exacerbating whatever—if anything—is problematic about their teaching. At some point, even a culture of
careful one-on-one (-on-one-on-one) mentoring may have little lasting
effect in the absence of other kinds of administrative action. At the departmental level, low pay, no chance for advancement, unpredictable hiring patterns, and generally scant resources leave our adjunct faculty members with
few motivations or rewards to support teacher change. At the institutional
level, there is a clear hierarchy (and a local oversupply of teachers) that
makes it possible for colleagues and administrators to state, variously, that
we do not have the resources—and/or do not have the need—and/or do
not have an obligation to mentor adjuncts. After all, we can barely mentor
the GTAs who are the department's top priority.

Meanwhile, and not coincidentally, the adjunct faculty review committee—comprising tenure-line faculty who are, via the departmental bylaws,
the only faculty allowed to be involved with personnel decisions—is chron-
ically understaffed and cannot provide enough feedback to the adjuncts it
reviews every year (via consideration of a one-class observation report and
an often slim teaching portfolio). In addition, because the well-intentioned
members thereof have, much to their credit, resisted easy evaluation checklists or single-member decisions about the fate of the faculty they review,
the process behind their committee-based decisions is somewhat opaque,
and not many details of their rating process make it back to the teachers or
mentors. Recent revisions to the official learning goals for composition
courses clarify some programmatic expectations, but the effects of those
changes will take several years to percolate through a widely distributed
instructor community. If teacher change is slow, institutional change happens in near-geologic time. Moreover, such change only rarely results
directly from the caring input of one concerned colleague, and it may cost
dearly in terms of personal and professional capital (of which a new WPA
has very little anyway). All of us caring together could leave us still facing
the writing program equivalents of angry robots and restless zombies, in
what seems to be an unmanageably large and forbidding set of unmen-
torable, unfeminist situations.

Does that sound more like a wail than a composed theory of administration? I laughed at Sally Forth and tacked the cartoon up on my bulletin
board, but I worry that my worrying will become disheartening and distracting. Kelly McBride suggests that "[m]any people [who] show up for
work their first day firmly rooted in a care-based ethical method . . . [later]
adopt the justice-based method prevalent in most businesses." She argues
that they do so by picking up behaviors from the prevalent corporate culture they see around them, but a sense of the unmanageability of care-based

practices may also contribute to this shift. I absolutely do not want to give up on either my feminist goals or my preferences and aptitudes for mentoring as a basis for program building. However, I need better ways to manage this caring and to ensure that the caring supports a range of management actions I might need or want to perform.

MAXIMIZING MENTORING: AN ALL-TERRAIN VEHICLE

Envisioned as a practice of one-to-one caring and individualized problem solving, a mentoring approach can actually exacerbate a WPA's sense that a program is unmanageable and that the WPA is not good enough. One way I could compensate would be by lowering my expectations for what mentoring can accomplish and developing other approaches or skills for solving other kinds of problems. Still, to try to approach each element of program administration with a different tool (some of which might move me away from the feminist goals I have) could be an equally unmanageable task. Walter Gmelch and Val Miskin, for instance, list 10 "Required Leadership Behaviors" and 38 "administrative duties and activities" en route to describing a department chair's job (19, 49). Even when these tasks are classified into five "key outcome areas," this kind of pageslong list still intimidates me.

What I want is a multipurpose, good enough, feminist administrative vehicle for the various kinds of caring, agency, and activism that I want to employ as a WPA, and I think that the concept of mentoring could be revised to serve that need well. Certainly working with an expanding, collaborative web of mentoring as I described earlier—something I

METACOUNTERNARRATIVES: RHETORIC

I submitted a proposal for this chapter in response to an invitation from collaborating feminist WPAs, who responded with acceptance and mentoring. I'm writing about my administrative experiences, which validates them as important and allows me to connect scholarship and action, experience and theory. I've been drawing on—and feeling quite drawn into—a community of feminists, including the other contributors to this volume, who are writing about composition, administration, leadership, and scholarship. I've had great conversations about the issues in this article with other academic women, from my mother, who helped grow me into the feminist I am, to new colleagues in a discussion group for women administrators, who can help support me into the feminist I am becoming. I'm experimenting with my own writing voice and genre, and I've used this time to reflect critically on my administrative experience and goals. I can begin to see myself setting the kinds of goals I describe and using them to help me feel a little more successful and a little less overwhelmed. Overall, writing this piece has been a healthy, empowering, feminist WPA experience.

think of as extensive mentoring—can help me increase the "terrain" or reach of my mentoring actions and principles. However, as I have already demonstrated, even extensive mentoring cannot manage all the caring or administrating in a writing program. In addition, then, I would like to briefly suggest three other interrelated mentor-based administrative modes—self-mentoring, mentoring-up, and mentor-leadership—that refashion common administrative roles from a feminist-mentoring standpoint. Each of these strategies can be used to enable action that goes beyond feminine nurturing to provide challenge, critique, and/or resistance. Moreover, each can be used to help mentoring be manageable, both by expanding agency and responsibility and by highlighting a few central principles rather than a broad list of tasks as markers of a successful WPA.

Self-Mentoring

I have two concepts in mind here. The first would help me focus on ways in which I can make it more possible for faculty in my program to be their own mentors: to value themselves and their relations to others, to set goals and recruit support as needed, and to resist being put down by (or through) an arbitrary hierarchy. The second, a close but easily overlooked corollary, is not to forget to apply the same strategies in mentoring myself. As Carol Gilligan notes, the concept of women's "ethic of care" was intended to give voice and power to women, not silence and drain them. In a 1993 article, she reminds us that backing away a little from "a language of selfless-

My original proposal was for an entirely impersonal article recommending strategies for other people to use when they mentored still other people in nice, neat mentoring programs. I'm pretty sure that the other article would have been easier for me to write, less risky (what will my colleagues say about this article at tenure review?), more scholarly, less conflicted, and less time-consuming: and thus "better." I found (again) in making these changes that I am a resistant mentee. (Be careful what you ask for . . . !) I accepted the challenge of writing this more personal article at the start of my first fall semester at my new job, and I spent not a moment on it until after Christmas, because even knowing I should not overestimate my capabilities or underestimate how long change can take, I did both rather splendidly. Unwilling to be seen writing from a purely personal point of view or be viewed as ill-informed or out-of-touch ("off with their heads!"), I then made a madcap January dash through dozens of previously unknown-to-me feminist texts, deliberately mining them for quotations I might use to shore up my own rickety sense of academic authority, more than savoring them for their support, wit, and intelligence. And though I found I had to begin by writing these personal counternarratives, I started right off putting them in special boxes in the margins of what I planned to become my "real" text. It worries me to no end to make recommendations to others that I have yet to put fully into

ness in relationship" is not the same as giving up on a caring ethic, but can instead be "a way of correcting an understanding of care that excluded, rather than included" a woman's self (Gilligan, "Response" 17–18). Certainly neither my self-mentoring nor that of my colleagues should replace more external relationships or leave members of a writing program to fend for themselves. Rather, supporting the agency of all the members of our faculty should go hand in hand with the other kinds of mentoring I describe.

> play for myself. So while I understand that it's useful, even vital, to articulate both plans and contradictions, I chafe at the untidiness—the un-rule-iness—of it all, and I have plenty of days when I think to myself: it's still a long, long way from here to feminist WPA-dom.
>
> But I (hope I) am (becoming) ok with that positioning: (I think) it's (becoming) good enough.

For instance, I would like to go back to the unmanageable issue of adjunct faculty review and evaluation, an event that often brings people like Lacie to my office. Part of Lacie's complaint was not knowing "what we wanted"; part of the adjunct review committee's difficulty comes from a nebulous review process. It is not a situation I can manageably ameliorate by traditional mentoring. If I approach it with a self-mentoring eye, however, I can see how creating a clearer set of highly visible expectations for our faculty can help adjunct faculty prepare for and control an initial review and help reviewers communicate their assessments. I have resisted establishing some sort of strict "Code for Teaching That Everyone Shall Follow," thinking it a selfish, unfeminist, and potentially morale-crushing approach to administration. Having *no* official list of expectations, however, violates a principle of fostering self-mentoring (and here I am reminded of how frustrating it was for me not to know "what they wanted" as I came up for pretenure review at my previous institution). Certainly I would want to attend to other feminist principles in creating a code or list of expectations: involving as many faculty as possible in its design, making the list and the evaluation process flexible enough to allow for and encourage diverse approaches and innovation, building in a relational aspect (perhaps an interview) to the evaluation process and allowing time for experimentation and feedback as we got started. Recognizing the need not just to rescue people through mentoring, but to enable their own abilities to mentor themselves (and others), may allow me to begin similar administrative endeavors without feeling as if I have sacrificed my commitment to feminist and caring-ethic principles, allowing me to engage in both kinds of self-mentoring at once.

Mentoring-Across and Mentoring-Up

Another aspect of rescue-mentoring that I would like to move away from is the idea, left over from male-gendered visions of mentoring, that all mentoring happens from higher status to lower status. McGuire and Reger's description of co-mentoring, in which equal-status partners work to "valu[e] cooperation over competition and collective success over individual success," expands the concept usefully (64). Mentoring-across is something I can do with my colleagues in composition and my other departmental colleagues. I am discovering that if I think of a committee meeting as a mentoring-across opportunity, it changes my outlook somewhat: This approach foregrounds the process over the tasks to be completed, reminds me that I am supposed to be learning as well as providing information, and helps me look for ways to enable "collective success." Marcia Dickson's suggestion that a feminist WPA should aim to "let others talk out their reservations, their problems and their discoveries" is a mentoring strategy that seems eminently exportable to a broader terrain (150). Nothing, of course, will magically change a rancorous meeting into butterflies and rainbows. Still, mentoring-across is a manageable mindset: Taking a mentoring-across approach may help me advocate for a larger collective success when I might otherwise be quiet, may help me find some nugget of useful learning in an otherwise frustrating meeting, and may help me feel that a meeting has been good enough on my feminist WPA scale even when progress toward an explicit goal has been minimal.[3]

Beyond mentoring-across, however, I am intrigued by the idea of overtly employing a strategy of mentoring-up. At once acknowledging yet disrupting the hierarchy of the institution, mentoring-up draws on the commonly accepted idea that even traditional mentors learn as much from the relationship as do the mentees. The surprised tone ("Who knew?!") in which this conclusion continues to be stated in reports on mentoring suggests that we are still considering the mentor as the sole repository of status and information. Even so, if it is true that higher status people benefit from their work with engaged and engaging mentees, I should be able to justify making mentoring a goal as I meet with others in the university, without worrying too much that I am stepping out of line. Essentially, as in mentoring-across, I can take an approach in which I arrive at a meeting as a co-mentor, ready to engage in a collaborative process (even if the person[s] on the other side of the table do not perceive or participate in that approach). My much-needed arguments (demands, requests, pleas) for better salaries for our adjunct faculty might take on a different color if I envisioned such meetings as a venue for mentoring-up: not "educating the heartless barbarians," but building relationships, listening actively, exchanging information, linking the professional with the personal, and providing support for difficult actions. Indeed, Kristine Hansen's efforts to procure better working conditions for faculty in her program sound a lot like mentoring-up: "I brought [our] administrators into a relationship with the part-time faculty because relationships are the venue for ethical action" (41). Again, this kind of strategy "softens" the hardball game I am sometimes reluctant to play while also strengthening my own sense that I have feminist ways of taking manageable, direct action within an institutional hierarchy.

Mentoring-Leadership

One concern I have about caring-based strategies for administration is that the administrator can be constructed solely as reactive and supportive, not enacting and visionary.[4] I have found that I need something more directly enabling on this count than Dickson's admonition that "the only [feminist] way to direct a program is to let the individual program shape itself according to the beliefs of the people who make it up and existing power structures of the institution in which it is located" (147). A related tension arises when such an administrator holds—and is expected to wield—institutional power: hiring, firing, voting, budgeting and holding others accountable. Taking an entirely or even predominantly reactive position can contribute to my feeling that my administrative position is unmanageable. In addition, feeling that some part of my job (enforcing program or institutional rules, firing instructors, cutting or redistributing budgets) is entirely separate from others could lead me to adopt prevailing justice-based action patterns for those crucial situations, rather than taking steps to integrate those actions into a feminist approach. Despite the accuracy of Enos's point that "many times an untenured assistant professor who is a woman is given the job of director of first-year English so that change is kept to a minimum" and that she may be "expected, or forced, to act as a caretaker *rather than* become an innovative administrator" ("Gender" 565; italics added), some kinds of caretaking can be incorporated into innovative administration. Indeed, Phelps argues that "it is healthy for women and vital for feminism to acknowledge desires for territory and self-realization as well as the intellectual and utopian motives in ambition" ("Becoming" 306). Accepting some responsibility for leadership—not just facilitation or spokesperson-ship—need not be opposed to practicing feminist or mentoring principles.[5]

Fine and Buzzanell describe some key aspects of the mentoring-leadership I am envisioning when they define what they call *servant leadership*:

> We suggest that the role of the academic administrator (or manager) is more productively conceived of as serving the faculty and students (or multiple stakeholders, particularly employees). On the most basic level, serving means doing things for others that enable them to do their jobs; serving means taking obstacles out of employees' way. (131)

From this definition, I want to unpack three elements a little further to help enable the mentoring-focused WPA to take action. First, it is crucial to keep in mind the wide range of stakeholders—including students and other campus entities—who need a writing program's leader to be attentive to relationships and committed to enabling their best possible work and growth. Second, a writing program itself, as Dickson points out, is an entity that requires nurturing: There is something greater than the individual teachers and classes that deserves attending to as a local entity, deserves protection from abstract hierarchies and too-distant principles. Finally, "taking obstacles out of employees' way" can be seen as already requiring a kind of vision and choice: What I see and identify as an obstacle may not be what others see or identify. Such a leadership stance also does not prohibit me from imagining other jobs or pathways not yet in the common range of vision and then removing obstacles from the new paths.

Bridging the gap between mentoring and leadership isn't quite as uncomplicated a shift for me as adopting the other mentoring approaches could be. Here I need to keep conflicts and tensions visible even as I try not to let them prevent me from initiating action. For example, in deciding that supporting the needs of students to have opportunities to become the best writers possible requires me to constrain or fire a teacher, I would need to be careful. In seeing the teacher as an "obstacle" in one sense, I cannot forget that at the same time she and I are individual humans in a relationship. (Building a mentoring-web and a more transparent, multi-step evaluation process can help me be more confident that I have attended to the humans on both sides of the office door.) Likewise, in deciding that the composition program needs a more definite, updated set of goals or outcomes, and in building a program assessment process, I would need to stay sincerely open to mentoring-across (and perhaps mentoring-up) from other people involved in the program who also have a stake in its success. Lastly, I need to remember my self-mentoring: How will I use these actions to create space for me to grow, rather than being eaten up by the daily challenges involved? How will I create space and time to acknowledge that good enough progress is being made by involving people in the discussions about moving forward, by taking small steps, even when inequities remain and individual people are distressed or even hurt despite my best efforts? As with each of the expanded definitions of mentoring that I have offered, mentoring-leadership is not a panacea: In a large, hierarchical institution, it is not unlikely that a WPA will face situations in which his or her actions are redirected, constrained, or even halted by institutional forms, traditions, resources, or politics. There is no quick fix to the interlinked problems that Lacie's story uncovers. Yet constructing my administrative work, even at its most independent, as integrally linked to mentoring structures and principles may, I hope, reduce the chances that I will be overwhelmed by the challenges in front of me and/or give up on the feminist philosophy that I consider a crucial part of my (WPA) identity.

MANAGING CARE

As I reach the conclusion of this chapter, I need to take my own advice, twice, by remembering that, as I write, I am mentoring-across, and that I originally set out to enable WPAs like me to feel that our work is good enough. I have made little progress toward either goal if, as you read, you find you cannot or do not want to step into my neat little mentoring shoes, attach yourself to my version of feminism, or cover your program's stories with mine. I know that as much as I need a usable set of guidelines for my own intentions and actions (and as much as I am enamored of my own rules), I am also the kind of person who tends to resist step-by-step self-help plans and other people's lists of "Six Guidelines for Coping with Stress" the way I resist infomercial weight-loss plans (and for many of the same, often feminist, reasons). Rather than concluding only by recommending "Four Fantastic Ways of Mentoring!", then, I would like to try to clear space for you to continue the discussion, to imagine and develop your own guidelines to being a feminist WPA—to do *as* I have done (and hope to do), rather than to replicate *what* I have done. Stepping back from my mentoring-paradigms and local paradoxes, then, I see three more general endeavors as crucial for new (and continuing) feminist WPAs to engage in and share with each other.

Develop a Philosophical Job Description

Beyond whatever formal documents we create to describe our tasks and responsibilities, we need descriptions of our principles, and I believe we need them earlier rather than later in our careers as WPAs. Leaders like Phelps—who first realized that she was "intuitively . . . referring to some kind of moral compass" and then took steps to "make it more explicit" ("Becoming" 314)—Hansen, and many of the contributors to this volume have developed their philosophies; their efforts have to be the beginnings, rather than the endings, of the mentoring-across that we owe each other. None of us can adopt others' goals all at once, nor can we perform as perfect feminist administrators on all counts all the time (because that, of course, would be an unfeminist expectation to hold of ourselves). However, we *can* articulate a limited set of principles of our own, rooted in our identities and responsive to our localities, to act on regularly. The process of "making it explicit" to ourselves (at least to ourselves at first) is creative, crucial, centrally feminist, as well as rhetorically sound. Moreover, focusing on just a few principles, a kind of "feminist shorthand," can help us take right actions without getting bogged down or overwhelmed.

Take Small, Conscious Steps

With an explicit set of goals in hand, we can attend to and apply these principles regularly on a personal level, strategically at a keep-the-program-running level, and occasionally in forays into larger institutional issues, sticky situations, or quixotic struggles. We can also attend to and encourage these feminist principles in others to help create and foster a culture of feminist thinking and action to support our own endeavors. Additionally, although it is important to feel true to the standpoints we have taken, to feel that we have not become strangers to our feminist selves, I think it is equally important to note that "attend to and apply" does not mean "succeed at to the acclaim of all." Likewise, we need to acknowledge that bringing ourselves into a wider range of relationships and facilitating or instigating change is likely to increase the number of conflicts and resistances we face. In such a setting, aiming for enough peace and harmony is actually better than aiming for complete peace and harmony.

Reflect on and Reward Our Endeavors

Implicit in the prior two statements is the need to set aside time, formally, to review and reflect on the principles we chose and the many sites and actions in which those principles have come into play. Fine and Buzzanell suggest that "expressing contradictions, tensions, and emotions to themselves and others is the very way that [women] grow and challenge traditional notions" (148), and Jane Gallop calls for women's identity to be "continually assumed and immediately called into question" (cited in Ritchie 86). However, continual questioning or attention to paradoxes can be overwhelming, disheartening, or even disabling. Informal, perhaps daily or hourly review can slip into self-chastisement and feelings of unworthiness or can provoke us into changing (or, worse, adding to) our list of principles or goals before we have had a chance to clearheadedly assess the need for such change.

Instead, we need to grant ourselves the assessment processes that we encourage others to take: processes that require us to list and value our achievements—even the small ones, even the incomplete ones, even the ones where the best we could manage was to remain true to our principles when all those around us were not—as well as challenges or failures, and to do so at enough distance to be able to see the forest as well as the trees. Using the occasion of a term end, project completion, or annual review may prove to be advantageous timing, as long as we remember that our reflection needs time and space separate from the project report or the university's review form. Such assessment also allows us to be reasonable: The impossible, as the song goes, will indeed take a little while. Finally, formal reflection and review allow us to make informed choices about when and how to "raise the bar" for our feminist administration, either by revising our core list of principles or by extending—just a little—the ways in which we attend to or perform them. Continuing to extend ourselves, without overextending ourselves, also brings us into right relation with ourselves and helps us feel satisfied as good enough feminist WPAs.

I want to state explicitly that, unlike the success-story women who populate diet-plan infomercials, a feminist administrator in a composition program should not embark on any of these steps with the goal of "fixing herself" to save or drastically improve her program. Such an attitude is neither healthy nor wise. Although I have paid little attention in this discussion to the pressures of institutional and cultural politics, other authors in this collection attend very carefully to these pressures, and additional analyses are plentiful in the field of composition studies. We know that the systems in which we work are often incomplete, ill-balanced, or broken; while we may bear a principled responsibility to challenge or seek to repair them, those external conditions should not be a primary motivator for self-reflection or personal change. Feminist WPAs are not broken. We need strategies to manage our caring on our own behalf so that we feel good about the incredibly challenging work that we do, and so that we can set reasonable goals and measure reasonable progress without abandoning principles that make us feel whole. What is crucial to recognize is that caring—or a feminist administrative philosophy based on a caring or mentoring model—is not in itself unmanageable, nor will it necessarily lead us into unmanageable situations. Conversely, managing care does not undermine its relational or transformative power. We can enact caring in a wide range of ways that can all be good enough, manageable, flexible, and locally successful—in ways that can fully engage our feminisms to help us and our programs grow and prosper.

10

DEFINING MOMENTS

The Role of Institutional Departure in the Work of a (Feminist) WPA

Kathleen Blake Yancey

Oh no, not stories.
— Patricia Bizzell

As a thought experiment, do you stay or do you go?

Thought Experiment 1: Directing a composition program where you altered the curriculum from literature and composition to academic writing and where you have increased the number of lecturer lines from 3 to 8 (and decreased the number of part-time positions accordingly), you are tenured as an assistant professor. You would like to be promoted to associate professor, but you have been advised that, to be eligible for this promotion, you need a book—and not a textbook, either, but a university press book. Given your commitment to WPA work and the 4/4 institutional teaching load, which translates into a 3/3 load with 1/1 for the full range of administrative tasks, you can not imagine when you would have the time to write the book. You were content with the fact that you would not ever be promoted to professor, but to remain always an assistant professor?

Do you resign the position and stay on, writing the book and becoming an associate professor? Alternatively, do you consider moving to another institution where the work as you define and value it might be rewarded?

Thought Experiment 2: Directing a WAC program, you find yourself reporting to a new provost whose priorities do not include writing. Your budget is cut, and you are unable to host the workshops and provide the undergraduate tutors who have fueled what has largely been regarded as a successful program. You are invited to coauthor a proposal to reinvigorate general education, which includes funding for service learning, learning communities, and a new WAC workshop series focused on the use of digital technology. The faculty senate, despite the institution's enthusiasm for graduate research, endorses the proposal. The provost funds all parts of the proposal except the WAC component.

Do you resign given the apparent dearth of support? Do you move to a school that values the WAC work that has defined your career?

Although these two scenarios are not mine, together they illustrate another of the (many) lessons we do not learn in graduate school: If we stay with WPA work long enough, sooner or later a moment of definition will arrive, prompting the question, do you stay or do you go? In this question, I do not mean the moment of WPA departure, the time when we rotate out of an administrative position or move permanently to faculty status, although that also is a moment worth inhabiting. I do mean the moment of institutional departure.

In my career as a WPA, I have had three such defining moments, and each time I have chosen to leave. In each case, I had powerful reasons for staying: I identified with the institution; I cared about my colleagues and friends; and, by staying, I could have continued to serve students and program. Nonetheless, in each case, I chose to leave. In describing and reflecting on each decision, I hope to articulate both what I learned about WPA work in general, with specific reference to a feminist iteration of it, and what I found within what I am calling *defining moments.* As important, reflecting across them, I hope I can speak to what makes them important for those of us interested in feminist administration.

So, a brief forecast. Institutions value us or not. They support our work or not. But through thick and thin, they expect us to stay—in part, I suspect, precisely because we are women, and women are expected to stay inside relationships regardless.

I do not share this expectation and this way of seeing the world.

＊ ＊ ＊

> *To understand his or her work*
> *as a writing program administrator,*
> *an author . . . might draw on knowledge gained*
> *as a parent, feminist theorist,*
> *poet, post-structuralist. . . .*
> *[S]uch combinations are necessary*
> *because, to be a good administrator,*
> *. . . you must draw on everything you know.*
>
> —Bizzell

SCENE 1

I have to save our resources for faculty.

Directing Purdue University's Office of Writing Review (OWR), a testing center for writing, I walk into the office of the head of the English Department. I am there to ask for support to attend a conference, and I am expecting a yes. Although I'm on a half-time administrative appointment for a writing certification program in a literature-dominated department, Dr. ———, the department head, has always been supportive of my efforts. When I wanted to attend the National Testing Network conference in Minneapolis last year, he paid for the full price of the trip; and his two evaluations of my administrative work have been positive, if not glowing. He and I both know that I have this appointment because none of the tenure-line faculty wants it. Jim Berlin kindly tries to make me feel better about this situation by pointing out that, unlike the faculty, I get paid for the labor I do. At the same time, we both know that my pay is barely more than a grad student's while my workload exceeds that of many of the faculty.

"Looks like you're busy, Dr. ——-."

"Kathi, good to see you. How are things at the OWR?"

"Also busy, Dr. ———. But good. The graduate students who work in the office are terrific. It's really a pleasure to work with them. And the undergraduates are coming along nicely, too: we've had a couple of problems, but working with the Writing Lab, we've been able to see them through. But [looking at the piles on his desk], I don't want to keep you too long. I need to ask you if you can support my attendance at the CCCC in the spring. I'm on the CCCC Assessment Committee now, so one thing I need to do is attend that meeting; that of course is good for Purdue, I mean, to have someone from our department on that committee. In addition, I'm trying to make connections between the OWR and the national testing and evaluation community. So this trip seems like a logical one to support. I thought before I sent you the memo making this request, I'd ask you in person first. I won't have another funding request this year, but I think this one can help the office and perhaps even the department."

"Kathi, I'd really like to help you. But finances are tight this year, and I've had many more requests than in years past. I simply have to save our resources for the faculty. I'm very sorry."

* * *

When I completed my PhD, I chose to accept an adjunct position that developed into a part-time administrative position, and I did so for personal reasons. My husband and I had one small child and wanted to have another. Although I had seen many smart academic women "do it all" and do it all well, I had serious reservations about my own ability to earn tenure while birthing a baby. Before the expression "Mommy Track" was invented, I attempted to do just that—create a space where I could continue to teach without assuming the responsibilities of a tenure-line position. I knew that the pay, prestige, and working conditions would be lower, but I accepted that as the price of the decision and—to be frank—felt fortunate that my family had the financial capacity to make this decision. Many families do not.

I began my adjuncting career by working both in the Office of Writing Review and in the Writing Lab, basically coaching students who needed to pass a writing test. After a year, the OWR director returned to faculty status, and another faculty member—this one with credentials in Old and Middle English—took his place. For 3 years, I served as his assistant, this time taking on many of the administrative responsibilities for an undergraduate testing program and a graduate one: setting the schedule, and coordinating the various programs inside the office, running interference with advisors and other staff; mentoring the graduate student staff members, both doctoral and master's. When this director too wanted to return to faculty status, no other faculty member volunteered to direct the OWR. I had a job. Literally, the position was shifted from faculty to staff; a new staff job description emphasizing a background in composition, rhetoric, and evaluation was posted locally. I applied, and I was in.

In administering this office, I had the pleasure of working with many graduate students, about 18 in all, in fields ranging from linguistics to American Studies, from rhetoric and composition to literature. My job was to ensure that students could write well, which involved creating writing prompts, administering the test, scoring the essays, informing students, and being sure that they got the help they needed so they would pass the test. I also changed the testing protocol, refined the scoring system, and researched a test for international English as a Second Language (ESL) graduate students. It was good work.

The graduate students (who were the staff of the OWR) were the primary resource of the office, of course, although as in the case of the non-funded trip to the CCCC, I had no money for rewards, I had no promotions to award, and I had no prestige to share. What I could do was perhaps in some ways more important: help make their working conditions intellectually engaging and their social situation affirming. In the 3 years I directed the office, we lost only 3 of 20 staff. The graduate student staff, in reapplying to retain their positions, talked about the value of a TA-ship with intellectual work at its heart. Specifically, they referred to our weekly staff meetings when we discussed (and often argued about) language issues, the relationship of syntax to cognition, and how a student's inability with invention surfaced in a text as a difficulty with organization. We also celebrated birthdays achieved, prelims passed, and dissertations completed. In summary, together we created an intellectual and social home.

When I approached the head of the English Department for CCCC conference support, I expected him to say yes. The year before, I had asked for one trip, which he had readily funded. It really had not occurred to me that he would say no; it was such a reasonable request, I thought. But the issue, of course, was not reasonableness; it was faculty status. Regardless of how good or ill my performance, the real politic was that I was not tenure line.

This refusal was a defining moment for me. I knew that I was working at least as hard as many faculty. I thought I was doing a good job; and I thought I was making a contribution. I think everyone else—or anyone else who cared—thought so, too. That was beside the point, however; the point was rank and constituency. I had no rank, and I was not a member of the departmental constituency—when it came to money (and to votes as well). I could see that the future would hold more of the same. If I really wanted to make a difference, at least at this kind of institution, I needed faculty status and tenure.

At that moment, I decided that no administrator would ever again decline a request from me because I was not faculty. The next year I went on the job market.

* * *

The administrator must consider
issues of budget, curriculum planning,
personnel management,
technological support . . . .

—Bizzell

SCENE 2

If we let them use technology, they won't read and write.

As tenure-line faculty member of an English Department in a comprehensive university reaching for doctoral status, I have served in various roles. In a faculty role, I focused exclusively on teaching my three sections a term—standard-issue kinds of courses like first-year composition and expository writing; English teaching methods courses for preservice middle and high school teachers; MA courses in rhetorical theory and writing assessment; and special topics courses like "Voice, Genre, and Technology." In another role, I taught and participated in various kinds of WPA work—chairing our Teacher Ed Committee, whose task (among others) is, through a program audit, portfolio, and interview, to certify the readiness of prospective student-teachers (and help them if they aren't ready); working with others to design a multiyear writing assessment program; and coleading and then directing our site of the National Writing Project (NWP). I like being a faculty member. I love the multiplicity of roles that are available for me to assume. This year, my ninth, I am especially enjoying the assessment projects and the NWP directorship.

Every year, the department meets for an annual retreat, this year held in February and intended to address new directions in the major. I sit in a break-out group with three colleagues, one in literature, one in linguistics and composition, and another in tech writing.

> "The question we have to deal with is technology," our group leader says. "How might we include technology in the major?"
>
> One colleague laughs, "As though!"
>
> "Greg uses technology all the time in his teaching. I'm sure he can give us some ideas," I say.
>
> Greg replies. "I do. In tech writing, it's a fundamental part of the course; students complete web pages as often as print documents. But of course our students don't major in tech writing, although some minor in it."
>
> "And," say I, "when we did our departmental assessment, we saw evidence of this kind of work. Those of us on the committee had disks to review instead of papers. It was interesting, although I don't think we are prepared yet for the shift that already seems to be happening for students."
>
> "Kathi, students just don't seem to read anymore. Even you said that when you talked about our students preparing for student teaching."
>
> "Well, yes, I did. But what I really keyed on wasn't so much their reading habits—though we could talk about those—as about our cur-

riculum, which sometimes, to me, seems to privilege short stories at the expense of longer genres and which excludes technology altogether. In a world in which even canonical print texts are going online, that seems silly to me. So that returns us, I think, to the question about how we could use technology inside our major."

A valued colleague replies, sadly, "I can't let them use technology. If we let them use technology, they won't read and write." And he believes it.

* * *

At UNC Charlotte, I learned two principal lessons. The first had to do with K–12 teacher preparation and was rooted in our certification process for students preparing to student teach. In concert with their faculty advisor, students carefully planned a program of study; one term before they planned to student teach, they compiled a portfolio of their work and sat for an interview, the purpose of which was to be sure that students could talk teacher talk, could think on their feet, could access resources, and could raise good questions. It was not a rubber stamp exercise, and once or twice and with good reason the committee turned an applicant down. In two instances, the deans of the colleges (Arts and Sciences and Education) got involved,[1] but I was tenure-line, at least, and the exigence—the need to have good teachers in our schools—was too strong to resist and the evidence too difficult to refute. The combination of curriculum and assessment keyed to real-world needs can be powerful.

When I directed the UNC Charlotte site of the NWP, I learned a second lesson—about how to work with peers. Nodghia Fesperman, a high school teacher with 30 years of North Carolina teaching experience, had much to teach me: about the schools in the region; about the teachers who work with kids there, about the state curricula and the NWP Summer Institutes, and about yearly follow-up. I learned that what I had to offer was WPA material: how to design workshops, how to connect to and speak to the university, and how to manage a budget. Perhaps most important, how to manage a budget. It is the budget that in some important ways confers authority and independence, and that was the one aspect of the project that until then had been veiled. Hence, the women who populated the NWP site carried out most of the work, but never saw the connections between the work and the budget. Much as when I had to ask for conference support in my earlier position, they were forced to ask—to host conferences, to be paid a summer stipend. If they were to take hold of the project, I thought, they needed to take hold of the budget. We worked on it together. I showed them what our basic expenses were, where our discretionary income was, and how we could change both numbers by shifting our priorities. Together we made decisions that the budget could support, we talked about new directions that would increase the budget, and we dedicated new monies that we would earn ourselves. Not least, with this group, new technologies presented not a threat, but rather an opportunity. We offered several "Saturday Morning Seminars" so that teachers could experiment with digital technology and consider together how we might use it to enhance and expand kids' literacies.

Soon after the February retreat, Clemson University—an institution with digital technologies at the heart of it and an English Department that understood such technologies as a "natural" evolution in the history of literacy—asked me to join them. I hesitated. I loved the mission of UNC Charlotte, an urban institution filled with nontraditional and first-generation college students. Clemson did not have that mission. I loved the NWP work, and that work would not be part of my responsibilities at Clemson. But what Clemson did offer was an opportunity to make a difference. Given the professorship they were offering, I thought that perhaps they would hear me in a way that UNC Charlotte did not. As important, given Clemson's commitment to digital technology, I thought that perhaps there technology would not be something to be resisted, but instead be an important part of what we would do as we developed new digital practices forecasting the literacies of the 21st century. In fact, to serve students more generally—in my department and across campus and through national efforts—I thought this might be the most important work I could take up.

Reluctantly, I left UNC Charlotte.

* * *

> *Perhaps the most difficult administrative skill*
> *of all is the ability always*
> *to see the big picture,*
> *to keep the vision in mind*
> *of what your program and*
> *our college wants*
> *to accomplish academically. . . .*
>
> —Bizzell

SCENE 3

I'm interested in your opinion:
Would we be better off with an inter-disciplinary Ph.D.,
or one in which there are disciplinary tracks,
one in health communication and one in spaces of learning?

I've been at Clemson for nearly 6 years, 5 of them as director of the Roy and Marnie Pearce Center for Professional Communication, a faculty development center for communication across the curriculum. We host workshops, we sponsor projects like our year-long PowerPoint project (focused on ways that PowerPoint can enhance teaching and learning) and our Symposium on the Visual in Learning, we sponsor sessions for graduate students making poster presentations at Clemson's April Focus on Research events, and we took the lead on Clemson's electronic portfolio. We invented the Clemson Digital Portfolio Institutes and partnered with departments and centers on campus and with external organizations like the Greenville Advertising Club. Working with the Clemson Foundation, we raised $1 million for a new Studio for Student Communication, a site we opened in January 2004 where students from across the campus can work on communication tasks from writing to electronic portfolios, from speaking to PowerPoints and posters. I invented and delivered a new class intended to prepare undergrads and graduate students to work in the Studio as Studio Associates. With my colleague, Morgan Gresham, I presented on the Studio at WPA and published on it in the WPA journal.

This administrative work has been rewarding. I team with a wonderful group of writing colleagues, and I find satisfaction in being able to work with faculty across the curriculum. With majors ranging from health administration and business to engineering and communication studies, the Studio Associates bring diverse disciplinary experiences with them to our new Studio. It is fascinating to learn with and from them as we explore how the new spaces and technologies of the Studio can change the way we learn to communicate. On my best days, I feel as if, in charting new communication practices for the 21st century, I have found what I had sought.

Not all days, however, are best. Something is not quite working. I feel a bit like the writing faculty member of the future, described by David Smit in *The Ends of Composition*, whose job is twofold: expertise in writing, and expertise in disciplinary writing (e.g., in biology, or engineering, or history). Only in my case, it seems to involve many disciplines, and it does not seem to include just writing. It is not only that it is fragmenting, although it is that. As much as I have enjoyed this cross-curricular work in visual, oral, and written communication, I have missed work in writing all by itself. In part because of my administrative responsibilities, I have not taught a course in plain-vanilla-brand writing since my first term on campus, and I am eager to return to composition—in class, in scholarship, with students, and with colleagues. Unfortunately, the likelihood of my being able to do so, at least in the classroom, is lessening. During the last 2 years, the first-year composition program has been cut by half—from a two-term program to a one-term course that many students (perhaps as many as 25%) exempt on the basis of Advanced Placement (AP) scores or dual-enrollment grades.

So the overall institutional valuing of and commitment to composition have been reduced. Moreover, even for the one FYC course we do have, teaching assistants are the instructors of choice. Ironically, as a full professor whose credentials are in composition and rhetoric, I will have less, not more, priority. Not least, we are preparing to offer an interdisciplinary PhD, which operates at the intersection of art, English, and communication studies. The expectation is that I will participate in that program, although how is not at all clear. I am not on the search committee for the new director of the program, nor am I on the implementation committee, and information about the program is hard to come by.

What also has happened is that Florida State has approached me about a position that is focused specifically on writing and that includes working with undergraduate and graduate students: The ad copy reads, in part:

> Associate or Full Professor. Composition and Rhetoric. Opportunity to rebuild and lead our graduate programs (M.A. and Ph.D.) in C/R. Broad knowledge of composition and rhetorical theory, plus commitment to research on improving writing instruction.

Clemson says they want me to stay, and I meet with the dean to discuss a counter-offer. At that meeting, we also discuss the Clemson PhD.

> "Kathi, a number of us are discussing the new Ph.D., in Rhetorics, Communication, and Information Design. Some of us think that the degree itself should be interdisciplinary and draw on all the involved departments. Others think that Ph.D. should act more as an umbrella, and under that, there should be two tracks. One would be in health communication, and another would be in learning environments for communication. I'm curious as to what you think."
>
> "Well, it's tricky. As you probably know, a number of the job candidates [for the directorship] have pointed out to the faculty how difficult they think it may be for graduates of the program to find a job in an academic department, given that this is an inter-departmental degree. I hadn't actually thought that through; it's worth considering. What I had thought about was a different problem, that it's not clear where the research these students produce will be published. It's hard enough to get papers in press, and these may be more difficult still. And a third is the re-tooling issue. I don't get a clear picture of the junior faculty trying to re-tool right now, especially given their need to get published. So how will they be prepared to work with students in this new (and still undefined) area? In other words, there's a writer in comp studies, Stephen North, who argues for this kind of approach, but the assumption is that the faculty and students will learn together and make it work. And they are working inside of the same depart-

ment, so that's different than this inter-departmental model. Besides, while people are trying to get tenure, they need to focus on the discipline they do have."

"So you think the tracks would be better?"

"Well, I'm not sure how we got to those tracks. I don't work in health com, so I have no idea if that's a good idea. I am thinking and writing a little about new spaces for learning, largely because of the Studio, but I wouldn't say that I have a lot of expertise on the topic yet. And honestly, I don't see myself re-tooling for this new degree. For sure, not in the next three years: I already have writing commitments that take me out that far, and I do have a discipline that I like working in. Of course, I do understand that this is an argument against making any kind of change, and I don't like taking that position."

<We both smile.>

* * *

When I began teaching at Clemson, I taught in the MA program in professional communication. I had read most of the basic texts defining the program before joining Clemson, and I found in the intersection of rhet/comp and professional communication a source of invention and insight. I loved the way the bad boy Ramus of rhet and comp fame became a leading Renaissance visual rhetorician. I loved the role of document design and ways that its vocabulary could become part of a more generalized writing curriculum. I learned about communication plans, website design, and theoretical approaches to the field. Principally, I enjoyed these additions for themselves, but also always in the larger context of my rhetoric and composition intellectual home.

We all work in context. At Clemson—home to a graduate degree in professional communication, to the Pearce Center for Professional Communication, and to the Pearce Professor of Professional Communication, each one of which is housed in the English Department—communication is a God word that subsumes writing. Right or wrong, I accommodated myself to that assimilation of writing, but over time felt that accommodation tugging at me. Perhaps I was too long away from writing courses myself—always for good reasons, of course, but away nonetheless. Perhaps these disjuncts were amplified by the development of a PhD that initially was located in an English Department, then by administrative fiat located more narrowly in Professional Communication and Communication Studies, and then further morphed, again by administrative direction, into a departmental collaboration among Professional Communication, Communication Studies, and Art. For certain, I knew I wanted to return to a discipline. Correction: I wanted to work in *my* discipline. I think we do have one, and I think on any campus, the WPA is the institutional leader of that discipline, and it is W: writing. Moreover, the dean's question made the point about composition's devaluing obvious to me. If tracks were possible inside the PhD, then some disciplines (like health communication) were acceptable. What clearly was not acceptable was my discipline.

In deciding to move to Florida State, I made the decision to return to the discipline, to focus on rhetoric and comp. My WPA work, at this defining moment, is in the context of a tenured faculty and administrative appointment focused on redesigning and directing a doctoral program that will engage both undergraduate and graduate students in writing.

In deciding to go to Florida State, I decided to go home.

* * *

The claim of reflective practice is that, in reviewing and reflecting, we make knowledge. If that is so, what have I learned here about feminist WPA work? Something, I think, about how we can make choices; perhaps something about how to work with people, especially when you do not have material rewards to offer; and perhaps something about defining moments as exigencies for an agency that are often at odds with cultural narratives.

Women of Academe: Outsiders in the Sacred Grove provides one helpful lens for thinking about choices. There Nadya Aisenberg and Mona Harrington outline and contrast two archetypal plots: the marriage plot and the quest plot. The marriage plot is familiar to women, even today, and it certainly was familiar to me: "what women *should* want, the way they *should* behave, and the choices they *should* make" (6). The quest plot, typically taken up by men, is often not available to women. Even when women choose not to pursue the marriage plot, the domestic sphere still intervenes: They have parents to care for or siblings needing help. The ideal of self-sacrifice is embedded in the marriage-qua-family plot, and that plot is embedded in the culture. According to Aisenberg and Harrington, the result is that many academic women have "deflected" careers, characterized as false starts, failure to complete, and failure to tenure. The ubiquitous marriage plot, in other words, preempts alternatives.

In my case, although I did not have the language at the time, I wanted both plots. The only way I could imagine pursuing both, at least initially, was sequentially: pursuing the PhD quest, creating a family sphere, and then pursuing a dual quest—career *and* family (yes, those children grew up: one now a graduate student in math, another studying to be an MD). For me—and this is a luxury that the academy affords (if you can otherwise afford it)—the ability to sequence alternately while I learned to pursue a dual quest was a gift. It allowed me to chart a path to both quests that initially was sequential and that then became intertwined. Even in deciding to leave, each time, the personal has constrained. Initially, we moved to the Southeast, where our families also lived. Later, with almost-grown children in the Southeast, positions across the county stretched the personal too far.

The specifics tell other stories.

I was offered the first administrative job because no one else wanted it, to be sure, but at the same time I learned about how to run an office, how to make WPA work intellectual in practice and representation, and how to let people know that they were valuable. This last—learning how to retain a staff that you could not materially reward—helped me develop practices that are part of my administrative portfolio today. Not surprisingly perhaps, those practices include bringing together the academic and the social, affirming each of us, and finding a way for each to be valued. I would like to think that this way of organizing work—with the domestic and intellectual spheres overlayering each other—is by design both feminist and humanitarian.

A second WPA position, working with colleagues in the NWP site, also was mine because no one else applied, and it taught me another lesson: how knowledge about how the money works can foster responsibility as it provides agency. Historically, the marriage plot has meant that the husband-father controlled the family budget and the wife the pin money; and that way of conducting organizations has spilled over into much WPA work (e.g., Lynn Bloom's "I Want a Writing Director"). If we want to manage the money, we may have to assume more responsibility, and make some tough decisions. Those decisions, however, bring with them control—of one's program and one's life. Philosophically, that approach is what I tried to share, and collaboratively we developed the practices that would make the philosophy material.

A third lesson has to do with the role of the discipline in WPA work. It may be that, again, the marriage quest informs more than we know. Perhaps I played the wife to Clemson as husband, enthusiastic about the opportunities, but maybe too eager to fit into a culture of communication that did not fully accommodate my intellectual commitment to rhetoric and composition. Perhaps had I identified this misfit earlier, it would have made a difference, perhaps not. In fact, I do like interdisciplinary work (and the colleagues engaged in it) very much, although not to the exclusion of composition. That became a tipping point, ever more so in the context of a job opportunity where I would focus on comp. Perhaps the relationship worked at one moment, but not at another. This lesson is still in process; what I do know is that, for me, moving (back) to composition has been invigorating.

Finally, what I have also learned is that, for me, each decision to depart was a move on a continuing path of WPA work, different at each campus, but each participating in the larger WPA project. In each case, although I could continue the WPA work at the local campus, I was positioned to lose a part of the larger project by staying—choosing to stay, for instance, in a nontenurable position in the knowledge that, as the Portland Resolution argues, tenure is fundamental for administrative work; and losing the chance to weave digital technology into the curriculum, those digital processes and representations now being developed for a new technology plank for the WPA Outcomes Statement; and losing the disciplinary center of all writing program administrative work: writing. For me, WPA work includes both: the local and the national. It is important to say: That defining moment is not easy. Taken seriously, it obliges one to make a hard (and sometimes agonizing) choice. Once the choice to leave is made, it is difficult to leave—family, friends, students, and colleagues. Part of the difficulty, a big part, is of course personal. Another part, I think, stems from the way the departure disrupts the institution-qua-family narrative that still prevails. When a woman leaves an institution by choice, it is (still) unexpected given the undercurrent of a marriage quest where the faculty member is wife and poignantly so when the institution represents itself in the rhetoric of family. The implication, intentional or not, is that the WPA taking a job better suited to her—because of tenure or disciplinary issues—is leaving the family that needs her. Such a narrative needs to be identified and resisted; it serves the institution at the expense of the faculty member and at the expense of the WPA.

The fact that we have these defining moments does not, of course, mean that we always decide to leave. I suspect that most of us, most of the time, decide to stay, and there are values to that decision as well. For me, however, understanding these moments as defining has underscored the agency I do have, has enhanced my work as a WPA, and, through reflection, has brought a philosophy to my WPA work that, in turn, gives it a kind of coherence.

In the midst of postmodern change, such agency and coherence may be fleeting, but they provide a grounding especially welcome in moments of departure.

PART IV

Performing WAC and WC Work

Challenging Spaces in the University and in Feminist Theory

Expanding the opportunities for women and other traditionally disenfranchised groups in higher education, however, not only enhances the visibility of those groups but normalizes their roles.

—Cheryl Glenn
(personal email)

11

"WHERE ELSE SHOULD FEMINIST RHETORICIANS BE?"

Leading a WAC Initiative in a School of Business

Kate Ronald

Cristy Beemer

Lisa Shaver

> *It is the* power *of a movement that, finally, I covet for WAC . . .*
> *the power that movements sometimes have to change individuals,*
> *to change a culture.*
>
> —Barbara Walvoord,
> "The Future of WAC"

> *Kate, where's the boldness? I'm looking for a bold vision*
> *that will change the culture here.*
>
> —Dean, School of Business,
> conversation with Kate, April 2004

Boldness and power have become daily metaphors for our work as directors of a WAC project in a large School of Business. At the same time, humility and service have been our daily methodologies as we work with an overwhelmingly male faculty in six disciplines largely devoted to content and capitalism. Negotiating those tensions—between content and context, boldness and modesty, leading and serving—seems to us at the heart of an investigation into the relationship between feminism and administration, especially in the context of a WAC project. Oddly enough, both earlier epigraphs address the same issue: How can a WAC initiative change a culture? Barbara Walvoord's reading of WAC as a social movement organization, kin to the feminist or civil rights movements, points to her belief that WAC has the potential for widespread transformations—not just in individual classrooms, but in wider, social and political arenas. Echoing Walvoord's hopes for a WAC project that can change cultures, Harriet Malinowitz asserts that WAC should "all[y] itself with other force-fields within the academy that have also set out to dismantle existing systems of knowledge-production" (363–64). Her primary example of Women's Studies suggests that she would agree with Walvoord about WAC as a powerful social movement.

The Dean's comment also asserts the potential for powerful change in our WAC work. As in the corporate culture, "managing change," "thinking outside the box," and entrepreneurial initiatives, especially to attract funding, are highly valued in the School of Business. But his call for a "bold vision" would, we suspect, leave existing disciplinary structures pretty much intact. What he means by *boldness* is performance—our ability to inspire, coerce, or convince faculty to teach more writing—or, more cynically, our ability to "improve the quality of student writing" without, we again suspect, significantly disturbing workloads or changing pedagogies. That has been our charge over the last 8 years: to "improve the quality of undergraduate writing" in a leading School of Business. In 1997, Kate was hired into a professorship endowed by the Richard T. Farmer School of Business at Miami University. Although her appointment is solely in English, half her teaching is assigned to consulting with Business faculty on integrating writing more fully and more coherently into their curriculum. Cristy and Lisa served as her assistant directors in this project for 2 years, also splitting their time between English and Business. Named the Howe Writing Initiative after its donor (which we simply term the Howe), this project assists both Business professors in the teaching of disciplinary writing and Business students in acquiring a variety of academic and professional writing skills.

More specifically, we consult with faculty from six different disciplines (Accountancy, Economics, Finance, Marketing, Management, and Decision Sciences/Information Systems) about how (and why) to incorporate writing into their courses; we visit classes to determine what kinds of writing will best help students learn; we help faculty devise writing assignments that mirror actual business writing contexts; we read the textbooks and scholarship in these disciplines; we interview students about writing in their courses; we run a writing center where we work with students; we prepare materials for the website we have developed for faculty and students; and we talk to faculty, formally, at workshops or committee meetings and, informally, in the hallways, faculty lounges, or on sidewalks between the Department of English and the School of Business.

This chapter focuses on the tensions we negotiate in all these sites, especially how we negotiate leading curricular change in a school intensely devoted to content and how we help students succeed in established forms of capitalism and corporate communication. Further, this chapter examines the administrative and service dynamic inherent in our particular local context: a faculty of 100 professors, over 99% male, teaching 5,000 students, and we three women charged with changing the "culture of writing." The first tension lies between what WAC specialists call "writing to learn" versus "writing in the disciplines." Although most WAC scholars call for a mediated—even opportunistic—stance between the two approaches (Kirchst, Levine, and Reiff; Jones and Comprone; Walvoord), Malinowitz sees WAC at a stage in its history where it can and should reinvigorate its transformative agenda. She is more optimistic about the capabilities of writing-to-learn (WTL) to accomplish her feminist project—dismantling existing systems of knowledge production. However, the other major approach to WAC—writing-in-the-disciplines (WID)—embraces a political stance that is, she says, "if anything, counter-revolutionary" because of its accommodation to smaller, more prosaic goals (293). In other words, WAC should foreground its (radical) politics and abandon its (nonfeminist) tendencies to assist faculty and students in learning disciplinary discourse.

Malinowitz poses a serious challenge to feminists working in WAC, where most often the largest successes come from the smaller, more prosaic goals, such as convincing a statistics professor to require students to include an executive summary with their spreadsheets so that they might understand the purpose of their analysis and how differing audiences might be affected by their results. Moreover, our experience as WAC administrators is that we rely much more on persuasion than on power to accomplish our goals. From the beginning, the Howe has worked from the bottom up, sitting in on classes to study the disciplinary concepts and rhetorical structures that are valued in these six disciplines, talking to faculty about student writing and writing assignments, and doing the kind of outreach and "cold calling" that bring faculty and students to our office and us into their classrooms. We have operated much more as consultants and colleagues than as administrators with authority over personnel or curriculum.

CONSULTANTS MARKETING
A RHETORICAL VALUE ADDED

Consultancy is a popular business model, and it is the way we try to describe and perform our role in the Farmer School of Business (FSB). In fact, many FSB faculty members supplement their incomes and stay attuned to the business world by moonlighting as consultants. Just as they market their professional expertise outside of academia, we have set up shop in the School of Business to market our rhetorical expertise. Yet, for us, the Howe is not a capitalist venture, but simply an extension of our teaching. Consultants typically operate as independent contractors, yet they are ultimately judged by their ability to "move the needle" or deliver "value added" to an organization. Although some administrators and faculty in the FSB initially envisioned the Howe as an editing/proofreading drop-off or express service, intended to "clean up" students' writing, Kate determined that the Howe's "value added" would be rhetoric. The Howe would impact Business School pedagogy by promoting rhetorical concepts such as audience, purpose, and rhetorical situation. First of all, because of the FSB's stated desire to integrate writing throughout the curriculum, rather than offer a menu of writing-intensive courses, the Howe relies on its own rhetorical skill and performance to convince faculty to include writing in their courses. Moreover, because the teaching load in Business is heavy (3/3 for all professors) and because class sizes are always increasing (60–150 in the core curriculum), we have to show professors why and how writing will improve student learning. Finally, because efficiency and brevity are core rhetorical values in business contexts, professors (and students) want results. Therefore, we have tried to help professors tailor assignments to business genres, rather than to academic ones. Indeed, to understand the concise style of business writing required for an executive summary or the segmented arrangement of a business proposal, students need to understand the purpose and context for these conventions.

In adopting a rhetorical approach, the Howe maintains a mediated stance between WTL and writing-in-the-disciplines (Kirchst, Levine, and Reiff). Overall, our goal has been to keep teachers and students attuned to the rhetorical contexts of communication within and among their disciplines; we keep asking professors questions about audience and purpose for writing, for example. Although we remain acutely aware of the political implications of working to help students succeed in established forms of capitalism, we take some measure of pride in seeing the word *rhetoric* on assignments more and more often. Keeping Malinowitz's cautions in mind, we believe that our emphasis on rhetorical contexts brings a feminist stance to the School of Business because it exposes disciplinary structures and values, because it means defining an audience and taking responsibility for meaning, and because it forces faculty to think about context and purpose.

To use David Russell's term, we wield our *rhetorical* skill to expose the *transparency* of business rhetoric to students and faculty. By *transparency*, Russell means the tendency of specialists not to see that the language/discourse of their fields is rhetorical (with particular audiences, purposes, forms, conventions, methods of proof, appeals to authority, values about what counts as evidence, what can and cannot be said, etc.). Russell carefully documents the reasons that "disciplines never acquired a conscious knowledge of the rhetorical conventions they used daily and expected their students to use" (17). Hence, the discursive strategies in any given discipline remain transparent, "so bound up with the activity of the discipline and acquired so subtly in the learning of the discipline that they were rarely thought of as writing instruction" (17). When students struggle with disciplinary conventions, faculty have tended to view such struggles as a lack of writing ability or sheer ignorance on the part of students, or as a failure of writing specialists to do their jobs properly. Russell argues that, "at the curricular level, if professionals are not aware of the role rhetoric plays in their own discipline, then they will see little need to teach it" (17). Therefore, one of our major goals as WAC leaders is to highlight and analyze—with faculty before they devise an assignment and with students as they complete it—the rhetorical assumptions, forms, stances, and styles embedded in the context of the task. In other words, we claim rhetorical authority and we use rhetorical expertise to further our agenda of exposing disciplinary structures. Performing as rhetorical consultants, we help the Business faculty develop writing assignments that enable students to put into practice the course concepts that they might otherwise simply memorize for a multiple-choice exam. A rhetorical approach to teaching writing in the FSB demystifies business writing, and it repositions students as researchers, analysts, and decision makers.

One example where our consultancy helped expose the rhetoric at work in business communication was the In-Basket Memo Exam. When students arrive at the 4-hour exam in their upper level Marketing Analysis course, they find a stack of five to seven memos on their desks. In addition to the memos, they also are provided with detailed information about the company they work for, including an organizational chart. Acting as the vice president of Marketing for the company (who has been away from the office for a conference), students reply to these memos written by their colleagues and provide relevant statistical calculations on the back. Acting as experts, students must put what they have learned into changing contexts where different people require different interpretations and answers from them. Students must make decisions, answer questions, and recommend alternatives. Therefore, they need to know more than simply how to perform an accounting, finance, management, or marketing function. For example, knowing how to do a statistical test is quite different than communicating results, recognizing subtleties, teaching subordinates, and using results rhetorically.

When the Marketing faculty asked us how to prepare students for the writing required during the exam, the Howe's rhetorical value added was introducing Aristotle's rhetorical triangle as a heuristic. We began teaching the Marketing classes how they could use the rhetorical triangle to consider their audiences, the manner in which the vice president of Marketing should address each audience, and the information they need to communicate. For example, with regard to the subject of each memo, we encourage students to identify the question(s) they are being asked, their audience's level of expertise, what information they will need to include in their response, how they should arrange that information, and how they can make their response as concise as possible—considering the time constraints of the exam as well as the conventions of professional communication.

To date, the Howe's rhetorical contribution to the In-Basket Exam has been well received by the faculty and students. Many students follow our advice and sketch a rhetorical triangle on the top of the exam memos to ensure that they remember that each memo is a unique rhetorical situation. Additionally, the Marketing instructors routinely invite us to come speak to their classes prior to the exam. Although we appreciate the repeat business and the opportunity to promote the Howe to students, we are concerned that the Marketing professors, who by now understand the rhetorical triangle, are simply opting to outsource the teaching of writing. As consultants who practice a feminist methodology, we are not interested in remaining the sole proprietors of rhetorical expertise in the Business School. We are concerned that this division of labor enables a split between disciplinary content and communication. We question whether our guest presentations imply that writing is an ancillary concern for business professionals. More problematically, does our presence suggest that writing is women's work? The Marketing faculty claims that our presentations emphasize the importance of writing, and we do want to support this exam. Yet we continually wrestle with the connotations of staging an all-girl writing road show in the Business School.

Another example of our consultancy's value added is our work with International Finance's Cross-Border Merger Analysis. Working in teams of two, students research and analyze recent multibillion dollar mergers between international and U.S. companies. Students examine the terms of the merger, the stock market's reaction, and any defensive strategies used by the firms. Students use the financial concepts they have learned in the course to perform analyses and write a 15- to 20-page report. The assignment is intended to familiarize students with the business report genre.

Again, context and purpose posed a problem. The instructor had difficulty getting students to change their perspective. Instead of adopting a business persona and using a business genre to address a business audience, students resorted to the familiar academic research paper, presenting the instructor with a narrative "show and tell" of everything they learned about the merger. To help students make this transition, the Howe advised the professor to clearly outline a rhetorical situation and audience for the assignment. The revised Cross-Border Merger Analysis specifies that students should act as outside consultants assigned the job of compiling a report on a recent cross-border merger for a company considering a similar type of merger. Specifically, they are asked to analyze the potential benefits and challenges for the company contemplating a merger. Initially, we described previous semesters' "best practices," composed supplemental handouts, and made guest presentations on writing effective business reports to the International Finance classes, but we have successfully transitioned that expertise to the course instructor. That transfer of expertise remains one of our feminist agendas. Now the Howe supports the Cross-Border Merger Analysis assignment by helping students in the Howe Writing Center.

In addition to advising FSB faculty, we also staff a writing center for Business students. Because the Howe conceives its role as promoting the use of rhetorical concepts in the Business School, we consider students important stakeholders. Through one-on-one consultations, we assist students in making the transition to business writing. Yet our consultations often involve an initial rhetorical turn. When students first visit the writing center, they often come in search of that elusive editing/proofreading drop-off service. We use these occasions to make a rhetorical turn. We ask students the business context for their writing project, their audience, the purpose, or how the information they are communicating will be used. In many cases, we also help them see the rhetorical function of the business genre their instructor has asked them to use. For example, we show them that constructing executive summaries or case analyses require decision making and prioritizing; they are not neutral, objective genres. In addition to repositioning the Howe, we believe we are repositioning students within the FSB. By demystifying the construction, function, and effect of business writing and business genres, we are preparing students to read and write more critically within the FSB, and we hope they will carry this expertise into their professional careers outside of the academy.

Although *consultant* is not a gendered term, the Howe Writing Center occupies a gendered space. A large handmade quilt hangs on the wall, greeting faculty members and students when they enter. We have plants and personal photos, and the focal point of the office is a round table where we meet with clients and each other. We also have a box of tissues handy because occasionally the Howe serves as a refuge. The most recent example occurred when a Management professor became frustrated trying to discuss a writing assignment with a student. His solution was to take the student by the arm and drop her off at our door. Understandably, the student was humiliated and immediately broke into tears when her professor left. After handing her the box of tissues, Kate and Cristy began diffusing the situation by laughing. Without accusations, their laughter prompted a rhetorical turn—gently shifting the student's embarrassment to the professor's awkward response. The student soon recovered, and the three of them got to the business at hand—discussing several different approaches to the student's profile of a corporate management structure. Although we refuse the label and role of *nurturing mothers*, with regard to people skills and treating individuals with respect, we are happy to serve as exemplars. Because we work with teachers whose model of leadership often comes from corporate hierarchies, rather than pedagogical theory, we believe that we perform models of teaching that counter a top–down structure of authority.

Ultimately, we view our consultancy as modeling feminist methodology, in the sense that we are continually unsettling and complicating notions about writing, teaching, and business in general. When we are talking to students about case studies, marketing plans, or cross-border mergers, we encourage them to consider aspects beyond the balance sheet. As consultants to the faculty, we also believe we have the obligation to voice uncomfortable comments, which often directly tie to our views as feminists. For example, when Cristy reviewed an instructor's assignment for class presentations, she questioned the advice for students to wear "suit and tie or the equivalent." The professor became defensive, but Cristy explained her concern about the message he was sending to female students as well as the confusion about what the professor considers equivalent to a suit and tie. Likewise, when Kate observed another instructor teaching a 100-student seminar, she noted the instructor's different approach to interacting with male and female students. The instructor liked involving students in his lectures with scenarios and questions, but he did not know his students' names. He attempted to work around this by asking male students their major, then referring to them as "Accounting major" or "Marketing major." Yet surprisingly, when the instructor called on female students, he usually designated them by their hair color or their apparel—"blondie" or "red sweater." Although the Business School faculty is overwhelmingly male, the business school students are not. Part of our role as feminist administrators in the FSB is challenging any notion or practice that portrays business as a male pursuit. Because we claim rhetorical authority as expert consultants, we can often perform critiques that colleagues, especially untenured women colleagues, might hesitate to voice. In that sense, we are emboldened by our status as outsiders. Likewise, our answer to our own colleagues in English, who sometimes behave as if we have sold our souls to capitalism, is always, "Where else should feminist rhetoricians be?"

MODELING AND MARKETING FEMINIST
ADMINISTRATORS

Most Business School faculty come from the business world of top–down power cultural norms that resist power sharing. As feminists, we believe in curricular and administrative leadership as bottom–up, collaborative, and based in local contexts rather than unilateral or top–down. Because the space we inhabit is a gendered space and we are sometimes viewed as caregivers to students in writing crises, our work mirrors the often marginalized space of women in business. However, the graduate students who work in the Howe take on roles of consultancy, wielding authority that is atypical for TAs in the FSB. As rhetorical consultants, the assistant directors of the Howe Writing Initiative are both outsiders and colleagues — leading and serving, advising and assisting professors. Our role as outside writing experts or consultants gives us the opportunity to advise faculty who may not be comfortable sharing power with their own TAs.

Rhetoric is the value added that we bring to the FSB, but the power-sharing model of feminist administration is perhaps the boldest concept we deliver to the school and to our work with one another. The colleague relationship the Howe has with the FSB faculty extends from the relationship between Kate and her assistant directors. Mentoring future WAC administrators, Kate prepares her assistant directors to be feminist curricular leaders by treating, trusting, and respecting them as colleagues. Kate employs what Goodburn and Leverenz outline as feminist principles for management: "Nonhierarchical collaboration, shared leadership, and the recognition of multiple sources of authority" (277). As Kate's colleagues, the assistant directors are received as colleagues by the faculty of the business school as well.

Most TAs in the FSB are master's Economic or Accounting students whose duties rarely extend beyond taking attendance and recording grades. In a faculty workshop led by Lisa and Cristy, one professor blatantly stated: "I wouldn't trust my TA to grade my student papers." This professor's candor in front of us demonstrates the distinction afforded Howe assistant directors. In our consultations, classroom presentations, and faculty workshops, the Howe graduate students have the *ethos* of colleagues. The authority Lisa and Cristy bring with them to these endeavors is a direct result of Kate's feminist pedagogical choice to resist the power inherent in her position and share power with her assistant directors. Kate enacts this feminist model of administration for the faculty by encouraging her TAs to invent and carry out their own consultant projects.

Lisa and Cristy came to the Howe in the second year of their PhD coursework. At their first consultation, a classroom presentation on effective team writing, Lisa and Cristy presented together. It has been Kate's experience that if she is in the room the graduate students would be ignored and her authority would override any authority the assistant directors may have. As the only representatives of the Howe, Lisa and Cristy were the rhetorical experts in the room. Perhaps more important, the professor turned his class over to them, sharing *his* power with the rhetorical experts.

In the same way that we demonstrate our value added to the FSB, Lisa and Cristy bring their own value added to the Howe. Beyond the everyday needs of a writing center, Kate did not lay out specific tasks or requirements for work with the faculty. Lisa and Cristy were proactive colleagues who sought out opportunities. Kate mentors her assistant directors through weekly meetings where we all share, collaborate, and consult one another on projects. We employ "shared leadership among group members, group goal setting, and a recursive rather than linear process of collaboration as the group continually works to consider each member's perspective" in these weekly meetings (Goodburn and Leverenz 278). Given the freedom to interview faculty and perform needs assessments, the assistant directors are able to pursue projects ranging from proposals to workshops to scholarly papers.

In their second year at the Howe, Lisa and Cristy began projects that resulted in faculty workshops and conference presentations. Lisa designed and initiated an IRB-approved study of writing assignment names used across the Business School. This study resulted in a faculty workshop and a white paper entitled, "Using Writing Assignment Names to Integrate Learning Across the School of Business." While Kate and the rest of the Howe team were there for support, Lisa led two workshops, asking faculty to consider the pedagogical effect of writing assignment names. Lisa published her findings in the *Journal of Business and Technical Communication.* One of Cristy's projects began as weekly e-mails to the faculty in a response to increasing class size. The e-mails, entitled "Howe to Keep Writing in Large Classes," provoked a sizeable response from faculty. The e-mails turned into a faculty workshop entitled "Writ Large: A Howe Writing Initiative Faculty Workshop on Using Writing in Large Classes" led by Cristy and a new Howe assistant director, Sarah Bowles, where participants were given a binder filled with handouts, lesson plans, and teaching resources.

From a graduate student perspective, working in a feminist WAC initiative provides various opportunities. The consultancy model and colleague relationship we have developed at the Howe have provided unique teaching experiences for the assistant directors. Lisa and Cristy have consulted with dozens of faculty members and presented to classes from the first year to graduate level. They have gained confidence and facility applying rhetorical concepts and adapting rhetorical expertise across many disciplines. Our work from a feminist model of collaboration and self-reflection also affords a unique professional development opportunity for future feminist administrators. Each of the previous Howe assistant directors has gone on to a tenure-track job, many of them in writing program administration. We believe that our work in the School of Business, therefore, impacts writing programs nationally.

Although a male-dominated Business School may appear an odd training ground for future feminist administrators, where else should feminist administrators be? The Howe Writing Initiative is, admittedly, a challenging space for women administrators, especially given the Business Dean's charge to *boldly* improve business writing performance alongside our own discipline's pressure to sustain movement toward institutional critique and change. Working as consultants in the Business School puts us in a space where these tensions become heightened at every meeting with students and every consultation with faculty. Just today, Kate had to explain to an Accountancy professor, again, that separating content evaluation from writing evaluation betrays the whole divisional project. At every turn, we have to argue and account for the expertise as well as the critique that we add to teaching writing in a capitalist curriculum and to helping students succeed as accountants and marketers. Although our goals might seem small and prosaic, even accommodationist to some, we believe that crossing the campus between English and Business constitutes, as Walvoord and Malinowitz would say, the power of feminist movement.

12

CENTERED WOMEN

Performing Gender and Power in the Writing Center

Carol Mattingly

Paula Gillespie

Many early notions of feminist pedagogy and administration seemed ideal for the writing center. Early feminist proponents supported a maternal or nurturing approach to students, a style that seemed appropriate to writing centers because then, as now, some students seeking help with writing were timid and lacking in self-confidence. Such approaches, suggested in Sally Miller Gearhart's "Womanization of Rhetoric" and Nel Noddings's *Caring: A Feminine Approach to Ethics and Moral Education*, focused on a warm, supportive approach to students. Directly or indirectly, these approaches found a home in writing center theory and practice. At conferences and on writing center listservs, scholars discussed ways to make students comfortable in the writing center and with their writing. Centers offered snacks and inviting chairs and sofas in colorful atmospheres, what Peter Carino dubbed "the three Cs of writing centers: coffee, cookies, and couches" (102). Similar theories that sought to diminish authority of "experts" in favor of a more equitable distribution of power—one that empowered students—also seemed to support the writing center's goals. To that end, writing centers often focused on retaining students' ownership of writing, with admonishments that the tutor should never mark on the writer's paper or take control of the mouse when working electronically with a student's writing. A questioning approach to tutoring that encouraged a student to make changes in her writing, rather than one where the tutor simply "fixed" the student's paper, also supported this empowering philosophy. Such notions of equity are especially evident in the early feminist pedagogy volume edited by Cynthia L. Caywood and Gillian R. Overing, as three of the five sections and 14 of the 20 chapters focus on promoting students' authority and equity.

Much of the support for these approaches found a home in conversations about collaborative learning, but not all collaboration is feminist. Drawing on such texts as Kenneth Bruffee's "Peer Tutoring and the 'Conversation of Mankind,'" Andrea Lunsford's "Collaboration, Control, and the Idea of a Writing Center," and Christina Murphy's "The Writing Center and Social Constructionist Theory," writing center theorists and practitioners argued that, because of its peer-to-peer instruction, the writing center offers the ideal collaborative space for undermining the patriarchal paradigm, empowering student writers, and removing the authority figure.

Such overly positive notions of collaboration have been questioned by more recent feminist and writing center theorists. Evelyn Ashton-Jones rightly questions blanket acceptance of collaboration as feminist. In fact, collaboration often reconstructs women's traditional, submissive roles. No longer do we believe that peer collaboration, by its nature, eliminates inequitable, hierarchical roles. We are more likely to question Carol Stanger's early optimism that "Student writer and peer critic" conferences by their very nature might "create a more natural and realistic writing situation" or that "male language doesn't dominate" in collaborative situations (42). Critics have argued convincingly that power relations in the culture at large often follow students into the classroom and writing center.

Nurturing practices generally have also come under scrutiny from those who believed that such approaches might further disempower women or, at the least, strengthen stereotypes and perceptions that relegated women to limited "maternal" roles in a hierarchical and patriarchal environment. Some have worried that, in not confronting patriarchal notions directly, feminists further promoted the hegemonic status quo. Such concerns were expressed most famously (or infamously) perhaps, in Dale M. Bauer's "The Other 'F' Word: The Feminist in the Classroom," but by other prominent scholars as well (Jarratt "Feminism"; Eichorn et al.).

Discussions drawing from these earlier debates have continued to the present, especially in disagreements over invitational rhetoric. Sonia K. Foss and Cindy L. Griffin have offered an extended version of Gearhart's theory, which saw an "act of violence in the *intention* to change another," by suggesting that we invite discussion rather than pursue coercion in our work with others. However, feminists remain divided on the value of such rhetoric, many trying to find a middle ground that permits persuasion to more equitable ideas without an assault on those whose perspective differs from or offends others.

Although early theories that promoted the writing center as a paradigm for feminist ideals may have been somewhat naive, complicating such theories can still be valuable for writing centers. The writing center may still support such ideals by openly examining issues that hamper the positive goals of greater equality and the empowerment of students. Because of its unique situation and one-to-one approach, the writing center often offers a unique environment where pedagogical approaches can present notable opportunities for increasing awareness of gender inequities. Many feminists, men as well as women, agree on basic premises essential to a feminist approach and believe that those principles are most at home in writing centers. For example, Meg Woolbright, drawing on early work by Schneidewind, calls for developing an atmosphere of mutual respect, trust, and community; shared leadership; a cooperative structure; the integration of cognitive and affective learning; and action. In this chapter, we hope to demonstrate how the writing center may extend such early feminist values by complicating and, perhaps, extending feminist principles into situations outside the writing center.

In their introduction to *Feminine Principles and Women's Experience in American Composition and Rhetoric,* Janet Emig and Louise Wetherbee Phelps note women "seldom enjoyed . . . opportunity to collaborate on intellectual and imaginative projects, exclusively with other women" (xi). Although not exclusively made up of women, writing centers may be the closest academic unit outside specific women's studies departments to achieving the comfort that Emig and Phelps envision, and certainly the most feminine within composition studies. Although writing programs tend to be headed and staffed predominantly by women, and writing classes generally reflect the university's male–female ratio, writing centers across all institutional categories are dominated by women. For example, the Writing Centers Research Project (WCRP) survey confirms the administration of writing centers as feminized. This international survey that establishes benchmarks for writing centers most recently (2004) found that 80% of writing center directors are women. The 2004 survey confirms earlier studies. In a 1994 survey, Dave Healy found that "writing center directors are disproportionately female: 74%" (30), and Childers and Gillespie's *Directory of Writing Centers, 1998-99* includes 76% women and 24% men. But women prevail in other categories as well. Bradley T. Hughes, Kirsten Jamsen, and Jody Cardinal researched gender balances and found that the staff and clientele of a range of writing centers was 70% female. Their research led them to agree with Margaret Tipper's findings about writing centers—that, more generally, in her all-male secondary school, male writers prefer not to seek help but enjoy tutoring others.[1]

Because women make up the majority of both tutors and writers, the writing center provides ample opportunity for administrators to share power with women, both writers and tutors, and to model relationships that allow the fostering of agency for both women and men.

LANGUAGE, GENDER, AND POWER

Stereotypes about women, men, and language have long influenced and justified beliefs and attitudes about gendered power relations. However, in recent decades, scholars have begun to challenge many of the stereotypes. For example, studies have demonstrated that, contrary to popular belief, men actually speak more than women (Spender); men interrupt both men and women far more often than women interrupt others (Le Masters; Philipsen; Abrahams; West and Zimmerman; Woods); and men control discussions and resist challenges to their hold on the floor (Savin-Williams; Maltz and Borker; Fishman). Further study has demonstrated that different conversational styles often create confusion about intended meaning (Tannen *Gender, You Just*; Kowalski).

These issues carry over into academic venues. In situations where teachers believed girls were talking more than boys, careful study demonstrated that boys actually talked more (Sadker and Sadker). Scholars have found that classroom speech and interaction at all levels favors patterns comfortable to boys and men (Treichler and Kramarae), and that female students not only received less attention from teachers but that the attention they received was less useful in educational value (Sadker and Sadker). Scholars have found that teachers' perceptions of conversational styles influenced classroom dynamics (Hull et al.; French and French; Sadker and Sadker). Others have found that students' misperceptions of one another based on language may cause dysfunctional groups (Andrews; Baird; Winter et al.), and that increasing computer use may heighten men's influence in groups because men usually take the role of computer expert in group writing tasks, relegating labor-intensive elements to others. Joanna Wolfe and Kara Alexander found that in such situations, although they do less work, men are often seen as contributing more.

Although some recent research suggests that status may be more powerful than gender in determining control of topics and discussions (Okamoto and Smith-Lovin), other research has found gender to be the more powerful determinant (Woods). Because dynamics of power and gender are interrelated, and because both are so important in one-to-one conferencing, examining both dynamics is useful for tutors, but little research has addressed gender and power dynamics in the writing center. Carolyn P. Walker and David Elias examined one-to-one conferencing in the writing center, for example; but while they examined numerous variables, they ignored obvious gender issues. Gail Stygall reexamined Walker and Elias' work in light of gender differentials and found that "successful" conferences tended to be those where the gender of both participants was the same. Laurel Johnson Black's research seems to support Stygall's findings. Black found that teacher/student conference dynamics change depending on the gender of tutor and writer. For example, Black recorded the following power moves: Women teachers used place holders such as "and" to maintain control of the dialogue twice as frequently with women as with men students, "you know" five times as frequently with women students, and "well" three times as often. She found evidence suggesting that gender can be a major influence in one-to-one conferencing, sometimes in unexpected ways: "[f]emale teachers dominate female students just as male teachers do. Female teachers are less likely to interrupt their female students than male teachers are, but they are also less likely to cooperatively overlap their speech. Female students initiate fewer revision strategies to female teachers and hear less praise from female teachers" (68). According to black, male students are more apt to use place-keeping markers with women teachers than with men teachers in order to hold the floor or to use "well" to foreshadow disagreement.

EMPOWERING PEDAGOGY

How do we make this theoretical material accessible to our tutors? How do we incorporate it into our daily practice? As administrators, our main tasks are to train tutors, facilitate the daily running of the writing center, and operate within the administrative structures of our institutions. To do so, we should understand and communicate to our staffs the relationship between language and power.

The writing center, by its very nature, is the forum for discussing language and interpersonal communications. We talk about writing with writers, but in our staff meetings we talk about how to talk about language and writing and how to do so effectively. We discuss ownership of writing and dynamics of power and comfort. Helping future leaders to consider deeply the nature of power and gender as it plays out in language and communications, as we do in the writing center, responds to Wendy Bishop's call for properly mentoring our "novitiate." Essential to that mentoring is the careful consideration of stereotypes and the examination of power relations so deeply embedded in our culture that we often do not notice them.

This examination can begin immediately as we plan and shape our training sessions. Finding just the right balance for tutor training is complicated by institutional histories, training course traditions, the nature and structure of staff meetings, the makeup of the tutor body, the amount of time available for tutor training, and other complex factors. But most of us require our tutors to read and discuss articles, during either the training period or ongoing staff development later. Some will argue that there is already too much to cover.

Isn't it enough—isn't it too much, really—just to train tutors to talk effectively about writing? Nancy Grimm disagrees. Her program, described in *Good Intentions: Writing Center Work for Postmodern Times*, puts feminist and other issues of power and language at the center of her tutoring program, working with her staff to articulate and understand unstated positions that affect the way we work with others, with a goal of listening more critically and more rhetorically. Other programs simply integrate a reading or two from our scant list of feminist writing center offerings. But we feel that the study of gender should be integrated into the curriculum early so that, as tutors are learning how to listen well to texts and generate good questions in response to them, they also come to understand that gender and power influence everything, including their interactions with writers. How should we do that?

Finding the right readings can be a challenge. An early version of the tutor-training course at Marquette required that undergraduates read Catherine Lamb's "Beyond Argument in Feminist Composition." This article, similar to those about invitational rhetoric, argues that training writers in mediating skills embodies a feminist ideal and an alternative to argument—a skill she conceives as hierarchical. But writing center tutors are seldom in a position to persuade students *not* to create a strong argument if the assignment calls for one. The Lamb article helps tutors to think critically about the nature of argument and about ways to persuade writers in one-to-one conferences when such persuasion is needed. But it leaves them frustrated when they are required by their teachers to create strong arguments. Lamb's article is more appropriate for instructors who are creating assignments than for tutors, addressing assignments and requirements over which they have no control.

Meg Woolbright's article, "The Politics of Tutoring: Feminism Within the Patriarchy," provides a discussion of feminist tutoring, but turns into a description of only one case study, a failed attempt at feminist tutoring that ended in an unsatisfactory proselytizing session. Nonetheless, Woolbright provides us—and tutors—with important definitions of feminist practice.

Other readings, mentioned earlier, might prepare tutors for concrete research activities that deepen understanding about gender. In our experience, tutors often enjoy an exercise that asks them to observe others in conversation. After appropriate readings regarding research on gender issues—which gender talks more or more likely interrupts or which is more supportive by offering nods, uh-huhs, or other backchanneling—tutors test these theories by observing conversations in the student union, restaurants or bars, or whatever locations they typically haunt. Their observations offer rich discussion at our next meeting.

At the University of Louisville, in preparation for another activity to understand gender and power dynamics, we read Black's *Between Talk and Teaching*. Black effectively discusses her own fears of inadequacy as a student before a critical male teacher. Tutors usually find Black's narrative compelling. In discussions of the work, they become aware that gender (male tutor, female writer; female tutor, male writer; etc.) may influence the effectiveness of their own sessions. Black's work also is useful as a model because she offers coded transcripts of one-to-one conferencing. As part of their training, our new tutors videotape at least one of their own sessions for self-observation and transcribe portions that demonstrate features of previous seminar discussions. After they have looked for many of the traditional session features we have discussed—was the writer introduced to our procedure, did the writer maintain ownership of her paper, and so on—they watch the video a second time for signs that gender and power have influenced sessions. They are often surprised to find that they are performing subtle power and gender issues of which they had been unaware.[2]

One additional activity helps to create awareness about gender issues. This activity might be used to set the stage for readings on gender, later to examine papers through the lens provided by the readings and discussions, or both. Most tutor-training programs do small- or whole-group discussions of student papers to provide tutors with practice in responding to texts before they actually meet with students. As we collect assignments that allow for such modeling, we gather some that will provide constructive discussions about gender. For example, we often use typical essays from first-year composition classes, especially those in response to a prompt about an important event or person in students' lives. In one essay, a young woman describes her boyfriend's importance to her; in another essay, a young man presents his role in a high-stakes football or basketball game. We also might include an essay in which a young man writes about his girlfriend. Tutors' responses to these essays often lead to interesting discussions about gender. Why do they respond positively to a young man's narrative about his girlfriend, but negatively when a young woman writes about her boyfriend? Do we feel that it is more or less appropriate for a young man to discuss his role as sports hero than as boyfriend? Why or why not? The discussion always brings us to question whether our reactions are to the writing or the topic; to the gendered nature of the essay or the way the narrative is told. Do the tropes and manner of addressing the topic by the man seem more acceptable? What makes for good writing in these essays? Such workshops also provide an opportunity to discuss papers that tutors might find offensive. If we have discussed a paper with misogynist overtones or offensive language, for example, tutors are better prepared to deal with the writers of such papers in the writing center.

MODELING STRENGTH AND PROFESSIONALISM

Wendy Bishop has called for more guidance for those good girls (and we would add good boys) who are likely to seek refuge in the writing center. Because primarily women directors mentor primarily women assistant directors (who mentor tutors as well) and because primarily women tutors work closely, one to one with primarily women students, writing centers offer ample opportunity for sharing power with women students, fostering agency, and furthering feminist principles. Bishop suggests that, instead of warring against change that is unlikely to happen among current faculty and administrators, we can create our own change by properly mentoring our students. The writing center, home to graduate student assistant directors and tutors who will become our future academic colleagues and administrators as well as leaders in the population at large, represents just such an opportunity.

Although we work hard with our undergraduates to help them become great tutors, we also look beyond the tutoring situation to their professional development. The many letters we receive from former undergraduate tutors show that their training does transfer in dramatic and dynamic ways. Research shows that undergraduates go into many and varied fields. Some become teachers. A few go on to graduate school. Some go to law school. Some become technical writers, editors, or public relations writers. Many go on to totally unrelated professions: cruise directors, waiters, or jazz musicians.[3]

Surveys from former undergraduate tutors tell us that they value the way they developed their abilities to listen actively, analytically, and critically; analyze texts; collaborate; speak comfortably and diplomatically with others; and multitask. They appreciate having developed patience and respect for others foregrounded in our training and practice. Men and women tutor alumni alike tell us they value these skills and attitudes. Such qualities take them far in the professional world, they tell us, and help them succeed.

But from observing us, they learn other skills and values. We model for them the role of professional: We deal with them equitably and fairly; we know how to assess power structures, and we make ourselves heard by those who hold institutional power. We show our staff how to represent our own interests and even our own selves to those higher in the hierarchies than we are. We show them how to succeed as academics, administrators, or both. We show them how we operate in a world where instructors ". . . control the curriculum, assign the work, and evaluate the results" (Trimbur, "Peer Tutoring" 290). We can talk to our staffs in detail about why we make the decisions we make. If we take the time to explain our choices, to share both our successes and our failures, our second attempts, our third and our fourth, it helps them understand what it means to become a professional.

CONCLUSION

Phelps reminds us that gendering of our programs "is not immutably fixed but is susceptible to transformation." Phelps wants women to "begin to pursue their intellectual projects and enact their values with confidence and some measure of institutional support" ("Becoming" 290–91). If we add some of the goals for tutorials set out by Marilyn Cooper ("Really") and Nancy Grimm, as they argue that tutors are in a unique position to foster increased awareness of agency in both men and women writers, we can locate the writing center in a central position and show an ability to intervene cooperatively and collegially in the writing and revision process, fostering a kind of literacy and awareness that can help writers locate their own positions.

Writing centers offer a unique space for promoting feminist goals—in how we train our tutors to engage in good pedagogy and in how we mentor future leaders and administrators as we help them internalize or become aware of feminist principles, empowering graduate students and peer tutors, helping them to be aware of the power dynamics in language and interpersonal activities. We must be aware of unconscious attitudes of directors, tutors, and, most of all, student writers. Jay Sloan resists the arguments of Cooper and others that the writer must be encouraged to resist the oppressive practices of universities. He argues that the most oppressive thinking processes come to college with the student and are part of the mass culture. It is a challenge to develop staffers who will be able to encourage new ways of looking at cultural issues and new ways of imagining the lives of those we might easily dismiss or ignore.

As professionals, we train our tutors to make mature judgments about when to leave the writing decisions up to the writer and when, as Carino points out, to use the power they have and share expert knowledge with writers who need it. Training manuals such as *The Allyn and Bacon Guide to Peer Tutoring*, 2nd edition, suggest that, rather than slapping pens out of tutors' hands, we might encourage them to exercise control and flexibility. If we carefully construct the experience of our writing center staff, we can indeed create our own "novitiate."

PART V

Performing Chair and Editorial Work
Challenging Institutional and Disciplinary Practices

Community renewal must begin with an examination of the paths of individual scholars [and administrators] who must then be heard as part of the collective history of the field of composition studies.

—Resa Crane Bizzaro ("Making Places
as Teacher–Scholars in Composition Studies" (493)

13

HERDING CATS

Feminist Practices and Challenges in Chairing an English Department

Linda Hanson

Pragmatists, then, believe in inquiry . . . and in belief . . . and in the symbiotic relationship between the two, symbiotic because the relationship itself yields new insights or third principles.

—Hephzibah Roskelly and Kate Ronald
Reason to Believe (87)

Responsibility to yourself means refusing to let others do your thinking, talking, and naming for you; it means learning to respect and use your own brains and instincts; hence, grappling with hard work.

—Adrienne Rich
"Claiming an Education" (233)

I am a pragmatist. I am a teacher. I am a rhetorician. I am a woman. Those multiple identities constantly inform each other, sometimes through conflict, always in reflection, as I define myself and my work.

As the first woman to chair our English Department, and in rare company within our college, I knew I was going to be under considerable scrutiny not only from colleagues (male and female) in the department, but from the "old boy network" that operated both within and outside the university channels of governance. Compounding my visibility as female was my association with the Basic Writing Program that in many eyes was more marginalized than the Writing Program[1]—which, after all, (male) literary scholars COULD direct. That association was doubly suspect because with a degree in literature I had resigned a tenure-line position to join my husband. I chose as a faculty wife to serve as a contract faculty member for 13 years, teaching and conducting research on writing, before I was hired in a national search in 1985 to direct the Basic Writing Program and join the fledgling Rhetoric and Composition faculty.[2]

To balance the potential negatives, what did I have going for me? Gender, experience directing and transforming the Basic Writing Program, and years of institutional knowledge. In other words, my potential liabilities also gave me sources of strength. I was working with situated knowledge in a context where I had been successful. I had the continuing support of contract faculty, many of whom had worked with me to transform the Basic Writing Program, and several of whom were enfranchised in 1992.[3] The previous chair had appointed me his assistant chair, so for 3 1/2 years I had had to work with everyone in the department on course assignments and scheduling, sometimes a contentious task, and had been acting chair through the chair's series of eye operations, so I had a track record on which to be elected. I also had an agenda of three major goals based on my assessment of the department's strengths and weaknesses. I laid my agenda out for the department because it would serve as my mandate if elected. I wanted the department to know what to expect from me and what I would expect from my colleagues during my 3-year term.[4] I wanted to transform the department, nothing less. Implicit in my agenda, but explicit in my message, was my method: collaborative decision making that would honor the diverse strengths of the department.

The role of the department chair is equivocal at best. The chair inhabits a pivotal space at the bottom of a hierarchical chain of command associated with a business model and at the forefront of a collegial model of governance. Elected by colleagues, the chair occupies a political position unlike that of other administrators. He or she is placed in a position of meeting differing, sometimes contradictory expectations of administrators and colleagues, a position that fosters a perhaps desirable ambivalence in straddling both administrative and academic expectations. The chair has responsibilities conferred on him or her, but often and certainly at my institution lacks authority to act unilaterally to meet those responsibilities. More than providing a conduit for information from above and within the department, the chair must be an advocate for the department on fiscal and academic issues. The chair must provide leadership for the department in research, teaching, and service. Least visible, the job entails an overwhelming service commitment, 90% of it devoted to human relationships—with administrative appointees, staff, individual faculty, students, and, in our case, long-standing disciplinary groups of faculty (area committees).

Embedded in my three goals were feminist thinking and practices that acknowledged the importance of human relationships to the work of our department and the university. My first goal was to transform our splintered department into a community that acknowledged the strengths in our diversity. The Writing Program, rhetoric and composition, linguistics, English Education, and British, world, and American literature designated not only disciplinary areas for faculty, but also multiple facets of English Studies. For the health of our programs, we needed to see them that way. Reexamining and revising our undergraduate curriculum from that perspective was the second goal. Reexamining and revising our faculty reward system to honor our "mosaic of talent" in light of Boyer's just-published *Scholarship Reconsidered* was my third goal (27).

My approach to chairing the largest department on campus[5] could be characterized with a list of words at the intersection of feminism,[6] rhetoric, and writing pedagogy—collaborative, inclusive, relational, faculty-centered, contextualized, dialogic,[7] recursive, positive, celebratory—but mapping progress toward each goal will best reveal the methods chosen to achieve them, the practical and theoretical support for those choices, the administrative issues that arose in the process, and their resolution (or continuing lack of resolution). With a 12-year perspective on my term as chair and other leadership roles since, I examine as well the long-term effects of feminist administrative practices in the culture of a department. Contextual knowledge is ultimately what we must learn from, and the context is not a single administrator's, but that shared by every member of the community. Conversation with a young colleague, husband to one of our recent PhDs, convinced me that only our narratives can offer to younger scholars that contextual knowledge and the map to use it.[8]

COMMUNITY

Community was both my central goal and the most broad ranging because it determines the ability of the administrative unit—whether a department, writing program, or college—to work effectively and project a coherent image. Shared work helps to create community, but for a community to survive beyond a single task, other bonds have to be established. The internal relationships create shared knowledge, expectations, and values; they enable collaborative decision making, mutual investment in or ownership of those decisions and ensuing implementation, and a context for valuing individuals through shared leadership. External relationships—with other departments, the college, university administrators, and even professional organizations—are facilitated by the energy that emanates from a strong community with a coherent vision. That energy empowers individuals speaking for the community, whether on campus, to prospective students or alumni, or within the profession.[9]

As I contemplated the state of our department while deciding whether to run for chair, I reflected on how, collectively, the Basic Writing faculty and I had changed the program and the culture by establishing a community of learners. Although initially I may have posed the questions and shared resources, we were all actively engaged in the inquiry about assessment that would enable us to transform the program. At the time, I did not realize what valuable experience I was gaining as I sought colleagues' help and collective power early in the 1980s. Advice from my father echoed in my head—that if I wanted to change something, I would have a better chance of changing it from within than from without. I have since come to understand the social and epistemic wisdom behind that maxim, but my only experience in social change at that point was tied to neighborhood activism and marching for social issues and human rights in the 1960s. I understood that personal investment, collaboration, and collective action could effect change, but my understanding was more intuitive than deliberate. My own investment in student learning, in providing the best possible learning experiences for my students, however, impelled me into leadership. I carried classroom practices, particularly shared inquiry and shared intellectual work, into the process.

One narrative of that multiyear process, "Pragmatic Politics," appeared in the *Journal of Basic Writing* in the spring of 1990. It focused on the program changes we effected. But by 1994, while I was applying my earlier lessons to department administration, I had begun to theorize my administrative practice for a session at the 4Cs, "Directing a Basic Writing Program: Encouraging Diversity Among Students and Instructors." From my current vantage point, I realize that I was describing my steps along the path toward self-actualization and "constructed knowledge," described by Mary Field Belenky, Blythe McVicker Clinchy, Nancy Rule Goldberger, and Jill Mattuck Tarule in *Women's Ways of Knowing*. I was trusting my own lived knowledge against external authority, but was ready to engage that institutional authority through inquiry to construct a viable program that would answer to my classroom knowledge as well as institutional knowledge:

> Having taught in the Basic Writing Program at Ball State University before I began directing the program in 1985, I knew how much I valued the autonomy I had been given over my own classroom and pedagogy. My responsibility was to my students. As long as they consistently achieved the competency levels set for the program, which they did, the director didn't question my methods or my priorities. But I was already seeking support for changing competency testing, so when the entire program became my responsibility, I had to address the discrepancies between my own philosophy and the program as it stood.
>
> To do that, however, I needed to build support for changing a smoothly running program that served approximately 1100 students each year (approximately 27% of the incoming class). By assuming responsibility for the program, I realized I was assuming responsibility for the message that instruction in basic skills constituted instruction in basic writing. (Hanson, "Directing" 2)

Both as a teacher of writing and as a rhetorician, I have become conscious of how much my pedagogical practices and rhetorical principles informed my initial approach to administration and shaped my term as department chair. Identifying the most productive questions to ask about Basic Writing meant reading the complex political and rhetorical context in the 1980s. The same held true for approaching both my curriculum and faculty reward goals as chair in the early 1990s. The context for Basic Writing revealed the multilayered problem we faced trying to make a single course pedagogically sound, suggested the work that needed to be done to solve it, identified the stakeholders who had to be satisfied, and suggested the forms of communication necessary to effect change:

> The climate in which I sought to alter the program was determined by legislative demands at the least for accountability and at most for the elimination of remedial courses at the university level, a dean and a provost whose orientations were quantitative, and a program with a successful track record: for ten years our continuing students had been averaging a C+ in ENG 103, a full half-grade higher than students placing initially in this first of two required writing courses. That track record, projected into the future, would satisfy demands for accountability.
>
> So why tamper with success? Because the basic writing teachers who were committed to empowering their students, to providing academic outsiders the tools for succeeding in an academic community, found themselves serving a schizophrenic master: public perception of the course allowed them some flexibility in writing instruction, but it demanded instruction in grammar and spelling. Pedagogically, the instruction in formal grammar and discrete skills was unsound. Publicly, we were perceived as teaching students to produce correct

texts. Politically, then, we needed quantitative data both to demonstrate
the irrelevance of discrete skills instruction to writing improvement
and assessment, and to shift the public perception of the course from
"remedial" . . . to "developmental," not different in type from our
required writing courses. The course did not belong in the profile of
"remedial" courses the legislature was seeking to eliminate from university level education. If we were ever to create a positive public and
legislative perception of basic writing courses—as a complex integration of listening, speaking, reading, thinking, and writing skills rather
than as a simplistic parceling of grammar, sentence construction, and
paragraph construction—we had to reshape our public messages. But
more, our public messages had to change because we were making
incompatible demands on teachers and students alike. (Hanson,
"Directing" 3)

The principles I identified as guiding my first administrative role were collaboration, respect for faculty, respect for students, and pragmatic politics,
which all contribute to building community. At the time, I was more interested in describing those principles in action than in placing them in a particular administrative model or theory, but a number of the descriptions
make clear the links to feminine, if not feminist, behavior and theory.
Under collaboration, I noted that "I needed help in spreading a new message" (Hanson, "Directing" 3). Using collaborative language reinforced the
principle: "When given the option, I chose the title Coordinator rather than
Director of Basic Writing because it emphasized a collaborative effort
rather than an authoritative hierarchical structure" (3). Finally, I recognized
the need for all voices to be heard, to contribute to the construction of new
knowledge, and to share ownership: "I determined to involve faculty from
the outset in making any changes. Any change in classroom behavior or
pedagogy MUST come from the faculty. If they are not invested in the
process, change will not occur in the classroom, and it certainly won't
occur quickly" (4). The major tasks we undertook to reconfigure the program, then, were truly collaborative ventures, and I relied heavily on that
experience when approaching my curricular and faculty reward goals for
the department.
    Respect for faculty—for individual strengths and differences—mani-
fested in collaboration, shared knowledge, and opportunities for faculty
development. Basic writing faculty at Ball State University are generally a
select group of experienced writing teachers whose flexibility in responding
to individual students' differences initially prompted each of them to
request or be invited to teach basic writers. As Basic Writing Coordinator,
I consciously and repeatedly selected faculty who respect students' individual strengths and differences. I also sought ways to both acknowledge and
foster respect for our individual differences in teaching and learning styles:

"Collaboration with its give and take of negotiation, of shared authority, functions on the same principles as those for decentering a classroom, implicitly valuing each individual's voice" (Hanson, "Directing" 4). Although our classrooms would become student-centered, the program would become faculty-centered. Human relations were central. Collaboration was more than task-oriented; it was a way of living and learning in the community.

Perhaps the most telling indicator of respect for faculty and their individual strengths and differences lies in our long-standing policy of relying on master syllabi in the Writing Program, rather than imposing a uniform syllabus for each course. That means we must rely on collaboration, on communally built assumptions and expectations, to maintain consistent quality in the program. To effect change, we would have to share in the construction of new knowledge, new assumptions, and new expectations. I observed that "Shared knowledge . . . could only strengthen the program and the impetus for change" (Hanson, "Directing" 4). In my analysis, I detailed the specific sessions during annual orientation and the in-house workshops and study groups during the academic year that were devoted to teaching and learning issues relevant to the Basic Writing Program, but the important point about them is that we shared responsibility and authority in developing and handling them. The study groups focusing on portfolios, rubrics, isolated grammar instruction, and spelling were most influential in shaping new expectations and assumptions and, thereby, in effecting change in the classroom, the program, and its public perception.

By setting community as a goal for the department, I was relying on my lived experience creating community among the Basic Writing faculty. By comparison, the task should have seemed more daunting than it did at the time because of the disparities in number of people, academic areas, epistemic assumptions, and established allegiances. But I presumed that we could find common ground on which to stand and forge connections that would honor our differences and strengths. The dialogic mode of collaboration identified by Lisa Ede and Andrea Lunsford acknowledges and values the realities of these multiple voices and shifting authority in the process of articulating goals and producing knowledge (132–35). I relied on both the group effort essential to dialogic collaboration and the resultant individual satisfaction to build community.

Simply bringing people together was the first task. Department meetings did not offer a site for the dialogues I envisioned. Within the 50-minute time frame, Roberts' Rules ruled. A department retreat—unheard of—seemed the best option. It had to be within the normal workweek to validate it as legitimate faculty work, so we set the December date early in the semester to give faculty time to plan around teaching responsibilities. The administrative team I had appointed deliberately included individuals from different disciplinary areas, so I relied on them to communicate with their areas as we made choices in planning the retreat. Our first choice was to reject suggestions to bring in an outside facilitator. Ours was not a task-oriented goal, but a community-building structured conversation among people who shared our department affiliation, but rarely talked. Having been in the department for 20 years, much of it as a contract faculty member, I was aware of the animosities, enclaves of power, gender and disciplinary biases, and allegiances that constituted our department. We had no coherent sense of our identity, no vision. I needed to disrupt what had become normal patterns of behavior to enable us even to discover our common ground. To facilitate that, I created table groups that mixed contract and tenure-line faculty, disciplinary areas, and, to some degree, interpersonal skills. I asked colleagues in Rhetoric and Composition, as well as the Assistant Chair and the three program directors (undergraduate, graduate, and Writing Program), to serve as table facilitators and to ensure that someone at the table was recording conversation. Each table had a laptop with a floppy disk (no networking at the site then). During breaks one of my Rhetoric and Composition colleagues transferred all the notes to a common file that served as the basis for full-group discussion. Working with one topic at a time, we used nonthreatening, open-ended questions about goals, what we valued, what we did well, and what we thought students looked for and valued in their learning experiences in our department. Table discussions always preceded the full-group discussion to guarantee each person a voice. Like quick writes at the beginning of a class to focus students' thinking, the table discussions and notes projected for all to see also empowered individuals who might not otherwise do so to speak up in the full group.

Our first annual Department Retreat on December 4, 1992, was a success. It provided us with the opportunity to articulate departmental goals; consider what students look for, what we can offer, and what we do well; and confront the possible relationships between the structure of our curriculum and the content. Discussion was illuminating. Outside our area committee system that separates literature from linguistics from composition from English education, faculty expressed similar goals for our major and minor programs, perceptions of what our best students do that we would like all our students to be able to do, and understanding of how students best learn. Faculty repeatedly emphasized that students learn through direct encounters with material—through writing, reading, speaking, thinking, discussing, reflecting, and responding. Noting with T. S. Eliot that students need a sense of tradition on which to build, they called for students and faculty to collaboratively examine the criteria by which literary canons are formed. They recognized the need to provide opportunities for reflection that encourage students to test the assumptions of the discipline against evidence from their own experience and other disciplines.

We had the common ground we needed. People continued to talk and enthusiastically accepted the challenges of pursuing the curricular questions raised by our discussion. As we worked toward the curricular and faculty reward goals within standing committees, special task forces, and two more department retreats, we had to continue to nurture and strengthen our communal bonds of shared knowledge and shared assumptions. Communication between area committees and task forces was crucial; we had to depend heavily on area representation to effect that dialogue. I revived the Department Newsletter as much to affirm for colleagues what we were doing (and to publicize accolades for faculty and student accomplishments) as to communicate our actions and presence across the university, to alumni, and to others in the profession.[10]

Respect for students, for their individual strengths and differences, was the third principle I had identified as guiding my Basic Writing Program administration, a principle we brought to communal consciousness through shared inquiry and negotiation about our public messages. The pedagogical effect on faculty and students was dramatic:

> Armed with knowledge of individual differences among student and faculty learning styles, faculty began to embrace portfolios as a more flexible frame for teaching and learning. In various guises they required journals and reflective writing in order to provide opportunity for students to gain perspectives on themselves as writers and on themselves in the context of community. In class after class, the emphasis was shifting from mastery of discrete skills to the development of students' writing abilities through a growing self-understanding of their own composing processes. (Hanson, "Directing" 6)

I hoped that the goals and values we articulated in our first Department Retreat would, through further examination, articulation in department documents, and continuing dialogue, help shape a more positive attitude toward and respect for all our students, not just the best and brightest. We deliberately recognized students' successes through the Department Newsletter, the English honorary society LIT, and an increasing number of scholarship and recognition awards. We took patterns of student complaints seriously, working with faculty and student alike for equitable solution. Although students should be at the heart of our teaching, evidence while I was assistant chair indicated that was not always the case. Our curriculum discussion summarized next provided the major way to reimagine our students, just as the focus on the Basic Writing course had enabled writing faculty to reimagine their students.

Labeling my fourth guiding principle pragmatic politics clearly acknowledges the public rhetorician: "Change what can be changed immediately; build a base to support subsequent changes when the opportunity arises; and work to create that opportunity through whatever channels are available within the department, college, and university—committees, sympathetic ears, even routine administrative reports which can be used to contextualize and to persuade" (Hanson, "Directing" 7). As rhetoricians, we need to be aware of not only the immediate, but also the larger and future contexts in which our words may be heard or read—public, legislative, administrative, academic.[11] The truism continues to hold.

CURRICULUM

Reexamining and revising our undergraduate curriculum was my second goal as chair. The Writing Program, rhetoric and composition, linguistics, English Education, and British, world, and American literature designated not only disciplinary areas for faculty, but also multiple facets of English Studies. For our students and ourselves, we needed to conceive and offer our programs as a coherent whole. A few of us with feet in two or more areas felt the divisions keenly. Again, context shaped the questions we asked of our own disciplinary identity. I analyzed the complexities for a 1994 MLA session on The Teaching of Writing and the Reform of the English Department Curriculum:

> According to *U.S. News and World Report*, the following fields [graduate level sub-disciplines] define our discipline: Medieval Literature, Renaissance Literature, 19th and 20th Century British Literature, 19th and 20th Century American Literature, Third World Literature, African-American Literature, Gender and Literature, Critical Theory. There is no mention of the graduate programs in Rhetoric and Composition, and Linguistics and English Education are viewed as having other homes—a different but relevant issue.
>
> In the public eye, we have succeeded in broadening the canon and in welcoming many voices. But the public debates about writing and literacy and the cry for national standards have not yet translated into recognition of Composition and Rhetoric as a field of study within English graduate programs.
>
> The omission is telling. It mirrors our own classifications of publications in the MLA Bibliography, the classifications that have been available for dissertations in Dissertation Abstracts, and the derivative search words that may be used to locate published materials. Expanding the canon can be and has been accomplished within the confines of the MLA Bibliography classifications—when American literature was finally accepted as appropriate for university study early [in the 20th] century, no new *type* of classification had to be added to

the bibliography. As a discipline, we have the tools and the language to handle the periodic revision of the literary canon without disturbing primary assumptions about who we are and what we do. To re-form English and the English curriculum, . . . we must disturb those primary assumptions. Despite the substantial evidence that composition has come of age as a discipline, such gaps as *U.S. News and World Report* exposed still reveal the hierarchical values and assumptions that make English curricular reform at best complex, at worst acrimonious and divisive. What we value professionally and in our graduate programs inevitably shapes our undergraduate curriculum. (Hanson, "English" 1–2)

It was our undergraduate program that sorely needed revision, but it did not exist in a vacuum. Rhetoric and composition had clear, related responsibilities to both the Writing Program and the graduate program, but there was not much in between. The place for writing in the university, too, remained ambivalent:

WAC programs, Writing in the Disciplines programs, growth in writing minors and majors, in upper division writing requirements in majors other than English, in hiring preferences for graduates who can write well—all indicate that people outside the discipline value the ability to write well. Yet there are no simple answers to what constitutes "English," what role English studies can and should play in a student's education, what constitutes a coherent and integrated curriculum for an English major or minor, how students best develop the sophisticated use of language we expect of our graduates. (Hanson, "English" 3–4)

The task of defining our profession—and thereby our undergraduate curriculum—has become progressively more complicated as we have become aware of both the diversity of inquiry within our field and the external political and social pressure to which the profession must respond:

Robert Pattison and Paulo Freire remind us that education in English functions within a sociopolitical framework—a framework that particularly in this country has tended to support a subject-based curriculum to match the "discipline models" of science and math. The "discipline model" for English, comprising separate subjects of literature, language, and composition to be mastered, continues to flourish despite the pedagogical acceptance in composition of a "growth model" that recognizes the individual student as an active participant in his or her learning.

Joseph Harris suggests that the conflict between the "growth model" that has become associated with composition and the "disci-

pline model" associated with literature is a conflict between teaching
and research, between meeting the needs and expectations of students
and the public versus those of other scholars. I would suggest that
more fundamental differences separate the two models, differences in
their concepts of knowledge and language. The pedagogy, theory, and
historical practice associated with each area—literature and composition—rest on opposing epistemological assumptions. Committee discussions, policy statements, even course descriptions can mask epistemological assumptions, but the classrooms provide the inevitable proving ground. (Hanson, "English" 5)

At the national level of the profession, then, the debate between writing
and literature had widened, rather than being resolved. Individual departments would ultimately have to confront the composition/literature controversy because no two departments share the same history, the same
range, or the same vision:[12]

The local impact of a national policy statement depends upon resident
assumptions about appropriate domains of inquiry, methodology, epistemology, and theory. And the way that impact plays out depends
upon the administrative structuring of the discipline at any given institution as well as on external demands for accountability—from the
public, from the legislature, from accrediting bodies. (Hanson,
"English" 5–6)

Recognizing and valuing the diverse voices within the department and
engaging large and small groups in the intellectual work of rethinking our
curriculum, we were participating in what anthropologist Clifford Geertz
describes as a fundamental "refiguration" of the topologies of knowledge:
"a phenomenon general enough and distinctive enough to suggest that what
we are seeing is not just another redrawing of the cultural map—the moving of a few disputed borders, the marking of some more picturesque
mountain lakes—but an alteration of the principles of mapping. Something
is happening to the way we think about the way we think" (165–66). We
identified criteria that our curriculum would have to meet for both students
and faculty, recognizing that currently it neither addressed mutually
informing conflicts, as Gerald Graff proposes in *Professing Literature* and
Beyond the Culture Wars, nor encouraged integration and collaboration, as
Ernest Boyer urges in *College: The Undergraduate Experience.*

If we are to engage students in the issues of the discipline, we need to
admit them to the discipline as participants rather than as observers.
Our comprehensive curriculum reform seeks to favor integration and

to acknowledge—in classrooms as well as in professional journals—our epistemological, theoretical, and interpretive conflicts. By confronting our differing perceptions about the nature and origin of knowledge, we confront the assumptions that shape our pedagogies. Our faculty represent the full range from a positivist model of teaching centered on the transmission of skills (composition) and knowledge (literature) to a transactional model of teaching that engages the student as an active participant in his or her learning, working in collaboration with other students and the teacher. Our goal is to enable all faculty to use their talents as effectively as possible while we empower our students to place into perspective their knowledge gained through active inquiry. (Hanson, "English" 7)

Key to our working definition of English was renewal of the dialectical relationship between poetics, the study of interpreting texts, and rhetoric, the study of creating texts. Through dialogic collaboration, we developed four new courses and an embedded portfolio requirement to embody that reconception and provide opportunity for all our majors to develop as writers while they grow as critical readers. The four-course English Studies core would serve as the skeleton on which all of the majors would be fully revised in the next 2-year catalog cycle.

FACULTY REWARDS

One of my colleagues told me that I had ruined the word *opportunity* for him because I had looked for and offered so many to colleagues when I was chair and because they usually meant work. But looking for opportunities to grow, learn, and impact the quality of our students' learning was already a habit and one other mark of respect for my colleagues. As Basic Writing Coordinator, I looked for grants to support program, collaborative, or individual research and funds to support travel to conferences. Because travel funds were becoming increasingly dependent on acceptance to present a conference paper, and nontenure- as well as tenure-line faculty all became eligible for departmental travel funds in 1986, the impetus to disseminate their work beyond the classroom increased significantly. As chair in 1992–1995, I encouraged and supported grant applications and looked for every opportunity to increase our funds for professional travel. After seeking faculty help to create the most equitable policy for distribution, I managed our allocations along with messages about our productivity so that every spring our college dean reassigned funds undesignated by other departments to us—a significant boost to our allocation and one measure of respect for colleagues.

Providing or recommending opportunities for colleagues and publicly recognizing accomplishments, while contributing to individuals' satisfaction within the community, paled next to my goal of revising our primary faculty reward system. Anticipating an increasing number of retirements through the 1990s, I wanted to have a clear concept of faculty expectations and rewards to offer to potential faculty hires. On our campus, salary documents originate in departments, whereas promotion and tenure documents originate at the university level. With a heavily tenured department in 1992, we had a significant number of tenure-line faculty who would never or rarely have to construct a full promotion and tenure document again. Some were engaged in nontraditional scholarship. I hoped to enlist broad support for radically revising our salary document, but I knew that would entail reimagining scholarship. Boyer's *Scholarship Reconsidered*, true to Emerson's notion of scholarship as a mosaic of discovery, integration, application, and teaching, seemed to capture the whole of a scholar's life of inquiry. The scholarly work involved with administration, faculty development, curricular development, or writing texts had a place in the mosaic. The traditional *service* category could then capture a scholar's good citizenship in the scholarly community. Reimagining scholarship, however, would not happen easily: There had been too many acrimonious battles over criteria and documentation requirements for salary committee deliberations, and too many faculty members still sported bruises. I turned to shared inquiry again, distributing copies of *Scholarship Reconsidered* to the salary committee that first fall. I requested that they familiarize themselves with the concepts before beginning the salary-review process based on our current document and, following the review, to be prepared to discuss how those concepts might have altered their appraisals of any of their colleagues' work. We repeated the process for the next 2 years, expanding the number of people in the department familiar with the concepts with the intention of drafting a document reflective of the Boyer model in the spring of the third year—1995. The opportunity to bring Charles Glassick to campus that spring, substituting for the ill Ernest Boyer, delayed the draft but expanded discussion, particularly toward issues that appeared in Boyer's last project, the 1997 *Scholarship Assessed*. The following summer, the colleague who had chaired the third salary committee drafted the initial version of the document we adopted that fall, during the first year of his term as chair.

To measure how thoroughly we reimagined scholarship, we can look to department documents. We still largely use the salary document adopted in November 1995. Its preamble places scholarship within a Boyer-like plan; it exemplifies scholarship throughout by reference to discovery, integration, application, and teaching; and it requires each tenure-line faculty member to submit an "Individual Scholarship Plan" based on both Boyer's *Scholarship Reconsidered* and a Ball State document, "A Different Dawn,"[13] which further spells out a Teacher-Scholar model for Ball State University. A recent internal report on "The Teacher-Scholar at Ball State University as Reflected in the Department of English" notes, "This [salary] document illustrates the most specific use in the department of Boyer's concept of scholarship, and its use over the years has resulted in the department's attempt to look both at Boyer's 'mosaic' of talent in the department, and to recognize the benefits of having faculty members reflect on their scholarship plans, goals, and results." Assigned time requests and reports ask faculty members to place projects for which they are requesting assigned time within the context of their Individual Scholarship Plans. Neither the Promotion and Tenure document nor the Graduate Faculty Application document specifically mentions any part of the Boyer model, but in practice the committees have broadened their understanding of "research" by respecting and giving credit for scholarship that has undergone peer review.

The internal report also comments on our influence beyond the department, an influence that we may well not have had without intentional shared intellectual work:

> The history and current health of the "teacher-scholar" model at Ball State University is intricately connected to the role that concept has played in shaping the Department of English since the late 80's, but specifically since 1989. Beginning with the role Linda Hanson played as assistant chair and continuing through her years as chairperson and those of the colleagues who succeeded her, the department has worked to infuse key principles of the "teacher-scholar" model, and specifically of the Scholarship of Teaching, into the decision-making principles of the department. Then, even more critically, to make sure that those principles are followed in hiring, promotion, tenure, salary, and assigned time decisions.

LEGACY

What lasting impact did my feminist practices have on the department? The legacy is mixed. Our undergraduate curriculum is stronger and more coherent than it was; we have a more coherent, holistic concept of our professional lives embedded in some of our personnel documents and in our practices; and faculty work together and talk across disciplinary areas. However, succeeding chairs did not intentionally nurture communal knowledge through the dialogic collaboration essential to integrate new faculty into the department, and the second stage of curriculum reform faltered as a result. That same internal report recognizes the need for such feminist methods: "A department culture that understands, supports, and practices the Scholarship of Teaching may be intentionally established, but it needs continual nurturing if for no other reason because faculty and students regularly enter and leave the department." Such nurturing depends on situated knowledge and must be intentional, fed by recursive habits of inquiry and critical reflection.[14]

14

COMPUTERS AND COMPOSITION ONLINE

Performing Feminist Community Amid the Politics of Digital Scholarship

Kristine Blair

Lanette Cadle

Kris Blair: As a computers and writing specialist, I can partially trace my entrance into the field to a joint meeting Pam Takayoshi and I had with Gail Hawisher and Cynthia Selfe at CCCC's conference in 1995, not long after our graduations from Purdue University, where both scholars had been frequent visitors to our doctoral program in Rhetoric. Encouraging our desire to edit a collection that later became *Feminist Cyberscapes*, both Gail and Cindy spoke of the way in which the proposed book would not only make a contribution to the field, but also help to create a sense of feminist community. Since that time 10 years ago, the positive mentoring model that Gail and Cindy provided has stuck with me because it suggests a nonhierarchical, coequal model among colleagues despite the differences in rank and stature within the profession, as well as continued mentorship from Gail and Cindy as I assumed the editorship of *Computers and Composition Online* in 2002. Part of this mentorship resulted from the continued ethics of care that Gail and Cindy have provided to me, believing that the national profile the full editorship would bring me would in fact enhance an upcoming promotion to full professor.

199

At the same time, however, scholarship such as Hawisher and Selfe's May 2004 *CCC* article and their more extended *Literate Lives in the Information Age* suggest a type of nonhierarchical collaboration with research subjects, as well as former and current graduate students, who become coauthors and cocontributors to the scholarly dialogue. As Janice Lauer suggests, this process of mentoring and graduate student professional development contributes to an ethic of care: "A graduate program makes a field's tone palpable for students, modeling the way in which members of the profession relate to each other whether at conferences or in print" ("Graduate" 234). Lauer notes the forums in which such mentoring can take place include "collaborative projects and papers, working together as a faculty, and meeting weekly with students as they work on dissertations" (234). Admittedly, as feminist teachers and researchers within our discipline assume administrative responsibilities, it is vital that we not reinscribe the structures we hope to subvert, but rather perform feminist administration in ways that impact both our local and disciplinary communities. Although Lauer acknowledges the importance of a feminist ethic of care, she simultaneously advocates and problematizes mentoring processes, questioning their viability in light of the increased scholarly demands of the discipline, including more pressure to professionalize and publish in graduate school and a continued emphasis on single-authored academic stardom, in which traditional agonistic stances against theories and theorists are commonplace. Lauer does not mention journal editing. However, Hawisher and Selfe's discussion of the edited collection as a genre in the same volume notes that both journal and collection editing allow graduate students to become part of a network of colleagues. Indeed, I can recall Cindy's words to Pam and to me about *Feminist Cyberscapes*: "Do this; you'll meet lots of people." As both Hawisher and Selfe contend, editorial roles on journals are exceptionally helpful in that graduate students are more comfortably and successfully able to dialogue with new or more established colleagues when "they had some additional and previous contact with the individual and when they had already worked with them in some context" ("Edited" 117).

Since the publication of the collection in which Lauer's and Hawisher and Selfe's chapters appeared, much has changed on the academic publishing front. More and more opportunities and expectations exist for multimodal literacies in the scholarly publication process, with graduate students and faculty alike possessing varied levels of technological competency to enable more digital design and delivery. At the same time, not that much has changed in traditional expectations for the academic job market, as well as tenure and promotion. The emphasis on single-authored print scholarship in departments of English remains a privileged benchmark, and admittedly my initial inclination was to submit this chapter as a single-authored piece, particularly in light of other coauthored pieces with current and former female graduate students. Despite this privileging, I ultimately realized I could not ethically advocate and chronicle within this chapter a mentoring model in the administration of *Computers and Composition Online* and not include the voice of the senior editor, Lanette Cadle, then a doctoral student in Rhetoric and Writing. Cadle has guided the development of the journal and has had the most active role in leading the editorial team at Bowling Green, as well as continuing her work with contributors new to digital authorship as an assistant professor at Missouri State. Thus, our collaboration on this chapter is a performance of the feminist practices we advocate and from which we have both benefited in our own careers through the mentoring we have received. In this sense, we also are aligned with Judith Butler's original charge for feminists to view the performative as an opportunity for subversion, disruption, and agency (*GT* 147). Moreover, for Theresa Enos, such a relationship between Lanette and me represents a form of (wo)mentoring, a process that moves away from hierarchical concepts of the master, tutor, or model to that of advisor, supporter, and sponsor ("Mentoring" 138), with these latter terms suggesting a reciprocity among individuals and groups.

As we stress within this chapter, online journal editorship provides a unique opportunity for the feminist mentoring of both male and female doctoral students in rhetoric and composition. Not unlike the learning community model set by both Gail and Cindy at the University of Illinois and Michigan Tech (and now, at Ohio State University) respectively, the evolution of *Computers and Composition Online* at Bowling Green State University has actively involved doctoral students as designers and editors, stressing not only collaborative administration of the journal, but also collaborative, interactive forms of hypertextual scholarship that is better aligned to a feminist agenda than traditional print scholarship. Such approaches also extend to the peer review process as we attempt to encourage new voices in new media to publish their work. Inevitably, these collaborations move away from isolating hierarchical models of mentoring and publishing within the academy (Ede and Lunsford) to promote a learning community of teacher-scholars within computers and writing at both the local and national levels. Therefore, this chapter profiles the process of establishing the *Computers and Composition Online* community at Bowling Green State University, theorizing the ways that a feminist approach to journal administration helps prepare technologically literate future faculty and new media scholars while acknowledging the institutional power relationships within the university and within academic publishing that often hinder this mentoring and community-building process.

AN INTRODUCTION IN A SECOND VOICE

Lanette Cadle: My own entrance into the field of computers and writing was similar to Kris'. Liz Monske and I met with Kris Blair, Gail Hawisher, and Cynthia Selfe over hot cocoa and coffee at a wet Watson conference in 2002. The redesign and rebirth of *Computers and Composition Online* had barely begun, but we were excited about the potential it had, both as a venue for scholarship and an opportunity for service to the field. Of course my interest in technology and writing as a graduate student was already a clear trend. My classroom work as a PhD student had a constant connection to the digital realm—especially blogs—and my previous journal experience as an associate editor for *Mid-American Review* most likely contributed to that interest. However, that meeting with Cindy and Gail was especially significant to me because it marked the point where my efforts and interests were seen as acts by a scholarly peer. The top–down mentoring I was familiar with from my years in the business world gave way to a new concept—a more feminist incarnation that treats significant contribution as significant worth. I was finally in a world without a glass ceiling.

That kind of mentorship—the kind that takes "the concept of collaboration a step further" (Tulley and Blair 60)—is part of their strategy in "Ewriting Spaces as Safe, Gender-Fair Havens: Aligning Political and Pedagogical Possibilities," which, more than coincidently, is coauthored. Although the article has a pedagogical focus, the feminist classroom practices described extend well outside the walls. Using the article as a case in point, Christine Tulley, at the time the article was written, was a recent PhD who in the past had worked in the traditional sense with Kris Blair, her dissertation director. Taking the idea of mentorship even further, the 2004 *CCO* article from the *Professional Development* section, "Class Review: What Video Games Have to Teach Us About Learning and Literacy (James Gee)" (Tulley et al.), is a true example of when coauthorship springs more from the feminist concept of a community where all members, including undergraduates, have significant contributions to offer than from the agonistic authorship hierarchy more common in the sciences, making the article a performative result of mentoring. Others in the field of composition see value in such collaborations, notably Andrea Lunsford in "Rhetoric, Feminism and the Politics of Textual Ownership." Lunsford describes "a new rhetoric of authorship" and advocates an alternative to what she sees as a trend toward the corporate author and the commodification of scholarly work:

> I hope that, working together, feminist rhetoricians can create, enact, and promote alternative forms of agency and ways of owning that

would shift the focus from owning to owning up; from rights and enti-
tlements to responsibilities (the ability to respond) and answerability;
from a sense of the self as radically individual to the self as always in
relation; and from a view of agency as invested in and gained through
the exchange of tidy knowledge packages to a view of agency as resid-
ing in what Susan West defines as the "unfolding action of a discourse;
in the knowing and telling of the attentive rhetor/responder rather than
in static original ideas." (190)

If our works and thoughts are to be seen as only so much lucre on the road
to tenure or promotion, then, yes, single authorship is the top tier of a
golden pyramid. However, if what we do as avowedly feminist scholars is
more than that, if building community truly works to benefit all, then we
need to not break the chain of women helping women, and people helping
people, and we need to help others as a matter of course. Sometimes it really is about the whole being greater than the sum of its parts—it is about
performing community, not just preaching it.

BUILDING A COMMUNITY PRESENCE

Since the publication in 1997 of Todd Taylor's "Politics of Electronic
Scholarship," in which he notes that the grammars, shapes, and styles of
electronic discourse have yet to be defined and presented as an alternative
to print scholarship, our discipline increasingly embraces more multimodal
literacies in teaching and scholarship at a time when disciplines across the
board are experiencing a "crisis in scholarly publishing." Because this crisis
includes skyrocketing costs of academic journal subscriptions and the
financial collapse of academic presses, it leaves fewer places to publish the
traditional scholarly article or book-length project. Thus, it is vital that we
work to create new digital communities that acknowledge this shift and
prepare future faculty to produce digital scholarship in multimodal genres.
Of course, online journals in the larger field of rhetoric and writing and the
subdiscipline of computers and writing are not new. The grassroots, graduate student-driven design and development of *Kairos: A Journal of
Rhetoric, Technology, and Pedagogy* is a long-standing prestigious forum
for both new and established digital rhetoric scholars to publish their electronic scholarship. Although the *Kairos* editors may not necessarily refer to
their approach as feminist, the principles of disrupting the privileging of
print and the hierarchical model of publishing established as opposed to
newer voices in the field creates an inclusive space that is certainly consistent with various feminist pedagogical models, in which the administrative

leadership is shared among graduate students, pretenure and nontenure-track faculty, in addition to established voices in the field who serve on the editorial board.

Moreover, what makes a journal such as *Kairos* unique in its editorial process is the move away from a strictly blind, hierarchical review process that has typically kept newer voices from finding homes for their work. Instead, *Kairos* has relied on a two-tiered process in which all editorial board members, regardless of institutional or professional rank, have a chance to weigh in online with their assessment of a submission's strengths and weaknesses with those who are successful in receiving a positive review in this first tier moving toward a more collaborative editorial relationship with two members of the editorial board to strengthen the piece in form and content. Although there has been concern expressed about the value and rigor of online scholarship because of the presumed lack of a clear refereeing process, *Kairos* and other journals are clear about the peer-reviewed nature of their submission process.

Certainly, the development of *Computers and Composition Online* attempts to mirror the collaborative editorial stance of both the print version of the journal as well as *Kairos,* and our origins are rooted in collaborative, team-development models of project management. Building an online presence and promoting it to the external community was and is a vital collaborative task. Our initial efforts to build this presence were supported by a number of individuals at Bowling Green, in particular Lanette, who was asked to come on board early in the process because of her existing editorial experience on another journal housed at Bowling Green, the nationally recognized *Mid-American Review,* as well as her growing and continuing interests in web-based writing and newer genres such as blogs. Together, both of us collaboratively developed the mission statement for the journal, as well as the journal sections: *Theory into Practice, Virtual Classroom, Print to Screen, Professional Development,* and *Reviews,* with the blog to be added later.

Although experienced in web design, neither one of us necessarily felt that the journal interface was a two-person job, and thus we worked with a group of graduate students enrolled in an online documentation course taught by instructor Angela Haas, now an Assistant Professor at Illinois State University. Admittedly, this collaboration initially mirrored a traditional project management process in which the students viewed us, in the context of their class, as "clients." The students reviewed the existing interface that was in place at the University of Texas at Austin, who graciously hosted the online component from 1997 to 2002, listened to the goals Lanette and Kris had, and came up with two beta-versions as part of their final project for their course. Perhaps this aspect of project management might not necessarily be considered feminist. Yet our collaborative efforts with Angela Haas to work with her graduate students on a project that mirrored the actual workplace practices in which several of them would engage upon graduation did constitute mentoring. Enos urges that we "define mentoring so that its activities are not split between nurturing (female) and real work (male)" ("Mentoring" 142), and "plan for graduate students to meet weekly with one or more faculty members for purposes of introducing students to the profession" (143). Hence, this process was beneficial in helping students in our scientific and technical communication program to establish a professional identity not only through authentic client tasks, but also in a way that equipped them to assume collaborative leadership roles. Indeed, some problems did occur when it became clear that one member of this original design team was assuming more leadership responsibility, in effect becoming a spokesperson for design choices that did not necessarily reflect the consensus of the group.

Because of this minor, but noticeable problem in establishing coequal relationships, we worked to alleviate these hierarchical models by assigning an editorial role for each of the sections of *Computers and Composition Online* (CCO) outlined above, encouraging each editor to write mission statements for each section that we then collaboratively reviewed and edited in a Blackboard discussion forum. Understanding that issues of site maintenance, design work, and file management required a special editorial role, we asked then doctoral candidate Richard Colby to assume the position of Design Editor. He was able to take the original suggestions of the original online documentation students and work collaboratively to recreate the logo, set up file directories, and collaboratively build the interface for the journal.

IF YOU BUILD IT, WILL THEY COME?
THE SUBMISSION PROCESS

So there we were, with a website all dressed up and ready to go. However, all the best design features and mission statements pale without that all-important feature—content. Early in the start-up process, we spent a fair amount of time drafting a call for submissions. The desire to "honor the scholarship of integration and the scholarship of application" from "teacher-scholars" (Gebhardt, "Scholarship" 44) was a central concern. The goal was to encourage all teacher-scholars in the field, regardless of stature, to submit their work. It was our hope that the inclusion of categories such as *The Virtual Classroom* and *Professional Development* would lend ample opportunities for voices within our field that may not have found expression in other journals. Theory definitely has a place in *CCO*, but pedagogy is equally honored as a site for research and as a jumping-off point for more theoretically based pieces. This purposeful deconstruction of the academic publication hierarchy of theory over pedagogy to a more egalitarian, coequal view of what is really the heart of who we are and what we do as compositionists would, we hoped, also lead to a stream of fresh faces submitting their latest and best work in computers and writing. We wanted submissions from the cutting edge, and that is often work from graduate students nearing completion of their degrees and from harried instructors teaching four classes a semester who find the time anyway to write about what they love best—computers, composition, and all the issues in between.

With that in mind, we distributed our first flyers at the Watson Conference in hopes of having our first issue ready in the spring. Looking back, we were wildly optimistic. That meant that almost immediate submissions, and very good ones at that, were needed to make the projected 3-month timeframe from submission to review to publication. Also, we had no idea what proportion of submissions would be web-publishable. In the past, authors would submit wholly text-based documents perhaps in hopes that the text would indicate the worth of the projected web piece to come. Our vision, however, meant that the article must be much more than text converted to HTML. It needed to be visually and hypertextually aware, preferably envisioned as a creature of the web right from the start, one that offers what Carolyn Handa calls "irresistible temptations to jump from one text to another" (169). Our submissions requirements indicated as much, but old publication habits die hard. The privileging of text in the tenure process can mean that academic authors see the web as a text-enabler, rather than a mode of expression of its own with uniquely visual and oral components. What Lanette calls the "endless scroll" article, one that unrolls text like a papyrus, has the same drawbacks for the web reader as it does for the one holding a physical scroll: It is unwieldy and cumbersome. We were ready for more than that.

As it turned out, the peer review process takes care of much of this. Our editorial board covers a broad range of subspecialty areas, and all members are web-savvy. However, telling web authors in an essay-like review what to do dimensionally sometimes falls short, and that is where editing and mentoring can blend together. The traditional view of an editor is one who "edits," who cleans up the niggling errors in the stream of words so that ideas can flow freely, a role that sets up an opposition of "expert" and "novice." As feminists, we shun that opposition and seek to collaborate with web authors to achieve the best possible work.

ACTIVE EDITING AS A MODE OF MENTORING

How might the review process become a form of feminist mentoring and still maintain the integrity of rigorous peer assessment? A parallel can be found in feminist classroom practice, where the instructor is seen as a facilitator, rather than a lecturer imparting wisdom. For example, an early submission to *CCO* that eventually became Michael Cripps' article "#FFFFFF, #000000, & #808080: Hypertext Theory and WebDev in the Composition Classroom" (Cripps) was visually beautiful from the start and used the module method of organization that commonly works well in web articles. However, the sections still functioned as just that—sections. Two things were missing at that point—more theory, the why behind the description of what was done in the classroom, and intertextuality, taking the existing text and stitching it together with cross-references within its text, as well as augmentations from other sources that hypertext makes possible. As editors, we firmly believed that this article in particular, because it was about hypertext theory, must not fail to use that theory as an object lesson in its own construction. That this collaborative dialogue benefited both author and editors was clear when Cripp's published piece in *CCO* received the *Kairos* Best WebText Award for 2004–2005.

At the same time, as a graduate student mentoring "up," this poses an interesting dilemma, one answered by the definition of comentoring as a practice "rooted in a feminist tradition that fosters an equal balance of power between participants, seeks to integrate emotion into the academic professional experience, and values paid and unpaid work" (McGuire and Reger 54). In this case, practice followed theory, and the author took the editor review comments to heart perhaps more easily because they were joined with assurances that Kris, Lanette, and the reviewers all loved the piece and what it had to say. The goal was to make it the best article it could be, not to reshape or twist it to match some arbitrary mark of achievement or to correct errors. The collaborative work done by e-mail between author and editors led to a richer, better piece.

Another area where feminist mentoring between editors and author can define the resulting article is the *Reviews* section. In that area in particular, author time constraints, typical of the heavy teaching/service load many compositionists share, mean that what should be the simplest and easiest article to complete for the web (the review) becomes the unrecoverable piece of procrastination that leads to a missed deadline. In a more traditional publication, that would mean the editors moving on to the next review in the queue or having an in-house writer take over the byline and complete the review.

At *CCO*, there have been times when an editor has literally become a silent collaborator for a reviewer and converted a review text to a web document simply because the reviewer was caught in a unavoidable, usually end-of-semester time crunch. At first glance, this may look more like mothering than mentoring, or one of Theresa Enos' "dangers of mothering in the academy" ("Gender" 65). However, because of the nature of reviews and the need for them to be timely, this type of collaboration, although not planned, benefits all—the reviewer still gets published, the journal gets a timely review instead of pushing it ahead 6 months, and the graduate-student editor gains valuable web-drafting experience. It must be emphasized that this sort of behind-the-scenes webwork is only possible in reviews where the structure is simple and elements that are in the forefront in other section articles such as hypertext, sound, flash, or any other graphically based elements are not a central part of the composition. Also, we maintain as feminist editors and mentors that it still would be better for all concerned if authors kept a lively interest in all phases of the publishing process. That is how the best work is done. All the same, the wish for what is best for the journal as a whole, rather than for personal credit or another vita line, lends additional flexibility when last-minute crises or unforeseen errors occur.

The concept of errors and the daunting task that proofreading becomes when hypertext is involved is yet another example of where feminist editing/mentoring has an advantage over a more traditional approach. In traditional journal editing, a common proofreading method with many variations is when the staff takes the article and pairs off, one person reading the manuscript text aloud spelling each word, placing each stop, and detailing every aspect of the text aloud. This process repeats several times as the text moves up the chain of command.

The paired proofreading method leads to a high degree of accuracy, but it also has some interesting implications about ownership and hierarchy. One implication is that, once the text leaves the authors' hands, they have no more responsibility for it. The other implication is that the important work of publishing is ours as editors and ours alone; authors are the novices who create the pieces, but the next step up, the experts, make it publishable. Both ideas are seriously flawed and, when taken into the multidimensional world of web publishing, quickly fall apart. For one thing, the staff for *CCO*, like many web journals, runs much leaner than the typical literary or scholarly journal. We do not have a staffroom full of 20 to 30 MFA or PhD students to do the page-by-page proofing. Instead, Kris does at least two holistic reads, Lanette does a line-by-line read, and our design editor does a thorough code check. When Lanette finds typos—and they are inevitable—instead of correcting them herself with the hierarchical implications that sets up, she writes down a line-by-line check sheet that is e-mailed back to the web author(s) for updating. That way, choices that may appear to be errors can be explained and kept, and responsibility for clean copy is retained by the author. As a result, even at the word and sentence level, mentoring can lead to a more efficient work environment and also has the potential for higher quality work in the future from authors who now see their work with an editor's eye due to our willingness to let them be part of the entire process.

FEMINIST MENTORING AS OPEN-SOURCE SCHOLARSHIP

A final issue that mentoring in publishing necessarily intersects is that of intellectual property. In today's increasingly corporate culture, who owns what is a pivotal concern, and the traditional print journal answers the question with first-rights copyright. How then does a more collaborative view of publishing, as we have described in this chapter, fit in this picture? The answer for many is the open-source model taken from software development. *CCO* acknowledges and embraces the collaborative and nonhierarchical view that the transplanted open-source movement in academia advocates. Early on we chose to publish Laurie Taylor and Brendan Riley's "Open Source in Academia" not only because of the timeliness and importance of its content, but also because of how well it fit with our own vision for the future of academia. As they point out, "nearly all print publications are released under traditional copyright, which requires written permission and/or fees for scholars wishing to reproduce such work. Such practices make some texts difficult to obtain or to teach" (online). The feminist principles of mentoring discussed in this chapter clearly give an answer to the problems that initiated this movement.

Fair use, first author/second author hierarchies, and other intellectual property difficulties cease to be issues when community is valued over a more corporate model. In fact, Lanette contends that the academic open-source movement is merely feminist practice in new clothes, unfortunately ones that often disguise the feminist concepts with combative, agonist rhetoric. For example, a common term for advocates of open-source publication is *copyfighters*, an obvious play on the word *copyright*. Using combative language like this to define self is far from coincidental, because there is a pervasive sense of "us against them" expressed within the movement (i.e., the old "let's stick it to the man" [meaning traditional copyright publishers] polemic). Agonistic invective does not mesh well with a collaborative, coequal building of a community of scholars aspiring for the building of knowledge. Especially when it comes to academic publication, the *them* railed against may well be *us*, making the ephemeral *them* a shadow bully.

To use *Computers and Composition Online* as an example, on October 27, 2004, a discussion thread at *Kairosnews* began by congratulating us on publishing "Open Source in Academia," but quickly questioned why the authors chose to publish it with us, rather than with a journal that uses the Creative Commons license. Interestingly enough, at that time, none of the journals in which the article could have been placed displayed the Creative Commons logo. The resulting request from the authors to use a Creative Commons license for the article was received positively, as, indeed, the collaborative process involved in producing the article had resulted in a dialogue between Kris and Lanette about Creative Commons and how to best incorporate its principles into the journal as a whole. The authors also had been debating which level of Creative Commons license to use. In other words, the discussion thread copyfighters ended up "winning" a "battle" that not only didn't exist, but also had already been "won." The process of feminist mentoring and publication had already placed value on this most practical incarnation of fair use, and it had done so without recriminations or setting up any straw men to get the job done. Keeping lines of communication open during publication and beyond, as well as valuing the input of all contributors to the publication process, helps solidify a true digital community where knowledge is more than a commodity.

A COLLABORATIVE CONCLUSION

Since moving *CCO* to Bowling Green State University, we have encouraged each of our in-house section editors to research and solicit submissions primarily through their attendance at national conferences—something that has led to the type of networks that Hawisher and Selfe chronicle with both edited collections and journal editorship. This process has been particularly beneficial in establishing a peer-mentoring network among graduate students here at Bowling Green and those at other institutions. For instance, Lanette has worked extensively with new graduate student authors to reshape their scholarship for an electronic venue. In a number of cases, graduate student authors, not unlike the leadership of the original graduate student editors at journals like *Kairos*, have clearly taken the lead in producing and submitting digital scholarship, equally high quality in both content and format, something that is not always as equally balanced in digital submissions. By encouraging web-based submissions from graduate students, we also are working to change an academic culture in which, despite increasing balance among print and digital scholarship, promotion and tenure documents still often fail to equally consider or value either collaborative or electronic scholarship, relying on a single-authored print model that has traditionally privileged more hierarchical publishing processes. Such efforts are inherently feminist. As Kathleen Blake Yancey has suggested, both feminist research and rhetoric are invested in recovering, re-reading, extrapolating, and conceptualizing (156), and all within formats that allow for the narration of and reflection on these performative processes that we have included within this chapter.

In assessing the feminist mentoring potential of administering a journal such as *CCO*, an important distinction to make is that any successful mentoring initiative will include an ideology of collaborative coequal administration, reward, and recognition for such work. For us this has recently included collaborative poster sessions at the CCCC's Computer Connection and the Editors' Roundtable for the preconference Research Network Forum. Perhaps a culminating moment for all of us here at Bowling Green occurred in Spring 2003, when both Gail Hawisher and Cindy Selfe met with most members of the editorial team who were in attendance at the CCCC to celebrate the inaugural online issue, a type of mentoring and support that mirrored the session Pam Takayoshi and Kris Blair had with Gail and Cindy at the CCCC nearly 10 years earlier. In this sense, feminist journal administration does indeed resonate with an ethic of care among a network of colleagues that is typical of the computers and writing community as a whole. The scope of this network is most recently evident in the "Community Voices" sections of James Inman's *Computers and Writing: The Cyborg Era*, in which new and established voices tell stories about, among other things, how they came to be active in the computers and writing community. That we at *CCO* are able to both benefit from and extend this model of community of teacher-scholars is a testament to its success.

AFTERWORD

Echoes From the Trenches and the Feminists Who "Dig" Them

Krista Ratcliffe

Rebecca Rickly

Because our "Introduction" opens with the 2003 Biennial Feminisms and Rhetorics Conference where this project originated, we felt it fitting that this "Afterword" conclude with the 2005 conference, where we, along with Chris Farris, presented a panel on this collection's findings. During that panel's question-and-answer session, Nan Johnson asked where better than this conference to confer about the troubled intersections of feminist principles and administrative practices. We agree. Consequently, we wish to thank all of our colleagues there who expressed ideas for and interest in this project and who inspired us to think more deeply about echoes from the administrative trenches and the feminists who "dig" them (pun intended).

But we also want to extend this conversation beyond the conference. Based on our conversations there, we decided that this "Afterword" should not simply summarize our contributors' voices, but rather supplement them. Given our desire to provide as many successful role models as possible, we solicited advice via e-mail interviews from feminist administrators too busy to contribute to this collection, five of whom responded. Given our desire to consider how feminism and administration are inflected by issues of diversity (e.g., race, class, and nationality), we culled (non)administration scholarship and reflected on our own administrative experiences and then laid both alongside the e-mail interviews. And given our desire to keep conversations about feminism and administration in play, we decided not simply to call for further research, but also to provide a website that supplements this book (cf. Appendix and www.femadmin.org). Laying solicited e-mail interviews alongside (non)administration scholarship and our own reflections with an eye toward continuing conversations on feminism and administration, this "Afterword" pays homage to the voices contributing and not contributing to this collection—voices that have inspired us, challenged us, humbled us, and become friends of our minds.

ADVICE FROM E-MAIL INTERVIEWS
AND (NON)ADMINISTRATION SCHOLARSHIP

Our e-mail interviews invited administrators not contributing to this collection to respond informally to five questions:

1. What administrative positions have you held?
2. What (if anything) prepared you for these positions?
3. How has being a woman/being a feminist (either one or both) affected your administrative activities, positively and/or negatively?
4. What do you consider essential qualities of a good administrator? As a good feminist?
5. What advice would you offer young women as they prepare to take on administrative positions for the first time?

Of all the e-mail invitations issued, five administrators responded: Cheryl Glenn (Professor, Penn State University), Gail Hawisher (Professor, University of Illinois), Andrea Lunsford (Professor, Stanford University), Carolyn Miller (Professor, North Carolina State University), and Carolyn Rude (Professor, Virginia Tech). We hope the patterns gleaned from their responses, laid alongside (non)administration scholarship and our own reflections, will provide pragmatic advice for budding and experienced administrators, whether feminist or not. In addition, we hope any gaps in the following discussions provide impetus for further reflection, conversation, and research.

1. What Administrative Positions Have You Held?

As expected, e-mail responses to this question vary because rhetoric and composition scholars fill myriad administrative posts. Traditional ones include: directors of first-year writing programs, directors/consultants of

WAC programs, directors of writing centers, and directors of graduate programs. These discipline-specific positions are usually held by tenured and/or untenured professors, with assistant positions often being held by graduate students. Because these jobs train professors and graduate students to be proficient administrators, they often serve as stepping stones to other institutional and national administrative roles. For example, rhetoric and composition administrators have also served their own institutions as vice provosts, directors of centers for teaching excellence, deans, department chairs, departmental vice chairs, and departmental consultants for issues as varied as curriculum design, assessment, teacher development programs, peer teaching evaluations, mentoring programs, and various interdisciplinary endeavors. Rhetoric and composition administrators have also served their national organizations, such as CCCC (Conference on College Composition and Communication), MLA (Modern Language Association), NCTE (National Council of Teachers of English), STC (Society for Technical Communicators), ATTW (the Association of Teachers of Technical Writing), TYCA (Two-Year College Association), and WPA (Council of Writing Program Administrators).

Given these opportunities, rhetoric and composition administrators benefit from considering intersections of theory and practice. Likewise, they benefit from considering these intersections in terms of feminism. Although in 1998 Amy Goodburn and Carrie Leverenz claimed that feminist WPA work remained "surprisingly undertheorized" (276), the journal *WPA: Writing Program Administration*, the online WPA archives, and the Shirley Rose/Bud Weiser collections function as mother lodes of information about theoretical and practical matters of writing program administration, and books by Susan Jarratt and Lynn Worsham and by Louise Phelps and Janet Emig provide chapters that theorize feminism and administration. This collection engages these discussions, and this "Afterword" also invites (non)administrative research voices into this conversation.

For example, rhetoric and composition administrators would do well to apply Malea Powell's question of imperialism to administration. She asks: ". . . can we take what we do best as a discipline—reflect, rethink, revisit, and revise the stories that create who we are? My hope is that we can begin to re-imagine ourselves, our pedagogies, our scholarship, our discipline [and, we would add, our administration] in relation to a long and sordid history of American imperialism" (428). Powell's hope invites administrators to consider how power differentials inform practical, theoretical, and political dimensions of administrative positions, particularly in terms of gender, race, ethnicity, and nationality.

The need for such consideration has been affirmed by Kris' experiences as a WPA. When a young man appealed his first-year writing grade, he claimed the instructor graded his work unfairly. What he did not say initially, because he did not want to be perceived as playing "the race card," was

that, as a young black man, he felt that the white instructor was inadvertent-
ly racist in ways that not only affected his papers' grades and comments,
but also hindered his performance in class. Admittedly, grade appeals cannot be judged solely on what students might have done in different situations. However, when another faculty member apprised Kris of the young
man's hesitancy to speak up, this appeal provided Kris the opportunity to
speak with the instructor about ways that gender and race intersect in the
classroom, especially in terms of differences between a teacher's intent and a
student's reception of that intent. This appeal also provided Kris an opportunity to speak with the student about ways to conceptualize race and personal performance in terms of deciding when and how to speak up. Just as
important, this appeal provided Kris a moment "[t]o come to terms with the
circumscribing nature of (our) whiteness" (Rich, "Notes" 219).

2. What (If Anything) Prepared You
for These Positions?

The e-mail respondents offer different responses to this question, but they
all agree that preparation comes in terms of people, personal initiative, and
training. As for people providing preparatory training for administrators,
the range runs from mothers to predecessors. According to Rude, her
mother taught her about making decisions within limited means, her children taught her to think of students as the "primary stakeholders in any
program," and her colleagues taught her to "value synergy and trust consensus." The value of support from colleagues—and also from friends—is
noted by Hawisher; also noted is the value of role models and mentors,
although the two may not always occupy the same body. For Hawisher,
mentors helped her to situate herself within academic administrative positions and to be cognizant of how best "to serve the generation of women
(and men) behind [her]." As Miller notes, the administrative staff in the
dean's office helped her learn her administrative jobs. As any WPA knows,
administrative staff in a department or writing program are instrumental in
providing administrators with information about running a program and
generating morale among the teaching staff. If a former administrator is
willing to provide transitional information, no one can be more helpful.
    According to several respondents, personal initiative and reflection on
its consequences are essential for administrative success. As Glenn reports,
networking to "ask for advice, help, direction, or money" is a valuable
administrative skill, as is employing research skills honed in PhD studies.
For Lunsford, initiative entails purposely taking leadership positions that
one can learn from and build on. For Miller, initiative means admitting
what you do not know and asking "whom to call, how to chase things
down, how to get an item to the attention of administrators and/or staff, . . .

how to run a meeting, how to motivate people, and how to follow through on something"—all of which may vary from institution to institution and from position to position.

As for training, Lunsford credits her graduate student work in writing program administration with training her to think like an administrator. Rude credits her rhetorical studies with providing her "a systematic was of reasoning about problems in communities and organizations," and Glenn credits attending university sessions on "personnel issues, academic policy, university budgets and strategic planning" with providing her a framework for understanding her university as a system. Unlike the respondents' experiences, current PhD students in rhetoric and composition programs benefit from graduate study in theories and practices of issues related to administration, such as program design, policy, diversity, and assessment. In answer to what, if anything, prepared her for her administrative positions, Rude has perhaps the most humorous, insightful, and succinct response: "Nothing and everything." Gleaning administrative lessons from all aspects of life (e.g., from parenting, coaching, socializing) is key to administrative success, because such reflections make administrators more aware of the metaphors that we administer by (e.g., mother/child, coach/player, friend), as well as the exigencies, constraints, and power differentials of such metaphors.

In the end, the question of preparation is difficult to answer because people and contexts differ. Each respondent's situation may be so different in mission, theory, design, and/or pedagogical method that finding a common administrative language across institutions can be difficult. What emerges, instead, is the feminist hope offered by Goodburn and Leverenz, who claim that, at their respective institutions, they "hope to create a language that the writing program staff can share for talking about resistance and conflict, not in personal but in institutional terms" (290). The acts of creating such a local language and acknowledging the theoretical assumptions undergirding that language are dependent on identifying and challenging existing terms, reinforcing the terms that work, revising the ones that do not, and constructing new terms that represent and promote the theoretical stance(s) built into the program while allowing room for individual teachers' own positions.

3. How Has Being a Woman/Being a Feminist (Either One or Both) Affected Your Administrative Activities, Positively and/or Negatively?

This question generated interesting reactions from e-mail respondents in terms of cultural and subject positions. When discussing current cultural positions of women administrators in the United States, Glenn notes two beneficial trends:

> Women can . . . take advantage of a special historical moment for
> women (and it's about time for this!!) at a confluence of two societal
> trends: more women are taking administrative positions, and we are
> recognizing a wider spectrum of administrative styles and successes
> (collaboration rather than authoritarianism, networking rather than
> hierarchy, and so on).

According to Lunsford, in this historical moment, women are recognizing
that "the glass ceiling is alive and well . . . though it isn't as thick as it used
to be." What is the best way to deal with this glass ceiling? Lunsford claims
that feminist theory provides grounds for action: When faced with an issue
to resolve or a problem to solve, she employs the heuristic—What would a
good feminist do?—a heuristic that often provides her an answer. Such
questions and answers, of course, beg questions of definition: What *kind* of
feminist? And good *for whom*? Both questions function as additional
heuristics, reinforcing once again the interconnectedness of feminist action
and theory and ethics.

In terms of particular subject positions, each e-mail respondent offers
advice for beginning administrators based on her own administrative experiences. Although this advice is grounded in particular times, places, and
experiences, it may be adapted by other administrators for their own situations when deemed appropriate. Some advice includes the following
injunctions:

1. Embrace incremental change. (Hawisher)
2. Believe that voiced and unvoiced opinions make a difference.
   (Hawisher)
3. Focus on helping students. (Rude)
4. Focus on serving the generation coming behind you. (Hawisher)
5. Recognize that women (must) frequently do their homework
   more than men for meetings. (Miller)
6. Do not take things for granted, be complacent, accept boundaries,
   or be self-satisfied. (Rude)

In addition, Rude identifies a diminishing, but still existent, problem facing
women in some institutions:

> Not every university culture will recognize the leadership of women.
> One way to deal with that unhappy truth is to work with it. At one
> point I realized that I could have quicker success negotiating with some
> male deans and the provost if I took my male chair to meetings. He
> might not say or do anything, but his presence gave the negotiations
> gravitas, and I could accomplish my objectives. In another university
> culture, such gaming might not be necessary.

Regardless of whether this particular gaming strategy is embraced, *gaming* is an apt metaphor for administration. It is a game with stakes and consequences for multiple players. But as a player in this game, an administrator should remember that her or his identity is not totally defined by the administrative position. As Kenneth Burke claims, all names (such as *woman, man,* and *administrator*) are synecdoches of identity (*Philosophy* 27-28), and every administrator has important parts of his or her identity that lie outside the workplace (e.g., family member, friend, community volunteer, researcher). In tough administrative times (and there will be some), keeping this idea in mind is an effective survival strategy.

When trying to survive and thrive in the academy, feminist administrators must resist the impulse of institutions to coopt or "other" them. In terms of the latter, feminist administrators would do well to heed the words of Renee Moreno when she speaks of how Latinos/as are othered in the academy: "Although the histories of U.S. Latinos/as are very different from histories of African Americans, Asian Americans, and Native Americans, I argue that within institutions these histories are often collapsed; we are all 'othered,' even objectified, our histories balkanized" (224). Moreno's words are pertinent here in three ways. First, they are obviously and importantly applicable to all Latinos/as in the academy. Second, although Moreno's claims focus on ethnicity, they may be read for this collection in terms of intersecting gender and ethnicity; that is, this book intends neither to balkanize feminists nor to erase our ethnic histories nor to deny the presumption of whiteness that haunts U.S. culture and, hence, administration. This collection does, however, intend to identify the gender balkanization that sometimes still exists within institutions. Third, Moreno's claims are applicable for feminist administrators, reminding us not to perpetuate gender or ethnic balkanization in the academy via our practices of hiring, curriculum design, textbook selections, and so on.

As a counter to ethnic and/or gender balkanization, feminist administrators would do well to embrace, instead, the idea of reciprocity. Reciprocity foregrounds the care for self-other identifications that is central to feminist ethics. Although Katrina Powell and Pamela Takayoshi define *reciprocity* in terms of researchers, their following claim could easily be adapted for feminist administrators: "Reciprocity requires that researchers [and administrators] pay close attention to their participants' needs as they evolve and be ready to embrace moments for reciprocity as they emerge. Thus, reciprocity requires an alert attention to context" (414). Powell and Takayoshi further develop the idea of reciprocity in terms of ethics:

> The classic rhetorical concept of *kairos* suggests at least two significant ethical dimensions to enacting reciprocal research [and administrative] relationships: (1) the appropriate form of reciprocity could be different

in different situations, and (2) moments of dissensus are generative indications of a need to pay attention to the purposes and needs of subjects that may not involve research [or administrative] aims. (415)

Reciprocity makes visible, once again, an oxymoronic linkage (i.e., the linking of agreement and dissensus, *both* of which may emerge from the grounds of reciprocity and *both* of which should be engaged).

4. What Do You Consider Essential Qualities of a Good Administrator? Of a Good Feminist?

This question generated e-mail responses that classify good administrators not just in terms of qualities, but also in terms of actions and goals. As for qualities, being curious and goal-oriented has served Glenn well. In addition, women's socialization can serve them well when it results in intellectual mobility and peripheral vision (Glenn). Such intellectual mobility enables administrators to "understand the persuasive power of both words and actions," and such peripheral vision enables administrators "to see, respect, and reward people around them, their work, experiences, talents, and time commitments" (Glenn). When combined with not being afraid to make decisions (Lunsford), such mobility and vision can help administrators construct a programmatic vision within which to teach and to learn, to mentor and to be mentored in return.

As for actions equated with good administrators, especially good feminist administrators, the e-mail respondents offered several options:

1. Listen. (Lunsford)
2. Collaborate. (Lunsford)
3. Prepare for meetings. (Hawisher)
4. Know the job. (Hawisher)
5. Develop a vision. (Hawisher)
6. Think about long-term consequences for people. (Rude)
7. Manage daily activities, such as keeping records, completing tasks on schedule, assessing, and planning. (Rude)
8. Perform "multiple roles—among them, advocate, mediator, motivator, delegator, instigator, supporter, colleague, organizer, leader, watchdog, gatekeeper, coordinator, officiator, auditor, lookout, forecaster, and probably mom." (Miller)
9. Assume good will on the part of all parties involved (even if they do not have it). (Hawisher)
10. Cultivate "patience" (even when you do not have it). (Hawisher)

Yet in addition to these injunctions, respondents offer a caveat: Women must still watch how they express emotion on the job because it still may be used to discredit them as weak, unstable, illogical, or bitchy.

As for goals, the most successful administrators, Glenn says, are those who "transform their individual goals into interests of the larger group—all of whom begin to work together toward a common goal" and who strive "constantly for inclusivity and invitation up, down, and across the university's population." Further, Glenn makes an important point about this inclusiveness: "Expanding the opportunities for women and other traditionally disenfranchised groups in higher education . . . not only *enhances the visibility of those groups* but *normalizes their roles*" (italics added). Only by normalizing such roles will the culture of any university or society change in ways that move beyond assimilation or tokenism.

Changing a culture presumes the existence of a community. When speaking about native Americans, Resa Crane Bizzaro makes the following claim about community: "Community renewal must begin with an examination of the paths of individual scholars who must then be heard as part of the collective history of the field of composition studies" (493). This claim may echo in the ears of feminist administrators in two ways. First, it signifies that feminist administrators must continue to publish their theories and practices of administration so as to be part of the discipline's scholarly conversation. Second, it signifies that whether designing programs, training teachers, chairing departments, or working as a vice provost, administrators must be aware of the histories they are writing as well as of who is being written in and out of these histories.

Contrary to popular belief, when writing such histories, feminist administrators do not focus on writing out men, but rather on inserting gender differences and gender equality into the story of administration. For example, the following claims by Bruce Horner and John Trimbur about the far-reaching effects of administrative decisions may be read for its potential inflections of gender:

> We might argue that composition courses and programs provide crucial opportunities for rethinking writing in the academy and elsewhere: spaces and times for students and teachers both to rethink what academic work might mean and be—who is and should be involved, the forms that work might take, the ends it might pursue, the practices that define it and which might be redefined. (621)

Thinking critically and creatively about such challenges and their gender inflections—indeed, thinking about such challenges and their inflections as possibilities—can make administrative work intellectually engaging and personally rewarding. These inflections of gender are complicated by inflections of whiteness, class, historical moment, and so on. Moreover, these inflections of gender and their intersections inform training, curriculum development, mentoring, pedagogy, and institutional program histories.

When writing such histories, feminists need to engage the role of women as administrators. Some women are appointed as token women administrators, not because of any administrative talent, and are tolerated accordingly. But that does not negate the fact that many women are, in fact, good administrators: They are well informed on the details of their programs; they can develop a vision grounded in these details; they can think systematically and system-wide when making decisions; they can act not just on what they want but on what the people being administered both desire and can actually do; and they are adept at multitasking. Even so, a woman administrator may find herself tokenized, perceived as different from other women, as one of the boys, even if she does not feel like one. The danger in such cases is that an institutionalized sexism may remain in place, celebrating its inclusiveness of one or two women, but continuing its tendency to make success difficult for many women via gendered assumptions concerning administration, teaching reviews, maternity leaves, and so on.

5. What Advice Would You Offer Young Women as They Prepare to Take on Administrative Positions for the First Time?

This question seemingly implies that feminists are only concerned with women, but that implication is false. As mentioned in the previous section, how young women are mentored in administrative positions is but one of many feminist concerns. For our e-mail respondents, this concern generated a list of 21 practical tips that may be employed by young women so that they may not simply survive administration but also excel at it. Of course, as with any advice, these tips must be adapted by readers—female or male, young or old, white or non-white—for their own administrative posts and local sites. These 21 tips focus on three categories: other people, the administrator, and institutional politics.

According to e-mail respondents, reflecting on other people is one of the best ways to learn administrative skills. Glenn advocates five ways to facilitate such learning:

1. Watch people.
2. Listen to how they talk to/about others.
3. Locate good role models and bad, and know the difference, especially if the good and bad inhabit the same body.

4. Locate a mentor or two, which may not be the same as models.
5. Rely on trusted friends from graduate school, whether they are former graduate students, former professors, or administrators.

Although tips 1 and 2 might be read as implying that administrators should watch and listen to role models, it is also incumbent on administrators to watch and listen to *all* people involved in an administrative system (e.g., students, teachers, administrative staff, higher administrators, and teacher/scholars in the field).[1] Indeed, administrators should be cognizant not only of differences among these categories but also of differences within each one. As tip 3 indicates, administrators can learn from good role models and from bad ones. The key is not replicating, unconsciously, performances of bad administrators and not presuming that one's past bad experiences are the sole grounds for making decisions in a current program. As tip 4 indicates, mentors are invaluable for initiating one into an academic field and fostering collaborative mentoring. The latter is especially important because the best mentor/mentee relationships are two-way streets, with each getting as good as she gives. Finally, tip 5 provides a safe distance for complaining, seeking advice, and/or keeping sane. In this manner, studying other people and then reflecting on that study will enable administrators to construct a theoretical framework of administrative principles, stances, and tactics, along with a flexibility for implementing this framework in daily life.

Although the prior advice focuses on relationships with other people, an administrator also must know herself. E-mail respondents provide tips that may help define an administrator's sense of self and, hence, her actions. Some important resolutions include:

6. Don't be afraid to share the work—or the credit. (Lunsford)
7. Don't be "afraid to make decisions." (Lunsford)
8. Develop sensitivity for problems and emotions of others and a thick skin about your own. (Miller)
9. Recognize that you can't please everyone all the time. (Miller)
10. Recognize that being an administrator may distance you from your friends. (Miller)
11. Focus on your strengths. (Rude)
12. Think rhetorically. (Rude)
13. Make the impact on students your priority. (Rude)
14. Respect your colleagues. (Rude)
15. Take care of yourself and the people who love you. (Rude)

As for tips 6 and 7, releasing fear about sharing work and making decisions is liberating in that one's identity as an administrator becomes grounded in one's own negotiated criteria for success, rather than in someone else's perceptions. Granted, administrators always have to report to superiors. However, once administrators negotiate their duties with their superiors, most superiors really just want administrators to make things work; that is, they *want* administrators to make decisions so they do not have to. Likewise with tips 8 and 9, recognizing that administrators cannot please everyone eases one's burden, yet in no way should this recognition be construed as accepting a haphazard, anything-goes program climate. Coming to terms with tip 10 (i.e., being distanced from friends) is sometimes difficult because administrative duties provide access to information that cannot be shared and responsibility for decision making that is not popular. As for tip 11, focusing on strengths is a reminder to resist U.S. gender socialization, which encourages women to obsess on imperfections in themselves. As for tip 12, thinking rhetorically allows women to adapt the gender socialization that encourages them to consider other people and put it to productive, not simply self-sacrificing, use. As for tip 13, making students the priority is the most important criterion. After all, student learning is (or should be) the central purpose of a university and its programs. Indeed, putting students at the center often provides clarity for decision making, especially when it is derailed by politics, such as disciplinary turf battles. As for tip 14 and 15, showing respect and care for others and yourself demonstrates not just the interconnectedness of self and other, but also the ethical decision making that can and should inform this interconnectedness.

Finally, e-mail respondents provide tips to help administrators be realistic about the politics of their locations—tips that may prove invaluable when navigating any university system:

16. Make sure that . . . someone in the university hierarchy . . . believes in you and your vision for the program, especially as you take on the position. (Hawisher)
17. DON'T DO IT WITHOUT TENURE!!! (Miller)
18. Make sure that your contract or employment agreement provides ways that your administrative work will be evaluated. (Miller)
19. Negotiate "sufficient reduction" in workload. (Miller)

Heeding tip 16, having support in the university hierarchy ensures that the needs of a program will often be met, which can determine whether a program will succeed. Such support can also protect administrators, especially non-white administrators, from being overworked by too many committee assignments. Such support also can protect administrators from being scapegoated. Heeding tip 17 by not accepting administrative posts without tenure guarantees more untenured time for scholarly activity, which is necessary to attain tenure and promotion. This tip is an oft-ignored maxim in rhetoric and composition studies because new administrators do not realize either the degree of work and commitment that administrative positions entail or the degree of politics inherent in administration. When work commitments are coupled with the nonwork commitments that many women have, the time in the day available for scholarly pursuits simply vanishes. Even with tenure, administration eats up valuable time that could otherwise be spent planning innovative pedagogy or writing scholarly books and articles. So regardless of whether administrators are tenured, they should heed tip 18 and negotiate ways in which administration will count toward tenure and promotion. Moreover, such negotiations should be put in writing and signed by a department chair or dean. During these negotiations, administrators should heed tip 19, too, and put workload on the table in terms of reduced teaching loads and reduced service loads at least on committees not related to the administrative position.

As we contemplated the previous tips, what echoed in our minds was Shirley Wilson Logan's injunction for the field, which we believe also may serve as an injunction for feminist administrators in rhetoric and composition studies:

> We must strengthen the links between language and democracy, text and street. During this present moment when various current national constituencies are "discovering" the importance of writing, let's make sure they understand what it means to teach writing and what learning and teaching environments best facilitate it. We have position statements that articulate those conditions. As language arts educators [and administrators], we ought to be at the center of all policy decisions that affect the teaching and learning of communication skills. Somebody needs to ask us the next time decisions are made about how facility with language will be assessed. Somebody needs to ask us before proclaiming a national crisis in the quality of college student writing. (335)

Two additional tips that we would like to offer from our own experiences include:

20. Turn administrative duties into scholarship.
21. Find ways to enjoy the job and make it intellectually engaging.

In terms of 20, publishing articles or books can benefit both the field and the administrator. Research not only enriches the field by theorizing that which is undertheorized, but also enriches an administrator's own performance and, let's be honest, promotion possibilities. In terms of tip 21, if intellectual engagement with administration is not possible, then seriously reconsider whether administration is a viable career goal. It is not for everyone, and there is no shame in such an admission.

CALL FOR FURTHER RESEARCH

Just as this collection adds to existing research on feminism and administration in rhetoric and composition studies, it leaves in its wake the need for further research. The following questions (generated by several people's conversations about this project) are offered as invitations to contemplate the important issue of feminism and administration within rhetoric and composition studies. Some of these issues have been addressed and simply need to be updated for 21st-century administrative contexts, whereas other issues are yet to be adequately addressed in terms of feminism:

- What are different ways that we define the status of administrators and GTA as well as contingent faculty, staff, and students? How do these definitions affect people occupying these positions and working with these positions?
- Who owns the stories we tell about administration? How do we benefit and not benefit from sharing our stories?
- What are multiple ways of training faculty administrators for the economic/financial side of their jobs?
- How can becoming an administrator be imagined as a productive career move, rather than as nonproductive, going over to the dark side, or selling out?
- What are the implications of the situation that WPAs function as administrators yet are not in charge of hiring who they want, at least in English departments with graduate programs, where the graduate studies committee is usually in charge of selecting GTAs?
- How may feminist administrators counteract pundits' visions of a utopian humanities of the mind and effectively foreground the political realities within contemporary universities?
- How well are administrators incorporating the areas of visual studies, multimedia, and technology into their 21st-century programs?
- What are the actual learning outcomes for graduate and undergraduate students in university programs, and how do these outcomes coincide and/or conflict with our field's theories and our individual ideals?
- What problems haunt researcher's use of lore as evidence (is lore really nontheoretical and nonrigorous)? Does it simply serve the graduate students to make teaching seem to be something they can do even if they are not rhetoric and composition specialists?

- How should administrators negotiate graduate students' desires for teaching with undergraduate students wants and/or needs for learning?
- What are the implications of designing first-year writing programs so that noncomposition graduate students can teach it?
- Should WPA work be a professional and/or paraprofessional degree?
- How conscious are administrators of their intents and the effects of their actions, especially as these effects impinge on all people involved in a program?
- What roles can unions play in feminist administration for all involved people?
- How do free-standing writing programs that have broken off from English departments—and their students—fare in comparison to English-based writing programs, especially in terms of professional development for teachers and scholarly contributions to rhetoric and composition studies?
- What does *not* work in administration in terms of qualities and actions?
- How does a community college mission and teaching load inform intersections of feminism and administration?
- To what extent are silence and listening, along with collaboration and other actions so designated as feminist, actually feminist administrative practices?
- What tropes, other than oxymoron, are useful for feminist administrative work? How do these tropes represent and/or construct attitudes and actions for all people involved?
- How may the conversation in this collection's chapters be complicated by issues of race and ethnicity, including the haunting presence of whiteness?
- What other troubled intersections between feminist principles and administrative practices exist?

These questions all suggest that performing feminist administration entails a consideration of how programs, people, and feminist principles intersect. Questions of intersections, in turn, presume the presence of boundaries. Consequently, we conclude with Min-zhan Lu's exhortation about the importance of boundary work and language use in composition studies: "Whether we realize it or not, whether we acknowledge it or not, we take part in this struggle through every decision we make on which English to use and how to use it. Composition is boundary work. How we go about using English matters" (24). In terms of this collection, Lu's exhortation suggests two ideas: (a) Performing feminist administration in rhetoric and composition studies is boundary work, and (b) how we use English in such administration matters.

If performance is a bodily site where cultural concept and concrete action meet, then performing feminist administration in rhetoric and composition studies means invoking feminist principles to underwrite administrative practices and, conversely, invoking administrative practices to challenge and/or reaffirm feminist principles. Reflection and action, action and reflection. Such performing is a recursive process, a process without end, a process that must be rendered anew each time it is adapted to a particular time and place. Yet rendering anew is not the equivalent of reinventing the wheel. Administrators may learn from one another's stories, theories, and knowledge. That is why the contributors in this collection are willing to share how they perform—sometimes easily, sometimes not so easily—feminist administration in their daily duties and in their scholarly conversations. We offer these chapters, as well as a continually evolving web presence at www.femadmin.org in hopes that such sharing will continue. Conversations such as these will benefit not only our field and our institutional programs, but also, and more important, *all* the people involved— both administrators and their colleagues—who, singly and collectively, may find themselves performing feminist administration in rhetoric and composition studies.

APPENDIX

The Supplemental Website:
www.femadm.org

The supplemental website to *Performing Feminism and Administration in Rhetoric and Composition* is a unique feature that allows for a more inter-active, participatory reading of this text. As issues introduced here become more complicated and as new voices join the ranks of administration, we need a way to allow the ideas introduced in this text to evolve, grow, and be revised. Our website is a rich collection of text-based, web-based, and human resources, including the following links:

- Links to information about current publications (books, collec-tions, and articles) that might be of interest to women administra-tors.
- Links to websites that provide information or resources for women administrators.
- Short video clips of women administrators offering sage advice in talks and interviews.
- Stories/narratives of women administrators.
- A "Day in the Life" series for women administrators along the lines of "A Day in the Life of a Technical Communicator" on the Society for Technical Communication (STC) website found at www.collegeview.com/career/careersearch/job_profiles/comtech /tw02.html.
- A resource for those working in administration seeking promo-tion and tenure along the lines of the "Tenure and Promotion Cases for Composition Faculty Who Work with Technology" found at www.hu.mtu.edu/~cyselfe/P&TStuff/P&TWeb/ Introduction.htm.

In addition to the more static linked resources, the website will feature a feminist blog, as well as links to other blogs by feminist administrators. Links to list resources (like the WPA and Fem Rhet lists) also will be included. Eventually, we hope to create an interactive discussion board (along the lines of the WPA list) for those interested in performing feminist administration.

•

NOTES

INTRODUCTION

1. In this collection, *feminist administration* signifies the performance of an ideology that foregrounds gender as a lens for interpreting and acting justly within the world while recognizing that gender always exists in the presence of other lenses, such as race, class, nationality, age, and region (Bem).
2. For descriptions of Kris and Becky's writing programs, see www.marquette.edu/english/first-year/index.shtml; Ratcliffe, "Coming Out"; and www.english.ttu.edu/comp/default.asp?serial=1465.
3. Feminist scholarship in education includes *Managing Women* by Sue Adler, Jenny Laney, and Mary Packer; *Gender Images in Public Education* by Camille Stivers; and *Gender Matters in Educational Administration and Policy* by Jill Blackmore and Jane Kenway.
4. Feminist scholarship within rhetoric and composition studies includes chapters in Louise Phelps and Janet Emig's *Feminine Principles and Women's Experience in American Composition and Rhetoric*; chapters in Susan Jarratt and Lynn Worsham's *Feminism and Composition Studies: In Other Words*; chapters in Shirley Rose and Irwin Weiser's *The Writing Program Administrator as Researcher*; and notable articles, such as Marcia Dickson's "Directing Without Power: Adventures in Constructing a Model of Feminist Writing Program Administration" and Jeanne Gunner's "Decentering the WPA."
5. Recent scholarship on writing program administration has defined these problems more clearly (e.g., Rose and Weiser's *The Writing Program Administrator as Theorist*; Irene Ward and William Carpenter's *The Allyn and Bacon Sourcebook for Writing Program Administrators*; Linda Myers-Breslin's *Administrative Problem-Solving and Writing Centers*; Carol Hartzog's

Composition and the Academy: A Study of Writing Program Administration;
Stuart C. Brown, Theresa Enos, and Catherine Chaput's *The Writing Program
Administrator's Resource A Guide to Reflective Institutional Practice*; and
Barbara L'Eplattenier and Jill Mastrangelo's *Historical Studies of Writing
Program Administration*).

6. Similarly, Writing Center scholarship includes administrative components, such
as Gary A. Olson's *Writing Centers: Theory and Administration*; Linda Myers-
Breslin's *Administrative Problem-Solving for Writing Programs and Writing
Centers*; Christina Murphy and Bryon Stay's *The Writing Center Director's
Resource Book*; and articles in *The Writing Center Journal*.

CHAPTER 1

1. In *The Theory of Social and Economic Organization*, Max Weber remarks that a
bureaucracy is characterized by concrete divisions of labor, a hierarchical organization of personnel in which managers supervise subordinates, and rigid rules of
operation that ensure bureaucratic control over production. In "The Feminist
Case against Bureaucracy," Kathy Ferguson argues that changing bureaucracy
requires not just the hiring of more women, but the introduction of feminist discourse into the discourse of bureaucracy.

2. For a more comprehensive introduction to the field of feminist ethics, see
Samantha Brennan's, "Recent Work in Feminist Ethics"; Eve Browning Cole
and Susan Coultrap-McQuin's, "Toward A Feminist Conception of Moral
Life"; Alison M. Jaggar's, "Ethics Naturalized: Feminism's Contribution to
Moral Epistemology"; and Margaret Urban Walker's, "Moral Epistemology."

3. As Hartsock makes clear in her introduction to *The Feminist Standpoint
Revisited and Other Essays*, her concept of a feminist standpoint is influenced
explicitly by the idea of the Proletarian standpoint in Marxist theory. Her goal is
to explore the ways in which the perspectives of men and women in a sexist society may parallel those of owners and workers in a capitalist society.

CHAPTER 4

1. The following are select collaborative presentations and publications incorporating profiles of writing instruction. These works grew out of collaborative
administration practices at Georgia State University. In addition, dozens of
individually authored presentations and publications were produced by those
of us involved in first-year composition instruction and administration at GSU.
Not included in this list are numerous collaboratively produced and disseminated reports, accreditation documents, assessment guidelines, and scoring
rubrics.

CHAPTER 6

1. We are indebted to Alice Gillam for leading our collaborative team to critically investigate the assumptions behind collaborative administration and for securing a WPA research grant to help make this investigation possible. We also would like to thank Laura Micciche, a fourth member of our collaborative team, for her contributions to this investigation.
2. Although their emphasis is slightly different from our own, Goodburn and Leverenz provide an important critique of the tendency to downplay conflict within collaborative administrative groups.

CHAPTER 9

1. Robert Boice reports that a primary reason that former academics reported being "significantly healthier and happier" than a matched group of their academic peers was "more than anything else because they were not regularly bothered by the feeling that they had not done enough" (133). A study by Gmelch and Miskin similarly puts "unrealistic self-expectations" in the top five stressors for department chairs (88). The prevalence of unworthiness feelings in academia at large, however, should not silence questions or concerns about whether (feminist) women in academia face this kind of stress in different or perhaps more intense ways.
2. In the list of traditional mentoring functions that Joyce Russell and Danielle Adams derive from the work of Kathy Kram, nearly all the descriptors depend on and even reify a power imbalance and/or anticipate a serious "lack" on the mentee's part. Mentoring provides "sponsorship, exposure and visibility [for the protégé], coaching, protection, . . . [it also serves to] enhance the protégé's sense of competence, identity, and . . . effectiveness . . . [and provides] role modeling, acceptance and confirmation, counseling, and friendship" (2).
3. Nel Noddings, in composing a generalized ethic of caring, asserts that caring is incomplete if the one who is cared for does not recognize or acknowledge the efforts of the one caring. Even in her ideal ethical universe, however, she allows that the one caring may not be to blame, and that we may not wish or need to call a halt to unrecognized caring (68–69).
4. Rebecca J. Rickly and Susanmarie Harrington, implementing a new mentoring program for TAs, found that "'administration' [i.e., traditional leadership] and 'collaboration' [a key aspect of feminist mentoring for them] seem[ed] often to be in conflict," as they worked to build a mentoring program for teaching assistants (111).
5. Fine and Buzzanell point out that when a woman adopts a "servant leadership" approach, as one way to stay true to her feminist, world-changing philosophy, she may be "acting in ways that are consistent with stereotypic women's roles" (146). The catch here is two-fold—that women's innovative leadership may go entirely unnoticed because, from a chauvinistic perspective, "for a woman,

enacting servant leadership is unremarkable" (147), and that if it is noticed, it may reinforce a gender stereotype, and thus lower her status in the eyes of other people. Thus, it seems particularly important for a pretenure feminist WPA to adopt a leadership philosophy that, although not succumbing to antifeminist values, can yet be recognized as leadership and will have agency even within conservative institutional structures.

CHAPTER 10

1. As in the case of the Office of Writing Review, I had *this* job, too, because no one else would accept it.

CHAPTER 12

1. Pam Childers has found that students in her all-boy high school regularly use the writing center when they find the writing center compelling: They use the 20 computers, and they workshop their college application letters. Childers recommends having a man and a woman tutor available at all times. A given writer will prefer one over the other depending on the stresses he is facing out of class.
2. Such an exercise is especially useful, too, because we have built an excellent library of videotaped sessions. Early in the semester, when we are less busy and new tutors are required to observe conferencing sessions, they have access to a library of sessions that are available at any time. Seeing others' tapes and realizing that not every other session is perfect also helps to alleviate anxiety about taping themselves. In addition, our video library offers a rich resource for research, which our students use often for research projects. Black's transcriptions provide a good model for students, but Gilewisz and Thonus provide a rationale and step-by-step instructions for transcribing that is useful for tutors. For a transcription scheme that also addresses gesture and body language, see Ragland.
3. The Peer Tutor Alumni Research Project's website is available at www.mu.edu/writingcenter/PeerTutorAlumniPage.htm.

CHAPTER 13

1. For the association between marginalization and feminization, see Connors, Enos, Holbrook, Miller, and Lauer. Connors, Enos, and Holbrook use similar data about institutional power, pay, and award systems to assert that the teaching of writing is primarily women's work. Lauer argues that the numbers indicate writing *instruction* has been feminized (evident too in expressive, nurturing,

student-centered pedagogies), but not *scholarship* in Rhetoric and Composition. Publications by males still outnumber those by females. Miller examines both the feminization of composition and the unwitting roles of composition teachers in the subordination of composition to literature.

2. For that story, see Enos, *Gender Roles* (49–52).

3. Contract faculty at Ball State University are so designated because they hold contract, rather than tenure-line, positions. Their renewable contracts may be for full- or part-time, academic-year or semester duration. The core of English contract faculty has provided a stable Writing Program faculty during the last 20 years, and the department has enfranchised those with more than 3 years of continuous full-time service.

4. The department policy, instituted in 1986 after a long-time chair was voted out of office while he was out of the country, stipulated a single 3-year term without opportunity for reelection. The policy also was extended to our other administrative positions (Assistant Chairperson, Graduate Program Director, Undergraduate Program Director, Writing Program Director) because they are appointed by the chair. Mine, however, was the first administration to begin with faculty new to each position; when my term ended, the enormity of the drain in situated knowledge began the sea change that first relaxed the terms of appointees to encourage continuity between administrations and finally, in 2004, saw the option of reelecting a chair for an additional 2-year term passed by a significant majority of the faculty.

5. During my tenure as chair, between 135 and 152 individuals were teaching in any given semester. Tenure-line faculty numbered 37 to 39, contract faculty close to 85, and graduate students the remainder. Our department was larger than five of the seven colleges on campus.

6. While admitting to strong beliefs in individual rights and equal opportunity underlying what Elizabeth Flynn identifies as *liberal feminism*, I find myself identifying more closely with what she calls *postmodern feminism*, with its rejection of binary constructions of gender and its association with social constructionism (202–5). Essentialized constructions of gender inadequately inform analysis of the social and political dynamics of collaborative decision making; recognizing and honoring multiple differences within a situated community allow for and in fact encourage a collaborative, rather than a hierarchical, administrative structure.

7. Drawing both from the dialogic process of making meaning advocated by Ann Berthoff and from Lisa Ede and Andrea Lunsford's notion of dialogic collaboration (132–35), the term incorporates several of the other descriptors, notably recursiveness and collaboration in making meaning or producing knowledge.

8. My own difficulties writing this piece stem from the conflicts John Trimbur identified in his Foreword to Gesa Kirsch's *Women Writing the Academy*. The academic genres I am accustomed to using and valuing leave little space for the personal narrative and reflection on experience. When I dared to submit a narrative of my academic life to Theresa Enos, it was on condition of anonymity. Yet repeated conversations with younger scholars have convinced me that we need to share our stories, and experiential knowledge not for its "academic exchange value," but, as Trimbur observes, for its social use. We need to acknowledge, as

Toni Morrison eloquently pointed out in her 1993 Nobel Prize lecture, that one
of the principal ways we absorb knowledge is through narrative (8). As I reflect
on the administrative and leadership roles I have played, some of them overlaid
on others, I see them as all of a piece, in gradually expanding domains, but
always grounded in teaching and learning.

- Basic Writing Coordinator — Writing Program, department
- Assistant Department Chair — department
- Department Chair — department, college, university, national
- Assessment — program, department, university
- Freshman Learning Council — university
- University Core Curriculum Task Force Chair — university
- Indiana Writing Project Site Director — department, university,
  schools, state Department of Education, national (NWP)
- NWP-IN State Network Director — multiple sites/universities, state
  DOE and Commission for Higher Education, national NWP

The passion for improving students' classroom experiences has driven each one
of these commitments — and decisions. I turned down the opportunity to serve
my college as associate dean because it would have taken me too far away from
the concerns of the classroom.

9. This statement may be truer for women than for men. Kirsch notes that the
   Perry scheme of development (based on young males) "posits stages . . . that
   eventually lead to commitment and membership in a community," whereas
   "Belenky and her colleagues found that 'for women, confirmation and community are prerequisites rather than consequences of development' " (*Women
   Writing* 16).
10. We also expanded our dialogue and visibility through IADE, ADE, and ADE
    summer seminars and then took our curricular concepts to state, regional, and
    national conferences to further enrich the dialogue.
11. Susan Jarrett's *Rereading the Sophists* illuminates the fifth-century Greek
    Sophists' theory and practice of socially constructed discourse, usefully support-
    ing dialogic collaboration, community building, and persuasive communication.
12. In "'Fitness for the Occasion': How Context Matters for JWPAs," Paul Ranieri
    and Jackie Grutsch McKinney, writing collaboratively, underline the importance
    of context, particularly the rhetorical context, of any administrative position.
    They see Rhetoric and Composition training as preparation that colleagues in
    other areas may not possess to address contextual issues surrounding any prob-
    lem, the ethical and rhetorical decisions that would enable them to address the
    problem, and communication of decisions. Their article also reflects the health of
    community in the department at points when they were asked to serve as
    JWPAs, one before and one after my term as chair.
13. Paul Ranieri, a Rhetoric and Composition colleague, served as the lead writer for
    the draft that would become the final report, "A Different Dawn — A Proposal:
    Scholarship Reconsidered for Ball State University."
14. Such habits of inquiry and critical reflection are most easily evident and at home
    in teaching, but the model is appropriate. An excellent example of such inquiry is

Jackie McKinney and Elizabeth Chiseri-Strater's "Inventing a Teacherly Self: Positioning Journals in the TA Seminar." Reflection on their course prompted their inquiry. For application of critical reflection and inquiry to administrative experience, see Amy Goodburn and Carrie Shively Leverenz's "Feminist Writing Program Administration: Resisting the Bureaucrat Within."

AFTERWORD

1. Listening techniques described in Ratcliffe's *Rhetorical Listening* may be applied to administration.

WORKS CITED

Abrahams, Naomi. "Negotiating Power, Identity, Family, and Community: Women's Community Participation. *Gender and Society* 10.6 (1996): 768-96.

Adler, Sue, Jenny Laney, and Mary Packer. *Managing Women: Feminism and Power in Educational Management.* Philadelphia: Open UP, 1993.

Aisenberg, Nadya, and Mona M. Harrington. *Women of Academe: Outsiders in the Sacred Grove.* Amherst, MA: U of Massachusetts P, 1988.

Andrews, Patricia Hayes. "Sex and Gender Differences in Group Communication: Impact on the Facilitation Process." *Small Group Research* 23 (1992): 74–94.

Anson, Chris M., and Robert L. Brown, Jr. "Subject to Interpretation: The Role of Research in Writing Programs and its Relationship to the Politics of Administration in Higher Education." Rose and Weiser, *WPA as Researcher,* 141–52.

Anson, Chris M., and Carol Rutz. "Graduate Students, Writing Programs, and Consensus-Based Management: Collaboration in the Face of Disciplinary Ideology." *WPA: Writing Program Administration* 21 (1998): 106–20.

Anzaldúa, Gloria. *Borderlands/La Frontera: The New Mestiza.* San Francisco: Aunt Lute Books, 1987.

Aristotle. *The Ethics of Aristotle: The Nicomachean Ethics.* Trans. J. A. K. Thomson. New York: Penguin Books, 1953.

Aronson, Anne, and Craig T. Hansen. "Doubling Our Chances: Co-Directing a Writing Program." *WPA: Writing Program Administration* 21 (1998): 23–32.

Ashton-Jones, Evelyn. "Collaboration, Conversation, and the Politics of Gender." Phelps and Emig 5–26.

Baird, John E., Jr. "Sex Differences in Group Communication: A Review of Relevant Research." *Quarterly Journal of Speech* 62 (1976): 179–92.

Barnes, Luann, and Donna LeCourt. "Writing Multiplicity: Hypertext and Feminist Textual Politics." *Computers and Composition* 16 (1999): 55–71.

Barr-Ebest, Sally. "Gender Differences in Writing Program Administration." *WPA: Writing Program Administration* 18 (1995): 53–72.

Bartlett, Laura. "Feminization and Composition's Managerial Subject." *Works and Days* 21 (2003): 261–81.

Bauer, Dale M. "The Other 'F' Word: The Feminist in the Classroom." *College English* 52 (1990): 385–96.

Bauman, Zygmunt. *Postmodern Ethics.* Oxford: Blackwell, 1993.

Belenky, Mary Field, Blythe McVicker Clinchy, Nancy Rule Goldberger, and Jill Mattuck Tarule. *Women's Ways of Knowing: The Development of Self, Voice, and Mind.* New York: Basic, 1986.

Bem, Sandra Lipsitz. *The Lenses of Gender: Transforming the Debate on Sexual Inequality.* New Haven: Yale UP, 1994.

Benhabib, Seyla. *Situating the Self: Gender, Community, and Postmodernism in Contemporary Ethics.* New York: Routledge, 1992.

Berthoff, Ann E. *The Making of Meaning: Metaphors, Models, and Maxims for Writing Teachers.* Upper Montclair, NJ: Boynton/Cook, 1981.

Bérubé, Michael. *The Employment of English: Theory, Jobs, and the Future of Literary Studies.* New York: NYUP, 1998.

Bishop, Karen. "On the Road to (Documentary) Reality: Capturing the Intellectual and Political Process of Writing Program Administration." Rose and Weiser, *WPA as Theorist,* 43–53.

Bishop, Wendy. "Learning Our Own Ways to Situate Composition and Feminist Studies in the English Department." *JAC* 10 (1990): 339–55. Rpt. in Kirsch et al., 496–511.

——. "On 'Learning Our Own Ways.'" *Feminism and Composition: A Critical Sourcebook.* Ed. Gesa E. Kirsch et al. Boston: Bedford/St. Martin's, 2003. 573–74.

Bizzaro, Resa Crane. "Making Places as Teacher-Scholars in Composition Studies: Comparing Transition Narratives." *CCC* 53 (2002): 487–506.

Black, Laurel Johnson. *Between Talk and Teaching: Reconsidering the Writing Conference.* Logan: Utah State UP, 1998.

Blackmore, Jill, and Jane Kenway. *Gender Matters in Educational Administration and Policy: A Feminist Introduction.* Bristol, PA: Falmer P, 1993.

Blair, Kristine, and Pamela Takayoshi. *Feminist Cyberscapes: Mapping Gendered Academic Spaces.* Stamford, CT: Ablex Publishing, 1999.

Blakemore, Peter. "An Intentionally Ecological Approach to Teacher Training." *WPA: Writing Program Administration* 21 (1998): 137–49.

Bloom, Lynn Z. "I Want a Writing Director." *CCC* 43 (1992): 176–78.

——. "Moving Forward: This Foreword." Brown et al., ix–xvi.

Boal, Augusto. *Theatre of the Oppressed.* New York: Theatre Communications Group, 1985.

Boice, Robert. "Coping with Difficult Colleagues." *Enhancing Departmental Leadership: The Roles of the Chairperson.* Ed. John B. Bennett and David J. Figuli. New York: Macmillan, 1990. 132–38.

Bousquet, Marc. "Composition as Management Science." *JAC* 22 (2002): 493–526. Rpt. in Bousquet et al., 11–35.

——. "A Discipline Where Only Management Gets Tenure?" *JAC* 22 (2002): 917–25.

——. "The Waste Product of Graduate Education: Toward a Dictatorship of the Flexible." *Social Text* 20 (2002): 81–104.

Boyer, Ernest. *College: The Undergraduate Experience in America.* Princeton: Carnegie Foundation, 1987.

———. *Scholarship Reconsidered: Priorities of the Professoriate.* Princeton, NJ: The Carnegie Foundation for the Advancement of Teaching, 1990.

Brady Aschauer, Ann. "Tinkering with Technological Skill: An Examination of the Gendered Uses of Technologies." *Computers and Composition* 16 (1999): 1–23.

Brennan, Samantha. "Recent Work in Feminist Ethics." *Ethics* 109 (1999): 858–93.

Brown, Johanna Atwood. "The Peer Who Isn't a Peer." George, 120–25.

Brown, Stuart C. "Applying Ethics: A Decision-Making Heuristic for Writing Program Administrators." Brown et al., 155–63.

Brown, Stuart C., and Theresa Enos. Introduction. Brown et al., 1–2.

Brown, Stuart C., Theresa Enos, and Catherine Chaput, eds. *The Writing Program Administrator's Resource: A Guide to Reflective Institutional Practice.* Mahwah, NJ: Lawrence Erlbaum Associates, 2002.

Bruffee, Kenneth A. "Peer Tutoring and the 'Conversation of Mankind.'" Olson, *Writing Centers,* 3–15.

Bullock, Richard. "When Administration Becomes Scholarship: The Future of Writing Program Administration." *Writing Program Administration* 11.1-2 (Fall 1987): 13-18.

Burke, Kenneth. *Attitudes Toward History.* 3rd ed. Berkeley: U of California P, 1984.

———. *The Philosophy of Literary Form: Studies in Symbolic Action.* Baton Rouge: Louisiana State UP, 1941.

Butler, Judith. *Bodies That Matter: On the Discursive Limits of "Sex."* New York: Routledge, 1993.

———. *Gender Trouble: Feminism and the Subversion of Identity.* New York: Routledge, 1990.

Cambridge, Barbara L., and Ben W. McClelland. "From Icon to Partner: Repositioning the Writing Program Administrator." Janangelo and Hansen, 151–60.

Carino, Peter. "Power and Authority in Peer Tutoring." *The Center Will Hold: Critical Perspectives on Writing Center Scholarship.* Ed. Michael A. Pemberton and Joyce Kinkead. Logan: Utah State UP (2003): 96–113.

Carpenter, William J. Introduction. Ward and Carpenter, 1–6.

Caywood, Cynthia L., and Gillian R. Overing, eds. *Teaching Writing: Pedagogy, Gender, and Equity.* Albany: SUNY P, 1987.

Childers, Pamela. E-mail to Paula Gillespie. 21 February 2005.

Childers, Pamela, and Paula Gillespie. *Directory of Writing Centers: 1998–99.* New Berlin, WI: Metagraphix, n.d.

Clement, Grace. *Care, Autonomy, and Justice.* Boulder, CO: Westview P, 1996.

Cole, Eve Browning, and Susan Coultrap-McQuin. "Toward a Feminist Conception of Moral Life." *Explorations in Feminist Ethics.* Ed. Eve Browning Cole and Susan Coultrap-McQuin. Bloomington: Indiana UP, 1992. 1–10.

Connors, Robert. "The Feminization of Rhetoric." New Directions in Composition Scholarship Conference. U of New Hampshire, Durham. October 1986.

Cooper, Marilyn. "From the Editor." *CCC* 56 (2004): 13–15.

_____. "Really Useful Knowledge: A Cultural Studies Agenda for Writing Centers."
   The Writing Center Journal 14 (1992): 97–111.
Council of Writing Program Administrators. *WPA: Writing Program
   Administration* Homepage. Oct. 17, 2005 <http://wpacouncil.org/journal/
   index.html?PHPSESSID=b7b8e78396ee33b86c75bdde3b51637>.
Creative Commons. 10 Jan 2007, www.creativecommons.org.
Cripps, Michael J. "#FFFFFF, #000000, & #808080: Hypertext Theory and
   WebDev in the Composition Classroom." *Computers and Composition Online*
   Spring 2004. 29 Sept. 2005 <www.bgsu.edu/cconline/cripps/index.html>.
Crowley, Sharon. *Composition in the University: Historical and Polemical Essays.*
   Pittsburgh: U of Pittsburgh P., 1998.
Cushman, Ellen. *The Struggle and the Tools: Oral and Literate Strategies in an
   Inner City Community.* Albany: SUNY P, 1998.
de Certeau, Michel. *The Practice of Everyday Life.* Berkeley: U of California P,
   1984.
DeVoss, Dànielle Nicole, Joseph Johansen, Cynthia L. Selfe, and John C. Williams,
   Jr. "Under the Radar of Composition Programs: Glimpsing the Future through
   Case Studies of Literacy in Electronic Contexts." Bloom et al., 157–73.
Dew, Debra. "WPA as Scholarly Change Agent." Conference of the Council of
   Writing Program Administrators. Newark, DE. 16 July 2004.
Dickson, Marcia. "Directing Without Power: Adventures in Constructing a Model
   of Feminist Writing Program Administration." *Writing Ourselves into the
   Story: Unheard Voices from Composition Studies.* Ed. Sheryl Fontaine and
   Susan Hunter. Carbondale: SIUP, 1993. 140–53.
"A Different Dawn — A Proposal: Scholarship Reconsidered for Ball State
   University." Muncie, IN: Ball State U, 1994.
Drew, Chris, Matt Garrison, Steven Leek, Donna Strickland, Jen Talbot, and A. D.
   Waldron. "Affect, Labor, and the Graduate Teaching Assistant: Can Writing
   Programs Become 'Spaces of Hope'?" *Works and Days* 21(2003): 169–86.
Duffelmeyer, Barbara Blakely. "Critical Computer Literacy: Computers in First-
   Year Composition as Topic and Environment." *Computers and Composition*
   17 (2000): 289–307.
Duffey, Suellynn, Ben Feigert, Vic Mortimer, Jennifer Phegley, and Melinda
   Turnley. "Conflict, Collaboration, and Authority: Graduate Students and
   Writing Program Administration." *Rhetoric Review* 21 (2002): 79–87.
Eble, Michelle, and Robin Breault. "The Primetime Agora: Knowledge, Power, and
   'Mainstream' Resource Venues for Women Online." *Computers and
   Composition* 19 (2002): 315–29.
Ede, Lisa, and Andrea Lunsford. *Single Texts/Plural Authors: Perspectives on
   Collaborative Writing.* Carbondale: SIUP, 1990.
Eichhorn, Sara Farris, Karen Hayes, Andriana Hernandez, Susan C. Jarratt, Karen
   Powers-Stubbs, and Marian M. Sciachitano. "A Symposium on Feminist
   Experiences in the Composition Classroom." *CCC* 43 (1992): 297–322. Rpt. in
   Phelps and Emig, 363–87.
Emig, Janet, and Louise Wetherbee Phelps. "Introduction: Context and
   Commitment." Phelps and Emig, xi–xviii.
Enos, Theresa. "Gender and Publishing Scholarship in Rhetoric and Composition."
   Kirsch et al., 558–72.

_____. *Gender Roles and Faculty Lives in Rhetoric and Composition.* Carbondale: SIUP, 1996.

_____. "Mentoring—and (Wo)mentoring—in Composition Studies." *Academic Advancement in Composition Studies: Scholarship, Publication, Promotion, Tenure.* Ed. Richard C. Gebhardt and Barbara Genelle Smith Gebhardt. Mahwah, NJ: Lawrence Erlbaum, 1997. 137–45.

Farris, Christine. "Stars, Apprentices, and the Scholar-Teacher Split." *Academe* 91.5 (2005): 19–21.

_____. "Too Cool for School?: Composition as Cultural Studies and Reflective Practice." Pytlik and Liggett, 97–107.

Farris, Christine, and Mary Favret. "Teaching the Teaching of Literature." *Peer Review* 6.3 (2004): 16–18.

Feenberg, Andrew. *Alternative Modernity: The Technical Turn in Philosophy and Social Theory.* Los Angeles: U of California P, 1995.

_____. *Critical Theory of Technology.* New York: Oxford UP, 1991.

_____. *Questioning Technology.* New York: Routledge, 1999.

_____. "Subversive Rationalization: Technology, Power, and Democracy." *Technology & the Politics of Knowledge.* Ed. Andrew Feenberg and Alastair Hannay. Indianapolis: Indiana UP, 1995. 3–22.

Ferganchick-Neufang, Julia. "Research (Im)Possibilities: Feminist Methods and WPA Inquiry." Rose and Weiser, *WPA as Researcher,* 18–27.

Ferguson, Kathy. *The Feminist Case against Bureaucracy.* Philadelphia: Temple UP, 1984.

Ferry, Christopher. "Theory, Research, Practice, Work." *Under Construction: Working in the Intersections of Composition Theory, Research, and Practice.* Ed. Christine Farris and Chris M. Anson. Logan: Utah State UP, 1998. 11–18.

Fine, Marlene G., and Patrice M. Buzzanell. "Walking the High Wire: Leadership Theorizing, Daily Acts, and Tensions." *Rethinking Organizational and Managerial Communication From Feminist Perspectives.* Ed. Patrice M. Buzzanell. Thousand Oaks: Sage Publications, 2000. 128–56.

Fish, Stanley. "Theory's Hope." *Critical Inquiry* 30 (2004): 374–78.

Fisher, Roger, and William Ury. *Getting to Yes: Negotiating Agreement Without Giving In.* New York: Penguin, 1991.

Fishman, Pamela M. "Interaction: The Work Women Do." Thorne et al., 89–101.

Fitts, Karen, and William B. Lalicker. "Invisible Hands: A Manifesto to Resolve Institutional and Curricular Hierarchy in English Studies." *College English* 66 (2004): 427–51.

Flax, Jane. "Gender and Publishing Scholarship in Rhetoric and Composition." Olson and Taylor, 58–72.

_____. "Postmodernism and Gender Relations in Feminist Theory." *Feminism/Postmodernism.* Ed. Linda J. Nicholson. New York: Routledge, 1990. 39–62.

Flynn, Elizabeth. "Review: Feminist Theories/Feminist Composition." *College English* 57 (1995): 201–12.

Foss, Sonja K., and Cindy L. Griffin. "Beyond Persuasion: A Proposal for an Invitational Rhetoric." *Communication Monographs* 62 (1995): 2–18.

Fox, Tom. "Working Against the State: Composition's Intellectual Work for Change." Olson, *Rhetoric and Composition,* 91–100.

Freire, Paulo. *Pedagogy of the Oppressed.* Trans. Myra Bergman Ramos. New York: Seabury, 1968.

French, Jane, and Peter French. "Gender Imbalances in the Primary Classroom: An Interactional Account." *Educational Research* 26 (1984): 127–35.

Gearhart, Sally Miller. "The Womanization of Rhetoric." *Women's Studies International Quarterly* 2 (1979): 195–201.

Gebhardt, Richard. "Administration as Focus for Understanding the Teaching of Writing." Ward and Carpenter, 34–37.

_____. "Scholarship and Teaching: Motives and Strategies for Writing Articles in Composition Studies." Olson and Taylor, 35–46.

Geertz, Clifford. "Blurred Genres: The Refiguration of Social Thought." *The American Scholar* 49 (1980): 165–79.

George, Diana, ed. *Kitchen Cooks, Plate Twirlers and Troubadours: Writing Program Administrators Tell Their Stories.* Portsmouth, NH: Boynton/Cook, 1999.

Gere, Anne Ruggles. "The Long Revolution." Bloom et al., 119–152.

Gerrard, Lisa. "Beyond 'Scribbling Women': Women Writing (on) the Web." *Computers and Composition* 19 (2002): 297–314.

Gilewicz, Magdalena, and Terese Thonus. "Close Vertical Transcription in Writing Center Training and Research." *Writing Center Journal* 24 (2003): 25–49.

Gillam, Alice. "Collaboration, Ethics, and the Emotional Labor of WPAs." *A Way to Move: Rhetorics of Emotion and Composition Studies.* Ed. Dale Jacobs and Laura R. Micciche. Portsmouth, NH: Boynton/Cook-Heinemann, 2003. 113–23.

_____. "Taking it Personally: Redefining the Work of the WPA." George, 65–72.

Gilligan, Carol. *In a Different Voice: Psychological Theory and Women's Development.* Cambridge, MA: Harvard UP, 1982.

_____. "Response to Tappan: 'Relational Voices and Moral Development: Reflections on Change.'" Kahaney et al., 15–18.

Glazer, Judith S. "Feminism and Professionalism in Teaching and Educational Administration." *Educational Administration Quarterly* 27 (1991): 321–42.

Glenn, Cheryl. "Re: Requesting your Voice." Email to editors. 5 August 2005.

Gmelch, Walter, and Val Miskin. *Leadership Skills for Department Chairs.* Bolton, MA: Anker Publishing Company, 1993.

Goodburn, Amy, and Carrie Shively Leverenz. "Feminist Writing Program Administration: Resisting the Bureaucrat Within." Jarratt and Worsham, 276–90.

Graff, Gerald. *Beyond the Culture Wars: How Teaching the Conflicts Can Revitalize American Education.* New York: Norton, 1992.

_____. *Clueless in Academe: How Schooling Obscures the Life of the Mind.* New Haven: Yale UP, 2004.

_____. *Professing Literature: An Institutional History.* Chicago: U of Chicago P, 1987.

Grimm, Nancy. *Good Intentions: Writing Center Work for Postmodern Times.* Portsmouth, NH: Heinemann Boynton/Cook, 1999.

Guillory, John. *Cultural Capital: The Problem of Literary Canon Formation.* Chicago: U of Chicago P, 1991.

Gunner, Jeanne. "Among the Composition People: The WPA as English Department Agent." *JAC* 18 (1998): 153–65.

———. "Collaborative Administration." Brown et al., 253–262.

———. "Decentering the WPA." *WPA: Writing Program Administration* 18 (1994): 8–15.

———. "Ideology, Theory, and the Genre of Writing Programs." Rose and Weiser, *WPA as Theorist*, 7–18.

———. "Identity and Location: A Study of WPA Models, Memberships, and Agendas." *WPA: Writing Program Administration* 22 (1999): 31–54.

———. "Letter from the Guest Editor." *WPA: Writing Program Administration* 21 (1998): 7–8.

Haas, Angela, Christine Tully, and Kristine Blair. "Mentors Versus Masters: Women's and Girls' Narratives of (Re)Negotiation in Web-Based Writing Spaces." *Computers and Composition* 19 (2002): 231–49.

Handa, Carolyn. "Teaching with the World Wide Web: Transforming Theory, Pedagogy, and Practice." Takayoshi and Huot, 166–81.

Hansen, Kristine. "Face to Face with Part-Timers: Ethics and the Professionalization of Writing Faculties." Janangelo and Hansen, 23–45.

Hanson, Linda K. "Directing a Basic Writing Program: Encouraging Diversity Among Students and Instructors." CCCC. Nashville. 17 March 1994. ERIC ED 369 085.

———. "English—The Second Hundred Years." Modern Language Association Convention. San Diego. 28 December 1994.

———. "Pragmatic Politics: Using Assessment Tools to (Re)shape a Curriculum." *Journal of Basic Writing* 9 (1990): 3–19.

Haraway, Donna. "A Cyborg Manifesto: Science, Technology, and Socialist-Feminism in the Late Twentieth Century." *Simians*, 149–82.

———. *Modest_Witness@Second_Millennium.FemaleMan_Meets_OncoMouse: Feminism and Technoscience.* New York: Routledge, 1997.

———. "The Promises of Monsters: A Regenerative Politics for Inappropriate/d Others." *Cultural Studies.* Eds. Lawrence Grossberg, Cary Nelson, and Paula Treichler. New York: Routledge, 1992. 295–337.

———. *Simians, Cyborgs, and Women: The Reinvention of Nature.* New York: Routledge, 1991.

Harding, Sandra. "A Socially Relevant Philosophy of Science? Resources from Standpoint Theory's Controversiality." *Hypatia* 19 (2004): 25–47.

Harrington, Susanmarie, Steve Fox, and Tere Molinder Hogue. "Power, Partnership, and Negotiations: The Limits of Collaboration." *WPA: Writing Program Administration* 21 (1998): 52–64.

Harris, Joseph. "After Dartmouth: Growth and Conflict in English." *College English* 53 (1991): 631–46.

———. "Meet the New Boss, Same as the Old Boss: Class Consciousness in Composition." *CCC* 52 (2000): 43–68.

Hartsock, Nancy. *"The Feminist Standpoint": The Feminist Standpoint Revisited and Other Essays.* Boulder, CO: Westview P, 1998, 105–32.

Hawisher, Gail. "Re: Requesting your Voice." Email to editors. 28 July 2005.

Hawisher, Gail E., Cynthia L. Selfe, Brittany Moraski, and Melissa Pearson. "Becoming Literate in the Information Age: Cultural Ecologies and the Literacies of Technology." *CCC* 55 (2004): 642–92.

Hawisher, Gail E., and Cynthia L. Selfe. "The Edited Collection: A Scholarly Contribution and More." Olson and Taylor, 103–118.

Healy, Dave. "Writing Center Directors: An Emerging Portrait of the Portrait of the Profession." *WPA: Writing Program Administration* 18 (1995): 26–41.

Hesford, Wendy. 1998. "'Ye Are Witnesses': Pedagogy and the Politics of Identity." Jarratt and Worsham, 132–152.

Hesse, Douglas D. "Politics and the WPA: Through and Past Realms of Expertise." Brown et al., 41–58.

____. "Understanding Larger Discourses in Higher Education: Practical Advice for WPAs." Ward and Carpenter, 299–314.

____. "Who Owns Composition?" Chair's Address. CCCC. San Francisco. 17 March 2005.

____. "The WPA as Father, Husband, Ex." George, 44–55.

Hindman, Jane E. "Writing an Important Body of Scholarship: A Proposal for an Embodied Rhetoric of Professional Practice." *JAC* 22 (2002): 93–118.

Hocks, Mary E. "Feminist Interventions in Electronic Environments." *Computers and Composition* 16 (1999): 107–19.

Holbrook, Sue Ellen. "Women's Work: The Feminizing of Composition Studies." *Rhetoric Review* 9 (1991): 201–29.

Holt, Mara. "On Coming to Voice." George, 26–43.

hooks, bell. *Feminism: From Margin to Center*. 2nd ed. Cambridge, MA: South End P, 2000.

____. *Teaching to Transgress: Education as the Practice of Freedom*. New York: Routledge, 1994.

Horner, Bruce, and John Trimbur. "English Only and U.S. College Composition." *CCC* 53 (2002): 594–630.

____. "'How I Learned to Love Larry,' So Why Can't We?" *Kairosnews*. Discussion thread. 27 October 2004 http://kairosnews.org/node/4022.

Hughes, Bradley T., Kirsten Jamsen, and Jody Cardinal. "Where the Boys Aren't: Gender Disparity in Seeking Help with Writing." CCCC. Denver. 15 March 2001.

Hull, Glynda, Mike Rose, Kay Losey Fraser, and Marissa Castellano. "Remediation as Social Construct: Perspectives from an Analysis of Classroom Discourse." *CCC* 42 (1991): 299–329.

Hult, Christine. "The Scholarship of Administration." Janangelo and Hansen, 119–31.

Inman, James. *Computers and Writing: The Cyborg Era*. Mahwah, NJ: Lawrence Erlbaum, 2004.

Jablonski, Jeffrey. "Developing Practice Theories through Collaborative Research: Implications for WPA Scholarship." Rose and Weiser, *WPA as Theorist*, 170–82.

Jaggar, Alison M. "Ethics Naturalized: Feminism's Contribution to Moral Epistemology." *Metaphilosophy* 31 (2000): 452–68.

____. "Love and Knowledge: Emotion in Feminist Epistemology." Ed. Alison M. Jaggar and Susan R. Bordo, *Gender/Body/Knowledge: Feminist Reconstructions of Being and Knowing*. New Brunswick: Rutgers UP, 1989. 145-71

Janangelo, Joseph. "Theorizing Difference and Negotiating Differends: (Un)naming Writing Programs' Many Complexities and Strengths." Janangelo and Hansen, 3–22.

Jarratt, Susan C. "Feminism and Composition: The Case for Conflict." *Contending with Words: Composition and Rhetoric in a Postmodern Age*. Ed. Patricia Harkin and John Schilb. New York: MLA, 1991. 105–23. Rpt. in Kirsch et al., 263–80.

———. "Feminist Pedagogy." *A Guide to Composition Pedagogies*. Ed. Gary Tate, Amy Rupiper, and Kurt Schick. New York: Oxford UP, 2001. 113–131.

———. *Rereading the Sophists: Classical Rhetoric Refigured*. Carbondale: SIUP, 1991.

———, and Lynn Worsham, eds. *Feminism and Composition: In Other Words*. New York: MLA, 1998.

Johnson-Eilola, Johndan. *Nostalgic Angels: Rearticulating Hypertext Writing*. Norwood, NJ: Ablex Publishing, 1997.

Johnson-Eilola, Johndan, and Amy C. Kimme Hea. "After Hypertext: 20 Years of Hypertext Theory & Practice." *Computers & Composition 20th Anniversary Issue* 20 (2003): 415–25.

Johnson-Sheehan, Richard, and Charles Paine. "Changing the Center of Gravity: Collaborative Writing Program Administration in Large Universities." *Technical Communication Quarterly* 13 (2004): 199–210.

Jones, Robert, and Joe Comprone. "Where Do We Go Next in WAC?" *CCC* 44 (1993): 59–68.

Jukuri, Stephen, and William J. Williamson. "How to Be a Wishy-Washy Graduate Student WPA, or Undefined but Overdetermined: The Positioning of Graduate Student WPAs." George, 105–19.

Keller, Katherine L., Jennie Lee, Ben W. McClelland, and Brenda Robertson. "Reconstituting Authority: Four Perspectives on a Team Approach to Writing Program Administration." *WPA: Writing Program Administration* 21 (1998): 33–51.

Kelley-Riley, Diane, Lisa Johnson-Shull, and Bill Condon. "Opportunities for Consilience: Toward a Network-Based Model for Writing Program Administration." Rose and Weiser, *WPA as Theorist*, 129–42.

Kimme Hea, Amy C. "Rearticulating E-dentities in the Web-based Classroom: One Technoresearcher's Exploration of Power & the WWW." *Computers and Composition* 19 (2002): 331–46.

Kirsch, Gesa. *Women Writing the Academy: Audience, Authority, and Transformation*. Carbondale: SIUP, 1993.

Kirscht, Judy, Rhonda Levine, and John Reiff. "Evolving Paradigms: WAC and the Rhetoric of Inquiry." *CCC* 45 (1994): 369–80.

Kowalski, Robin. "Complaints and Complaining: Functions, Antecedents and Consequences." *Psychological Bulletin* 119 (1996): 179–96.

Lamb, Catherine E. "Beyond Argument in Feminist Composition." *College Composition and Communication* 42 (1991): 11–24. Rpt. in Kirsch et al., 281–93.

Lauer, Janice M. "The Feminization of Rhetoric and Composition Studies?" *Rhetoric Review* 13 (1995): 276–86. Rpt. in Kirsch et al., 542–51.

____."Graduate Students as Active Members of the Profession: Some Questions for Mentoring." Olson and Taylor, 229–35.

LeMasters, E. E. *Blue-Collar Aristocrats: Life-Styles at a Working-Class Tavern.* Madison: U of Wisconsin P, 1975.

L'Eplattenier, Lisa, and Jill Mastrangelo, eds. *Historical Studies of Writing Program Administration: Individuals, Communities, and the Formation of a Discipline.* West Lafayette, IN: Parlor P, 2004.

Leverenz, Carrie. "Theorizing Ethical Issues in Writing Program Administration." Rose and Weiser, *WPA as Theorist,* 103–15.

Logan, Shirley Wilson. "Changing Missions, Shifting Positions." *CCC* 55 (2003): 336–42.

Lorde, Audre. "The Master's Tools Will Never Dismantle the Master's House." *Sister Outsider: Essays and Speeches by Audre Lorde.* Berkeley: The Crossing P, 1984. 110–13.

Lu, Min Zhan. "An Essay on the Work of Composition: Composing English Against the Order of Fast Capitalism." *CCC* 56 (2004): 16–50.

Lunsford, Andrea. "Collaboration, Control, and the Idea of a Writing Center." *The Writing Center Journal* 12 (1991): 3–10.

____. "Re: Requesting your Voice." Email to editors. 26 July 2005.

____. "Rhetoric, Feminism, and the Politics of Textual Ownership" *College English* 61 (1999): 529–44.

Maihofer, Andrea. "Care." Jaggar and Young, 383–92.

Malenczyk, Rita. "Administration as Emergence: Toward a Rhetorical Theory of Writing Program Administration." Rose and Weiser, *WPA as Theorist,* 79–89.

_____. "Fighting Across the Curriculum: The WPA Joins the AAUP." *WPA: Writing Program Administration* 24 (2001): 11–23.

Malinowitz, Harriet. "A Feminist Critique of Writing in the Disciplines." Jarratt and Worsham, 291–312.

Maltz, Daniel N., and Ruth A. Borker. "A Cultural Approach to Male-Female Miscommunication." *Language and Social Identity.* Ed. John J. Gumperz. Cambridge: Cambridge UP, 1982. 195–216.

Marciluiano, Francesco, and Craig Macintosh. "Sally Forth." Cartoon. *Washington Post* 26 September 2004: D6.

Marshall, Margaret J. *Response to Reform: Composition and the Professionalization of Teaching.* Carbondale: SIUP, 2004.

McBride, Kelly. "The Ethics of Justice and Care in the American Media: A Tale of Two Reporters." *Poynter Online.* 9 January 2002. 14 January 2005 <www.poynter.org/content/content_view.asp?id=4688>.

McGuire, Gail M., and Jo Reger. "Feminist Co–Mentoring: A Model for Academic Professional Development." *NWSA Journal* 15 (2003): 54–72.

McKinney, Jackie, and Elizabeth Chiseri-Strater. "Inventing a Teacherly Self: Positioning Journals in the TA Seminar." *WPA: Writing Program Administration* 27 (2003): 59–74.

McLeod, Susan H. "Moving Up the Administrative Ladder." Brown et al., 113–24.

Meeks, Lynn, and Christine Hult. "A Co-Mentoring Model of Administration." *WPA: Writing Program Administration* 21 (1998): 9–22.

Micciche, Laura R. "More Than a Feeling: Disappointment and WPA Work." *College English* 64 (2002): 432–58.

Miller, Carolyn. "Re: Requesting your Voice." Email to editors. 26 July 2005.

Miller, Hildy. "Postmasculinist Directions in Writing Program Administration Work." *WPA: Writing Program Administration* 20 (1996): 49–61. Rpt. in Ward and Carpenter, 78–90.

Miller, Janet L. *Creating Spaces and Finding Voices: Teachers Collaborating for Empowerment.* Albany: SUNY P, 1990.

Miller, Richard. *As If Learning Mattered: Reforming Higher Education.* Ithaca, NY: Cornell UP, 1998.

———. "Critique's the Easy Part: Choice and the Scale of Relative Oppression." George, 3–13.

———. "'Let's Do the Numbers': Comp Droids and the Prophets of Doom." *Profession 1999.* New York: MLA, 1999. 96–105.

Miller, Susan. "The Feminization of Composition." Bullock and Trimbur, 39–53.

———. *Textual Carnivals: The Politics of Composition.* Carbondale: SIUP, 1991.

Miller, Tom. "Lest We Go the Way of the Classics: Toward a Rhetorical Future for English Departments." *Rhetorical Education in America.* Ed. Cheryl Glenn, Margaret M. Lyday, and Wendy B. Sharer. Tuscaloosa: U of Alabama P, 2004. 18–35.

Moreno, Renee M. "The Politics of Location: Text As Opposition." *CCC* 54 (2002): 222–42.

Morrison, Toni. *Nobel Prize for Literature Lecture.* New York: Knopf, 1994.

Morson, Gary Saul. "Sideshadowing and Tempics." *New Literary History* 29 (1998): 599–624.

Mortensen, Peter, and Gesa E. Kirsch. "On Authority in the Study of Writing." *CCC* 44 (1993): 556–72.

Murphy, Christina, and Bryon Stay, eds. *The Writing Center Director's Resource Book.* Mahwah, NJ: Lawrence Erlbaum, 2006.

Murphy, Christina. "The Writing Center and Social Constructionist Theory." *Intersections: Theory-Practice in the Writing Center.* Ed. Joan A. Mullin and Ray Wallace. Urbana, IL: NCTE, 1994. 161–71.

Myers-Breslin, Linda, ed. *Administrative Problem-Solving for Writing Programs and Writing Centers: Scenarios in Effective Program Management.* Urbana, IL: NCTE, 1999.

Nelson, Cary. *Manifesto of a Tenured Radical.* New York: NYUP, 1997.

Noddings, Nel. *Caring: A Feminine Approach To Ethics and Moral Education.* 1984. Berkeley: U of California P, 2003.

Okamoto, Dina G., and Lynn Smith-Lovin. "Changing the Subject: Gender, Status, and the Dynamics of Topic Change." *American Sociological Review* 66 (2001): 852–73.

Olson, Gary A. Foreword. Ward and Carpenter. ix–x.

———. Preface. Olson, *Rhetoric and Composition,* xi–xvi.

Olson, Gary A., ed. *Rhetoric and Composition as Intellectual Work.* Carbondale: SIUP, 2002.

———, ed. *Writing Centers: Theory and Administration.* Urbana, IL: NCTE, 1984.

Orwell, George. *Animal Farm.* New York: Harcourt, 1942.

Pagnucci, Gian S., and Nicholas Mauriello. "The Masquerade: Gender, Identity, and Writing for the Web." *Computers and Composition 16* (1999): 141-51.

Payne, Michelle. "Rend(er)ing Women's Authority in the Writing Classroom." *Taking Stock: The Writing Process Movement in the 90s.* Kirsch et al., 398–410.

Peeples, Tim. "'Seeing' the WPA With/Through Postmodern Mapping." Rose and Weiser, *WPA as Researcher,* 153–67.

Phelps, Louise Wetherbee. "Becoming a Warrior: Lessons of the Feminist Workplace." Phelps and Emig, 289–339.

___. "A Constrained Vision of the Writing Classroom." *Profession 93.* New York: MLA, 1993. 46–54.

___. "The Institutional Logic of Writing Programs: Catalyst, Laboratory, and Patterns for Change." Bullock and Trimbur, 155–70.

___. "Lessons of the Feminist Workplace." Phelps and Emig, 302–29.

___. "Turtles All the Way Down: Educating Academic Leaders." Brown et al., 3–39.

___. and Janet Emig, eds. *Feminine Principles and Women's Experience in American Composition and Rhetoric.* Pittsburgh: U of Pittsburgh P, 1995.

Philipsen, Gerry. "Speaking 'Like a Man' in Teamsterville: Cultural Patterns of Role Enactment in an Urban Neighborhood." *Quarterly Journal of Speech* 6 (1975): 13–22.

Popham, Susan, Michael Neal, Ellen Schendel, and Brian Huot. "Breaking Hierarchies: Using Reflective Practice to Re-Construct the Role of the Writing Program Administrator." Rose and Weiser, *WPA as Theorist,* 19–28.

Powell, Katrina M., and Pamela Takayoshi. "Accepting Roles Created for Us: The Ethics of Reciprocity." *CCC* 54 (2003): 394–422.

Powell, Malea. "Rhetorics of Survivance: How American Indians Use Writing." *CCC* 53 (2002): 396–434.

Ragland, Nathan. *Nonverbal Communication and Gender in the Writing Center.* M.A thesis. U of Louisville, 2005.

Ranieri, Paul. "The Teacher-Scholar at Ball State University as Reflected in the Department of English." Department of English Internal Report. Muncie, IN. 19 April 2005.

Ranieri, Paul, and Jackie Grutsch McKinney. "'Fitness for the Occasion': How Context Matters for JWPAs." *JWPAs: Voices Above, Below, and Within.* Ed. Debra Dew and Alice Horning. Lafayette, IN: Parlor P, forthcoming.

Ratcliffe, Krista. "Coming Out: Or, How Adrienne Rich's Feminist Theory Complicates Intersections of Rhetoric and Composition Studies, Cultural Studies, and Writing Program Administration." *Teaching Rhetorica: Theory, Pedagogy, Practice.* Ed. Kate Ronald and Joy Ritchie. Portsmouth, NH: Boynton/Cook, 2006. 31–47.

___. *Rhetorical Listening: Identification, Gender, Whiteness.* Carbondale: SIUP, 2006.

___. "Rhetorical Listening: A Trope for Interpretive Invention and a 'Code of Cross-Cultural Conduct.'" *CCC* 51 (1999): 195–224.

Reynolds, Nedra. "Interrupting Our Way to Agency: Feminist Cultural Studies and Composition." Jarratt and Worsham, 58–73.

_____ . "Who's Going to Cross This Border? Travel Metaphors, Material Conditions, and Contested Places." *JAC* 20 (2000): 541–64.

Rich, Adrienne. "Claiming an Education." In *On Lies, Secrets, and Silence: Selected Prose 1966–1978*. New York: Norton, 1979. 231–35.

_____. "Notes Toward a Politics of Location." *Blood, Bread, and Poetry: Selected Prose, 1979–1985*. New York: Norton, 1986. 210–32.

Rickly, Rebecca. "The Gender Gap in Computers and Composition Research: Must Boys Be Boys?" *Computers and Composition* 16 (1999): 121–40.

Rickly, Rebecca J., and Susanmarie Harrington. "Feminist Approaches to Mentoring Teaching Assistants." Pytlik and Liggett, 108–20.

Ritchie, Joy S. "Confronting the 'Essential' Problem: Reconnecting Feminist Theory and Pedagogy." Kirsch et al., 79–102.

Roen, Duane, Barry M. Maid, Gregory R. Glau, John Ramage, and David Schwalm. "Reconsidering and Assessing the Work of Writing Program Administrators." Rose and Weiser, *WPA as Theorist*, 157–69.

Rose, Shirley K., and Margaret J. Finders. "Learning from Experience: Using Situated Performances in Writing Teacher Development." *WPA: Writing Program Administration* 22 (1998): 33–52.

Rose, Shirley, and Irwin Weiser, eds. *The Writing Program Administrator as Researcher: Inquiry in Action and Reflection*. Portsmouth, NH: Boynton/Cook, 1999.

_____.*The Writing Program Administrator as Theorist: Making Knowledge Work*. Portsmouth, NH: Boynton/Cook, 2002.

Roskelly, Hephzibah, and Kate Ronald. *Reason to Believe: Romanticism, Pragmatism, and the Possibility of Teaching*. Albany: SUNY P, 1998.

Rude, Carolyn. "Re: Requesting your Voice." Email to editors. 29 Sept. 2005.

Russell, David R. *Writing in the Academic Disciplines, 1870–1990: A Curricular History*. Carbondale: SIUP, 1991.

Russell, Joyce, and Danielle Adams. "The Changing Nature of Mentoring in Organizations: An Introduction to the Special Issue on Mentoring in Organizations." *Journal of Vocational Behavior* 51 (1997): 1–14.

Sadker, David, and Myra Sadker. "Is the O.K. Classroom O.K.?" *Phi Delta Kappan* 66 (1985): 249–61.

Savin-Williams, Richard C. "An Ethnological Study of Dominance Formation and Maintenance in a Group of Human Adolescents." *Child Development* 47 (1976): 972–79.

Schell, Eileen E. "The Costs of Caring: 'Feminism' and Contingent Women Workers in Composition Studies." Jarratt and Worsham, 74–93.

_____."Who's the Boss: The Possibilities and Pitfalls of Collaborative Administration for Untenured WPAs." *WPA: Writing Program Administration* 21 (1998): 65–80.

Schuster, Charles I. "The Politics of Writing Promotion." Ward and Carpenter, 331–41.

Selber, Stuart. "Hypertext Spheres of Influence in Technical Communication Instructional Contexts." *Computers and Technical Communication: Pedagogical and Programmatic Perspectives*. Ed. Stuart Selber. Greenwich, CT: Ablex Publishing, 1997. 17–44.

____. *Multiliteracies for a Digital Age*. Carbondale: SIUP, 2004.

____. "Technological Dramas: A Meta-Discourse Heuristic for Critical Literacy." *Computers and Composition* 21 (2004): 171–95.

Selfe, Cynthia L., and Gail E. Hawisher. *Literate Lives in the Information Age: Narratives of Literacy in the United States*. Mahwah, NJ: Lawrence Erlbaum, 2004.

Shamoon, Linda K., Robert A. Schwegler, Rebecca Moore Howard, and Sandra Jamieson. "Reexamining the Theory-Practice Binary in the Work of Writing Program Administrators." Rose and Weiser, *WPA as Theorist*, 67–77.

Sledd, James. "Where's the Emperor? or The Revolution That Wasn't." CCCC. Nashville, TN. 18 March 1994.

____. "Why the Wyoming Resolution Had to Be Emasculated: A History and a Quixotism." *JAC* 11 (1991): 269–82.

Sloan, Jay D. "Centering Difference: Student Agency and the Limits of 'Comfortable' Collaboration." *Dialogue: A Journal for Writing Specialists* 8 (2003): 63–74.

Smit, David. *The Ends of Composition*. Carbondale: SIUP, 2005.

Smoke, Trudy. "Collaborating with Power: Contradictions of Working as a WPA." *WPA: Writing Program Administrators* 21 (1998): 92–100.

Spender, Dale. *Invisible Women: The Schooling Scandal*. London: A. Wheaton & Co., 1982.

Stanger, Carol. "The Sexual Politics of the One-to-One Tutorial Approach and Collaborative Learning." Caywood and Overing, 31–44.

Stearns, Peter N. *American Cool: Constructing a Twentieth-Century Emotional Style*. New York: NYUP, 1994.

Stella Dallas. Dir. King Vidor. The Samuel Goldwyn Co., 1937.

Stivers, Camille. *Gender Images in Public Education*. Thousand Oaks, CA: Sage, 2002.

Strickland, Donna. "The Managerial Unconscious of Composition Studies." Bousquet, et al., 46–56.

____. "Taking Dictation: The Emergence of Writing Programs and the Cultural Contradictions of Composition Teaching." *College English* 63 (2001): 457–79.

Stygall, Gail. "Compromised Positionings: Women and Language in the Collaborative Writing Classroom." Jarratt and Worsham, 318–41.

Sullivan, Laura L. "Wired Women Writing: Towards a Feminist Theorization of Hypertext." *Computers and Composition* 16 (1999): 25–54.

Takayoshi, Pamela, Meghan Huot, and Emily Huot. "No Boys Allowed: The World Wide Web as a Clubhouse for Girls." *Computers and Composition* 16 (1999): 89–106.

Tannen, Deborah. *Gender and Discourse*. New York: Oxford UP, 1994.

____. *You Just Don't Understand: Women and Men in Conversations*. New York: Morrow, 1990.

Taylor, Laurie, and Brendan Riley. "Open Source and Academia." *Computers and Composition Online* Spring 2004. 29 Sept 2005 <www.bgsu.edu/cconline/tayloriley/intro.html>.

Taylor, Todd. "The Politics of Electronic Scholarship in Rhetoric and Composition." Olson and Taylor, 197–209.

Tiernan, M.L. "Writing Program Administration and (Self)-Representation: Paradoxes, Anomalies, and Institutional Resistance." George, 162–74.

Tipper, Margaret. "Real Men Don't Do Writing Centers." *Writing Center Journal* 19 (1999): 33–40.

Treichler, Paula A., and Cheris Kramarae. "Women's Talk in the Ivory Tower." *Communication Quarterly* 31 (1983): 118–32.

Trimbur, John. Foreword. Kirsch, ix–xi.

——. "Peer Tutoring: A Contradiction in Terms?" *The Writing Center Journal* 7 (1987): 21–28. Rpt. in *The Allyn and Bacon Guide to Writing Center Theory and Practice.* Ed. Robert W. Barnett and Jacob S. Blumner. Boston: Allyn and Bacon, 2001. 288–95.

——. "Writing Instruction and the Politics of Professionalization." Bloom et al., 133–45.

Tulley, Christine, and Kristine Blair. "Ewriting Spaces as Safe, Gender-Fair Havens: Aligning Political and Pedagogical Possibilities." Takayoshi and Huot, 55–66.

Tulley, Christine, and the Students of Web Writing for English Majors (University of Findlay). "Class Review: What Video Games Have to Teach Us About Learning and Literacy (James Gee)." *Computers and Composition Online* Spring 2004. 29 Sept 2005 <www.bgsu.edu/cconline/tulley1/Splash.htm>.

Turnley, Melinda. "Contextualized Design: Teaching Critical Approaches to Web Authoring through Redesign Projects." *Computers and Composition* 22 (2004): 131–48.

Vaughn, Margaret E. "Why Teachers Change—An Analysis of Consequences and Rules." Kahaney et al., 113–30.

Villanueva, Victor, Jr. "Considerations of American Freiristas." Bullock and Trimbur, 247–62.

Walker, Carolyn P., and David Elias. "Writing Conference Talk: Factors Associated with High- and Low-Rated Writing Conferences." *Research in the Teaching of English* 21 (1987): 266–85.

Walker, Margaret Urban. "Moral Epistemology." Jaggar and Young, 363–70.

Walsh, John F. Letter to the Connecticut State University AAUP. 27 September 2004.

Walvoord, Barbara E. "The Future of Writing Across the Curriculum." *College English* 58 (1996): 58–79.

Ward, Irene. "Developing Healthy Management and Leadership Styles: Surviving the WPA's Inside Game." Ward and Carpenter, 49–67.

Ward, Irene, and William Carpenter, eds. *The Allyn and Bacon Sourcebook for Writing Program Administrators.* New York: Longman, 2002.

Ware, Vron. *Beyond the Pale: White Women, Racism, and History.* New York: Verso, 1992.

Weber, Max. *The Theory of Social and Economic Organizations.* Trans. A.M. Henderson and Talcott Parsons. New York: Free P, 1964.

Weingartner, Rudolph H. *The Moral Dimensions of Academic Administration.* Lanham, MD: Rowman and Littlefield, 1999.

Weiser, Irwin, and Shirley K Rose. "Theorizing Writing Program Theorizing." Rose and Weiser, *WPA as Theorist*, 183–95.

West, Candace, and Don H. Zimmerman. "Small Insults: A Study of Interruptions in Cross-Sex Conversations Between Unacquainted Persons." Thorne et al., 103–18.

White, Edward M. "Use It or Lose It: Power and the WPA." *WPA: Writing Program Administration* 15 (1991): 3–12. Rpt. in Ward and Carpenter 106–13.

Willard-Traub, Margaret K. "Professionalization and the Politics of Subjectivity." *Rhetoric Review* 21 (2002): 61-70.

Williams, Linda. "'Something Else Besides a Mother': *Stella Dallas* and the Maternal Melodrama." *Home is Where the Heart Is: Studies in Melodrama and the Woman's Film.* Ed. Christine Gledhill. London: British Film Institute, 1987. 299–325.

Winter, Janet K., Joan C. Neal, and Karen K. Warner. "How Male, Female, and Mixed-Gender Groups Regard Interaction and Leadership Differences in the Business Communication Course." *Business Communication Quarterly* 64 (2001): 43–58.

Wolfe, Joanna L. "Why Do Women Feel Ignored? Gender Differences in Computer-Mediated Classroom Interactions." *Computers and Composition* 16 (1999): 153–66.

Wolfe, Joanna, and Kara Alexander. "The Computer Expert in a Mixed-Gendered Collaborative Writing Group." *Journal of Business and Technical Communication* 19 (2005): 135–70.

Woods, Nicola. "Talking Shop: Sex and Status as Determinants of Floor Apportionment in a Work Setting." *Women in Their Speech Communities.* Ed. Jennifer Coates and Deborah Cameron. New York: Longman, 1988. 141–57.

Woolbright, Meg. "The Politics of Tutoring: Feminism Within the Patriarchy." *Writing Center Journal* 13 (1992): 3–7.

Worsham, Lynn. "Writing Against Writing: The Predicament of *Ecriture Féminine* in Composition Studies." *Contending with Words: Composition and Rhetoric in a Postmodern Age.* Ed. Patricia Harkin and John Schilb. New York: MLA, 1991. 82–104.

WPA Executive Committee. "Evaluating the Intellectual Work of Writing Administration: A Draft." *WPA: Writing Program Administration* 20 (1996): 92–103. Rpt. in Ward and Carpenter, 366–78.

The WPA Outcomes Statement for First-Year Composition. *WPA: Writing Program Administration* 23 (1999): 59–66. Rpt. in www.english.ilsu.edu/Hessse/outcomes.html and *College English* 63 (2001): 321–25.

Yancey, Kathleen Blake. "On Feminist Research: What Do Women Want (Now)?, Or A Query Regarding Con/Textual Relationships." *Feminist Empirical Research: Emerging Perspectives on Qualitative and Teacher Research.* Ed. Joanne Addison and Sharon James McGee. Portsmouth, NH: Heinemann, 1999. 145–57.

_____, and Meg Morgan. "Reflective Essays, Curriculum, and the Scholarship of Administration." Rose and Weiser, *WPA as Researcher,* 81–94.

_____, and Michael Spooner. "A Single Good Mind: Collaboration, Cooperation, and the Writing Self." *CCC* 49 (1998): 45–62.

ABOUT THE EDITORS AND CONTRIBUTORS

Krista Ratcliffe is Professor and Chair of English and former Director of First-Year English at Marquette University in Milwaukee, Wisconsin, where she teaches undergraduate and graduate courses in rhetoric and composition theory, writing, and women's literature. She has served as the CCCC Representative and Chair of NCTE's College Forum and President of the Coalition of Women Scholars in the History of Rhetoric and Composition. Her research focuses on the intersections of rhetoric, feminist theory, and pedagogy. Her publications include Anglo-*American Feminist Challenges to the Rhetorical Tradition*, *Who's Having This Baby* (with Helen Sterk, Carla Hay, Alice Kehoe, and Leona VandeVusse), and *Rhetorical Listening: Identification, Gender, Whiteness* (2006 *JAC* Gary Olsen Award; 2007 CCCC Outstanding Book Award; 2007 RSA Book Award). Her work has appeared in edited collections, as well as in *CCC*, *JAC*, *Rhetoric Review*, and *College English*.

Rebecca J. Rickly is Associate Professor and former Co-Director of Composition at Texas Tech University, where she teaches undergraduate and graduate courses in rhetoric, research, and writing. She teaches the required research methods courses in Technical Communication and Rhetoric, Composition, and Rhetoric, and she also teaches the Feminist Research Methods course for Women's Studies. Her work revolves around rhetoric, but includes such diverse applications as technology, feminisms, methods and methodologies, literacy study, and administration. She has served on the CCCC Committee on Computers and Composition and NCTE's Assembly on Computers in English, and she has chaired NCTE's Instructional Technology Committee. Her publications include *The Online*

Writing Classroom (with Susanmarie Harrington and Michael Day), and her work has appeared in several edited collections, as well as *Computers and Composition, CMC Magazine, The ACE Journal*, and *Kairos*.

Cristy Beemer is Assistant Professor of English at the University of New Hampshire, where she teaches graduate and undergraduate courses in composition, rhetoric, and technical writing. Cristy completed her PhD in Rhetoric and Composition at Miami University in 2008, where she served as Assistant Director for the Howe Writing Initiative and Director of Writing Curriculum for Business 102 in the Richard T. Farmer School of Business. Cristy's research focuses on history of rhetoric, with a particular emphasis on women and the early modern period, WAC, and business/professional writing.

Kristine Blair is Professor and Chair of the English Department at Bowling Green State University where she teaches in the Rhetoric and Writing Doctoral Program and serves as Editor of *Computers and Composition Online*. Her work on gender and technology, distance learning pedagogies, and electronic portfolios has appeared in a wide range of journals and collections, and her co-edited collection *Webbing Cyberfeminist Practice: Communities, Pedagogies and Social Action* is forthcoming from Hampton Press.

Lanette Cadle is Assistant Professor of English at Missouri State University and Senior Editor of *Computers and Composition Online*. She was a doctoral student at Bowling Green State University when this chapter was written.

Julie Nelson Christoph is Assistant Professor of English at the University of Puget Sound, where she teaches courses in composition, autobiography, literacy, writing and gender, and rhetorical theory. While in graduate school at the University of Wisconsin-Madison, she served for two years as Assistant Director of the Writing Fellows Program. Her current research explores writers' uses of the personal in narrative, undergraduate essays, and scholarly writing. Her work has appeared in *College English* and *Research in the Teaching of English*.

Ilene Crawford is Associate Professor of English and Women's Studies at Southern Connecticut State University in New Haven. She has served as the Basic Writing Coordinator at the University of Wisconsin-Milwaukee, Co-Director of the Composition Program at SCSU, and Composition Faculty Development Coordinator at SCSU. Her scholarly work examines the relationship between economies, race, language, and emotion. She teaches undergraduate composition courses and graduate courses in feminist, rhetorical, and pedagogical theory.

Christine Farris is Professor, Director of Composition, and former Associate Chair in the English Department at Indiana University in Bloomington where she teaches courses in writing, rhetoric and composition theory, and literature. Her recent projects focus on the politics of writing instruction and the preparation of the English professoriate. She is the author of *Subject to Change: New Composition Instructors' Theory and Practice* (Hampton Press); co-editor with Chris Anson of *Under Construction: Working at the Intersections of Composition Theory, Research, and Practice* (Utah State UP); and co-editor with Judith H. Anderson of *Integrating Literature and Writing Instruction: First Year English, Humanities Core Courses, Seminars* (MLA).

Lynée Lewis Gaillet is Associate Professor of rhetoric and composition at Georgia State University and past Executive Director of the South Atlantic Modern Language Association. She is the Editor of *Scottish Rhetoric and Its Influences* and author of numerous articles and book chapters addressing writing program administration and the history of rhetoric/writing practices. Currently, she is co-editing two collections: *Stories of Mentoring: Theory and Praxis* (with Michelle Eble) and the 3rd edition of *Present State of Research in the History of Rhetoric* (with Winifred Bryan Horner).

Paula Gillespie is Associate Professor of English and Director of the Ott Memorial Writing Center at Marquette University (since 1985). She teaches the tutor training course and literature in the English Department and is involved with WAC initiatives. She has published on James Joyce's *Ulysses* but currently focuses on writing about issues of pedagogy, writing centers, and tutoring. She is the co-author with Neal Lerner of *The Allyn and Bacon Guide to Peer Tutoring* 2nd ed., and she has been researching and writing on the short- and long-term effects of peer tutoring on the tutors.

Sibylle Gruber is Professor in Literacy, Technology, and Professional Writing at Northern Arizona University. She directed the University Writing Program and worked with 40 graduate assistants, several instructors, and many undergraduate students for 5 years. She teaches graduate and undergraduate courses in literacy studies, rhetoric and cultures, and computers and composition. Her book-length projects include *Literacies, Experiences and Technologies: Reflective Practices of an Alien Researcher; Weaving a Virtual Web: Practical Approaches to New Information Technologies; Alternative Rhetorics: Challenges to the Rhetorical Tradition* (with Laura Gray-Rosendale); and *Social Change in Diverse Teaching Contexts: Touchy Subjects and Routine Practices* (with Nancy G. Barron and Nancy Grimm). Gruber's work on cybertheories, feminist rhetorics, composition, and cultural studies can be found in various journals and edited collections.

Letizia Guglielmo is Assistant Professor of English at Kennesaw State University and teaches first-year writing and world literature, both in the classroom and online. Her research and writing focuses on changing definitions of literacy, digital media in the composition classroom, and the impact of feminist pedagogy and feminist rhetoric on online learning. She is currently completing a PhD in Rhetoric and Composition at Georgia State University.

Jeanne Gunner is Vice Chancellor for Undergraduate Education and Professor of English at Chapman University in southern California. She has been a Writing Program Administrator at UCLA and Santa Clara University and works closely with the writing program in her current position, has been a member of the Council of WPA's executive and editorial boards, and was co-facilitator of the WPA Summer Workshop in 2001-02 and 2002-03. Writing program theory continues to be a primary research area, especially writing programs and ideology, and she is co-editing with Donna Strickland a volume on critical issues in WPA work. She teaches undergraduate writing and literature courses.

Linda Hanson is Professor of English at Ball State University, Muncie, Indiana. She has served as the Coordinator of Basic Writing (1985-92), Assistant Department Chair (1989-92), Department Chair (1992-95), and Site Director for the Indiana Writing Project (1995-present). She also serves as the Indiana Network Director for the 5 National Writing Project sites in Indiana. Her scholarly focus on romanticism, rhetoric, and writing includes pragmatic work on assessment as well as the reflexive links between theory and practice. At the undergraduate level she teaches Basic Writing and the Introduction to English Studies required of all new majors. At the graduate level she teaches British Romanticism, Nineteenth Century Theories of Rhetoric and Composition, Literary Theory, and a seminar in Theory, Pedagogy and Research in Basic Writing, seeking always the serendipitous connections. Her work has been published in several collections, the *Journal of Basic Writing*, and *Computers and Composition.*

Amy C. Kimme Hea is Assistant Professor in the Rhetoric, Composition, and Teaching of English program at University of Arizona. Her research interests include web and wireless teaching and learning, teacher training, and professional writing theory and practice. She has published on articulation theory and methodology, visual rhetoric, WWW design, hypertext theory, and service learning projects. Her work appears in the anthology *Working with Words and Images: New Steps in an Old Dance* and journals including *Computers and Composition, Kairos, Educare/Educare,* and *Reflections: A Journal of Writing, Service-Learning, and Community Literacy.*

Carrie Leverenz is Associate Professor of English and director of the New Media Writing Studio at Texas Christian University, where she teaches undergraduate and graduate courses in composition theory and practice, cyberliteracy, writing for publication, and the politics and ethics of writing instruction. She has served as Director of the Reading/Writing Center and Computer-Supported Writing Classrooms at Florida State and as Director of Composition at TCU. Her current research interests include administrative ethics, new media writing programs, and the history of research methodology in the field of composition. She is the former co-editor, with Brad Lucas, of the journal *Composition Studies*.

Carol Mattingly is Professor of English and Director of the Writing Centers Research Project at the University of Louisville. She has held administrative positions at three universities; those positions include Director of Writing Center, Director of Composition, Director of National Writing Project, and Associate Chair; she has also held administrative positions in the public school system. Her scholarship focuses on 19th-century women's rhetoric and writing centers (e.g., *Well-Tempered Women: Nineteenth-Century Temperance Rhetoric*; *Water Drops from Women Writers: A Temperance Reader*; and *Appropriate(Ing) Dress: Women's Rhetorical Style in Nineteenth Century America*). Her teaching includes seminars for teachers in the writing center and in the classroom, history of rhetoric, women's rhetoric and literature, and the rhetoric of U.S. slavery.

Rebecca S. Nowacek is Assistant Professor of English at Marquette University. She has worked as Assistant Director of the Letters and Sciences Program in Writing Across the Curriculum and Director of the English 100 Tutorial Program at the University of Wisconsin–Madison. She often teaches courses on rhetorical theory, literacy and society, and advanced composition. Her work work has appeared in *College English*, *JGE*, and *Research in the Teaching of English*.

Mary Lou Odom is Assistant Professor of English and Assistant Director of the Writing Center at Kennesaw State University. She previously held posts as the Assistant Director of the English 100 Program, the Director of the English 100 Tutorial Program, and Lead Writing Center Teaching Assistant at the University of Wisconsin–Madison. Her research and writing investigate the relationship between theory and practice in the training of writing teachers and issues of identity and ethics in writing center administration. She teaches both undergraduate and graduate courses in composition and writing center theory and pedagogy.

E. Shelley Reid is Assistant Professor of English and Director of the First-Year Composition Program at George Mason University, where she teaches writing as well as courses in composition theory and pedagogy. She has published articles on faculty development and TA mentoring in writing programs, the difficulty of teaching multiculturalism in first-year writing courses, and approaches to teaching composition pedagogy. She continues to investigate strategies for educating and mentoring composition teachers—and she is, all the while, preparing for tenure review.

Kate Ronald is the Roger and Joyce L. Howe Professor of English at Miami University, where she teaches graduate and undergraduate courses in composition and rhetoric and directs the Howe Writing Initiative in the School of Business. Her recent publications include *Reason to Believe: Romanticism, Pragmatism, and the Teaching of Writing*, co-authored with Hephzibah Roskelly (SUNY, 1998), and *Available Means: An Anthology of Women's Rhetoric(s)* (Pittsburgh, 2001), and *Teaching Rhetorica* (Heinemann, 2006), both co-edited with Joy Ritchie.

Lisa Shaver completed her PhD in Rhetoric and Composition at Miami University in 2006, where she has also served as Assistant Director for the Howe Writing Initiative in the Richard T. Farmer School of Business. She is Assistant Professor of English at Baylor University where she teaches courses in rhetoric and professional writing. Lisa's research centers on women's rhetoric, history of rhetoric, writing across the curriculum, professional writing, and literacy studies. Her work has appeared in *Rhetoric Review* and the *Journal of Business and Technical Communication*.

Bonnie Kathryn Smith is Assistant Professor of English at Belmont University in Nashville, Tennessee. At Belmont, she serves as the Director of the Writing Center and the Co-Coordinator of the First-Year Seminar. While a graduate student at the University of Wisconsin-Madison, she was the Assistant Director of the Writing Across the Curriculum program. Smith's teaching and research explores ways literacy informs life in the community. Currently, her exploration of literacy in community life revolves around a group of women in Nashville who are in recovery from prostitution and drug abuse.

Donna Strickland is Assistant Professor and a member of the Composition Staff at the University of Missouri-Columbia, where she teaches writing, rhetoric, and the teaching of writing. She previously worked as an administrator of writing programs at Southern Illinois University Carbondale, Butler University, and University of Wisconsin-Milwaukee. Her scholarship has appeared in a variety of journals, including *College English*, *JAC*, and *Works and Days*, as well as in the collections *A Way to Move: Rhetorics of Emotion and Composition Studies* and *Tenured Bosses, Disposable Teachers: Writing Instruction in the Managed University*. She is currently completing a book on the managerial affect of composition studies.

Melinda Turnley is Assistant Professor of English at DePaul University. Her research and teaching interests highlight issues of teacher development, media pedagogy, service learning, document design, and critical approaches to technology. Her work has appeared in journals such as *Computers and Composition, Technical Communication Quarterly, Kairos,* and *Rhetoric Review*.

Kathleen Blake Yancey is Kellogg W. Hunt Professor of English at Florida State University, where she teaches undergraduate and graduate students and directs the graduate program in rhetoric and composition. A past president of the Council of Writing Program Administrators, past Chair of the College Section of the National Council of Teachers of English, and Immediate Past Chair of CCCC, she is President of NCTE. She has taken up various WPA positions, including directing the UNC Charlotte site of the National Writing Project and directing Clemson's Pearce Center for Professional Communication, where she also created and directed the Class of 1941 Studio for Student Communication. With Barbara Cambridge, she founded and directs the National Research Coalition on Electronic Portfolios. She has edited, co-edited, or authored 8 books—among them *Voices on Voice; Reflection in the Writing Classroom;* and *Teaching Literature as Reflective Practice*—as well as many articles and book chapters. Her recent edited collection—*Delivering College Composition: The Fifth Canon*—examines the ways that technology, site of instruction, and faculty shape composition curricula and pedagogy.

AUTHOR INDEX

SUBJECT INDEX

Academic discourse, 28, 29
  Masculinist, as, 37, 46, 71
Adjunct faculty (contingent labor), 12, 71, 85, 90-91, 132, 146
Administration/Administrator vii
  Bad, traditional assumptions about, 44, 49
  Consultancy model, 162
  Good, feminist assumptions about, 17, 127, 145
  Good, traditional assumptions about, 14
  Metaphors of, 160
  Models, 22
  Practice, and, xiii
  Preparation for, 216-217
  Upper, 54
  Women, in/as, 154
Administrative genre of scholarship, xi, 19, 235(n8)
  Conventional, 19-20, 26
  Erotics of, 22, 27
  Supplements to, xi, 23, 26-29
  Utopian, 22, 31
Administrative staff, 216
Advice. *See also* Feminist administrators
Affective, the, xii, 83-88. *See also* Care
Age, vii
Agency, xii, xv, 12, 21, 27, 36, 109, 135, 156, 179
  Feminist, 124
  Limitations on, 12
  Teacher agency, 122

Technical, 110, 117.
  See also Technology
Allies, 12
Anger, 82-83
Assessment, 64, 89
Authority, vii, 37-38, 94, 100, 117, 121, 167, 168, 171, 172, 186
  Rhetorical authority 163

Boldness, xiii, 159-160
Boss compositionists, 70
Budget, 149
Bureaucracy, 232(n1)
Bureaucratizing of the affective, 84, 87.
  See also Affective, the
Bureaucratizing of the imaginative (K. Burke) 84, 87

Care, xi, xiii, xv, 4, 8-10, 86, 95, 96, 130, 141, 200, 233(n3)
  Criticisms of, 9, 131-132, 137, 172
  Managed care, 125-141
  Theory-Practice Tensions of, 126
Chair of department, xiv, 45, 184-198
Class, vii, 70, 90, 97, 213, 222
Collaboration, xi-xii, xiv, xv, 32, 37, 38, 39, 40, 45, 53-66, 104, 106, 111-112, 121, 168, 178, 189, 202, 206, 220, 235(n7), 236(n11-12)
  Active editing, as mode of, 207-209
  Flattened (decentered) structure, as, 56-57, 58-59, 106, 111
  Interruption of, xii, 77-91
  Pedagogy, 172

CPSIA information can be obtained
at www.ICGtesting.com
Printed in the USA
FFOW03n0639031215
19012FF